Intertemporal Planning, Exchange, and Macroeconomics

Intertemporal Planning, Exchange, and Macroeconomics

D. F. I. FOLKERTS-LANDAU

Graduate School of Business
University of Chicago

CAMBRIDGE UNIVERSITY PRESS

Cambridge
London   New York   New Rochelle
Melbourne   Sydney

Published by the Press Syndicate of the University of Cambridge
The Pitt Building, Trumpington Street, Cambridge CB2 1RP
32 East 57th Street, New York, NY 10022, USA
296 Beaconsfield Parade, Middle Park, Melbourne 3206, Australia

First published 1982

Printed in the United States of America

Library of Congress Cataloging in Publication Data
Folkerts-Landau, D. F. I. (David Fokke Ihno),
1949-
Intertemporal planning, exchange, and macro-
economics.
Bibliography: p.
Includes index.
1. Macroeconomics.   2. Equilibrium (Economics)
3. Time and economic reactions.   I. Title.
HB172.5.F64   339   81-38501
ISBN 0 521 23067 5   AACR2

To
EVA MARIA PLATZMAN

Contents

Preface

This volume presents the results obtained in a series of papers dealing with the microfoundations of macroeconomic models sustaining a dynamic general-equilibrium structure. We first characterize the individual's intertemporal planning and trading behavior when transacting is costly. Next we investigate the possibility of attaining a general monetary equilibrium and its intertemporal optimality. Finally, the analysis is extended to include non-Walrasian disequilibrium economies.

The choice of method and the scope of these investigations were motivated by a desire to provide a unified and coherent approach to the construction of microeconomic and general-equilibrium foundations of macroeconomic analysis through the explicit introduction of a transactions and market technology. Thus they reflect my conviction that the absence of such foundations is responsible for the failure of macroeconomic analysis and that the first step to remedy this shortcoming must be the analysis of general-equilibrium systems of rational individuals subject to transactions and information costs. The second step inevitably will then lead to an analysis of efficient institutional innovation arising from the desire to minimize transactions and information costs.

For persistent help, encouragement, and constructive criticism I am indebted to Professors W. H. Branson, D. M. Jaffee, M. Mussa, M. Rothschild and Drs. A. Brillembourg, T. Gylfason, G. Faulhaber, G. J. Schinasi, and D. M. Raff. I have also benefited from discussion and correspondence with Professors R. Barro, A. Blinder, E. Green, H. Kuhn, R. E. Lucas, D. Patinkin, and H. Sonnenschein, and I should like to thank Professor J. Niehans for his very early encouragement.

Several parts of this book were presented in seminars and workshops at Princeton University, Johns Hopkins University, the University of Chicago, the University of California at Berkeley, the University of Southern California, the University of British Columbia, the University of Texas at Austin, and the University of Rochester, as well as at various American Economic Association meetings and the Fourth World Congress of the Econometrics Society.

Last but not least, I should like to thank the students at Princeton University and the University of Chicago, who were subjected to my lectures on these topics, for their challenging questions.

D. F. I. Folkerts-Landau

Frequently used symbols

a	actual, ex post
$B(t)$	nominal stock of bonds held by households at time t
$b(t)$	stock of bonds in units of consumption goods held by households at time t
$B_C(t)$	flow demand for bonds in exchange for consumptions goods, denominated in units of bonds
$b_C(t)$	$\equiv B_C(t)/P_{CB}(t)$; flow demand for bonds in exchange for consumption goods, denominated in units of consumption goods
$B_M(t)$	flow demand for bonds in exchange for money, denominated in units of bonds
$b_M(t)$	$\equiv B_M(t)/P_{CB}(t)$; flow demand for bonds in exchange for money, denominated in units of consumption goods
$C(t)$	stock of consumption goods in physical units held by households
$C_B(t)$	flow demand for consumption goods in exchange for bonds, denominated in units of consumption goods
$C_M(t)$	flow demand for consumption goods in exchange for money, denominated in units of consumption goods
$d(t)$	$\equiv (C_M(t), C_B(t), b_M(t)\Pi(t))$
e	expected
G	government
i	individual household
$M(t)$	nominal stock of money held by households at time t
$m(t)$	stock of money in units of consumption goods held by households at time t
$M_B(t)$	flow demand for money in exchange for bonds, denominated in units of money
$m_B(t)$	$\equiv M_B(t)/P_{CM}(t)$; flow demand for money in exchange for bonds, denominated in units of consumption goods
$M_C(t)$	flow demand for money in exchange for consumption goods, denominated in units of money
$m_C(t)$	$\equiv M_C(t)/P_{CM}(t)$; flow demand for money in exchange for consumption goods, denominated in units of consumption goods
N	nominal
$P(t)$	$\equiv (P_{CM}(t), P_{CB}(t), P_{BM}(t))$

tracting, as well as the costs of establishing the equilibrium prices and exchanges. The choice and the use of a medium of exchange, together with the use of forward contracts, are endogenous decisions that depend on the properties of the transactions technology and the market-clearing mechanism. The agent's asset-accumulation behavior and market behavior are determined by its desire to achieve an optimal consumption path and optimal asset stocks for bequest. Its optimization problem is subject to its endowments, asset depreciation, and the generalized transactions costs embodied in the transactions technology.[4] The first-order conditions for an optimum of the intertemporal maximization problem are exploited to establish the marginal conditions describing the agent's optimal asset-accumulation behavior and market behavior.[5]

The curvature of the transactions technology determines the frequency of the agent's transactions and thereby determines whether its response to a disturbance takes the form of a continuous partial stock adjustment or a discrete stock shift.

A comparative dynamic analysis establishes the effect on the agent's asset-accumulation behavior and market behavior of an anticipated or unanticipated change in its exogenous variables, such as endowments, market prices, and the structural parameters associated with its utility function and transactions technology. In addition to the familiar wealth and substitution effects, it is possible to derive an intertemporal substitution effect of a change in prices. The effects of anticipated or unanticipated changes in the rates of inflation on the agents' planned intertemporal demands can also be ascertained, as can the effects of innovations in the transactions technology. The intertemporal demand functions are shown to possess the usual homogeneity properties.

In the second part of this book we shall analyze an aggregate general-equilibrium asset economy, which consists of overlapping generations of the finite-life agents described in the first part.

By aggregating linearly over all individual agents, we obtain the market demands and supplies. In the Walras-Debreu types of general-equilibrium models the equilibrium price vector is established by a costless and timeless tâtonnement process, and the agent's expected price vector equals the equilibrium price vector. If financial markets are complete, then the introduction of uncertainty about future states of the economy will not alter the properties of this equilibrium. One difficulty with such models is that they do not admit a medium of exchange in a meaningful way. All future exchanges are contracted in a complete set of contingent forward markets. A second difficulty is that the general-equilibrium models of Walras and Debreu do not lend themselves to an explicit analysis of the dynamics of assets accumulation. The model of an aggregate economy with overlapping generations of finite-life agents, on the other hand, allows for an explicit analysis of the dynamic properties of aggregate economies and facilitates the introduction of alternative transactions and market-clearing mechanisms.

We shall initially maintain the assumption that the recontracting process is timeless, but we dispense with the assumption that it is costless. The costs of establishing the equilibrium price vector and the set of equilibrium exchanges are allocated to the potential traders through the transactions technology. We assume that the price vector, which equates market demands and supplies, is attained in a tâtonnement process or is the previous outcome of a convergent learning mechanism.[6] Once this equilibrium price vector is established, the set of equilibrium trades among the agents is found.[7] Because the complexity and hence the cost of the process establishing the equilibrium trades decreases with the introduction of a medium of exchange, the requirement of efficiency dictates its use.

Furthermore, the requirement that the process establishing the set of equilibrium trades consumes real resources also implies that this process will take place at the time the exchange is to be executed. Hence the introduction of transactions and tâtonnement costs implies that forward contracts in complete markets do not entirely displace the use of a medium of exchange. When markets are not complete, there are, of course, additional reasons for the use of a medium of exchange.

The requirement that there exist no systematic opportunity for profits from arbitrage across the various barter and monetary markets is then employed to derive the necessary and sufficient conditions for an economy to use a medium of exchange.

An instantaneous temporary equilibrium in the overlapping-generations model exists, and it is optimal, stable, and unique. However, the agents' assets portfolios are not Pareto-optimal. In particular, the agents' portfolios can be moved toward socially efficient levels by a change in the stock of money that equates the rate of change in the nominal price of the physical good with the negative of the rate of time preference.[8] The agents' finite lives are the cause for a similar nonoptimality in their bond holdings. If the government can exploit productive opportunities such as the production of public goods, then an appropriate choice of financing this production can bring about a Pareto-efficient stock of debt instruments.[9]

It is also possible to show that the presence of nonconvex transactions technologies constitutes a necessary and sufficient condition for a Pareto-efficient institutional innovation in the form of intermediary traders. Furthermore, it is now consistent and exhaustive to characterize flow markets as markets with a convex transactions technology and stock markets as markets with a nonconvex transactions technology.

After analyzing the behavior of a dynamic general-equilibrium economy, we shall investigate economies in which the assumption of a timeless tâtonnement and complete markets has been suspended. Instead, the agents start with an expected price vector and update it as new information becomes available. The agents are endowed with an expectations-formation mechanism that is characterized by a set of inference rules for making conditional optimal forecasts. The agents also possess a learning mechanism that alters the inference rules as forecast errors occur. This process has been modeled qualitatively through the agents' converging reactions to forecast errors.

The necessity of an intertemporal optimization model to analyze the agent's reaction to mistakes is obvious. Its expectations about future prices affect its current consumption and portfolio decisions. Forecast errors alter those expectations and hence affect current behavior. In the model at hand, expectations and past mistakes find their way into current instantaneous decisions via the shadow prices of asset stocks. Agents may have inconsistent future plans even if spot markets clear instantaneously; the resulting temporary market equilibria derive their dynamic properties from the revision of expectations and from the agents' accumulation activities, as well as from changes in the average age of the overlapping generations (Grandmont, 1977).

We furthermore permit the spot market to be in disequilibrium. It is then necessary to distinguish between notional and effective demands. Agents may be unable to satisfy their notional demands or supplies, but instead may have their effective demands or supplies satisfied. Because there are costs associated with extracting information that signals nonzero demand, as well as other costs of price changes,[10] the movement of prices toward the Walrasian equilibrium may be retarded. When markets are in disequilibrium, agents form expectations about prices and quantities.

We derive the qualitative and convergence properties of the movement of market variables toward a temporary equilibrium. The properties of the expectations and price adjustment processes permit such an analysis. The current disequilibrium literature relies heavily on the assumption of fixed prices and investigates quantity adjustment alone. Furthermore, these models have failed to incorporate the intertemporal aspects of the agents' decision problems. Moreover, they ignore the distinction between asset markets and flow markets. Such a distinction is of some importance, because we establish that disequilibrium can occur in flow markets only, not in asset markets, when asset markets are defined as markets with a nonconvex transactions technology.

CHAPTER II

A model of the intertemporal household

II.1   Introduction

The economy under consideration is made up of n households whose economic life extends over the interval $[0, T]$. There exist three commodities, a consumption good, bonds issued by households, and non-interest-bearing government debt called money. The n households trade among themselves by exchanging one commodity for another in any of three markets (the bonds-cum-money market, the consumption-good-cum-money market, the consumption-good-cum-bonds market). These markets are assumed to clear continuously with the aid of an auctioneer, and the households act as price-takers. Time in this economy is not divided into periods but is allowed to flow continuously. An important further characteristic of this economy is that transactions use real resources.

Each of the n households receives an endowment of the consumption good and maximizes an intertemporal utility function by choosing a feasible path of consumption. In this process, the household allocates its endowment over time by holding inventories of money, bonds, and consumption goods. The utility maximization hypothesis implies that the household minimizes resources spent on transactions.

The purpose of this chapter is to define the maximization problem of a representative household.

II.2   The objective function of the household

The objective of the household is the maximization of utility from consumption. The standard mathematical representation of this general behavioral proposition is an optimization problem in which the household chooses, subject to a budget constraint, the bundle of goods that affords it the greatest utility. More precisely, the household finds the constrained maximum of a continuous and quasi-concave utility function that is defined on a closed and convex consumption set $Y \subset R^n$.[1] The existence of such a utility function is guaranteed by assuming that the household possesses a continuous, convex, and complete preference ordering on Y; for a proof, see the work of Debreu

(1959). The budget constraint forces the value of a given endowment to equal or exceed the value of the chosen consumption bundle and so defines a feasible set that is convex and closed. Symbolically, we have

$$\max_{X} U(X) \quad \text{subject to} \quad X \in \Omega \subset R^n$$

where U is the utility function, X is the consumption bundle, and Ω the feasible set.[2]

The consumption bundle in this problem can be interpreted quite generally; some components of the vector X may represent generalized consumer goods produced by the household with the aid of commodity and labor inputs, whereas others may represent flows of services from stock holdings.[3] Hence, this formulation of the maximization problem can be used to conceptualize stock holding as well as household production of goods. However, the role of time in this model is not well defined. An elementary intertemporal interpretation of this model is that it determines the steady-state value of the household's consumption vector. The household is assumed to be infinitely lived, and it not only views all prices as persisting at their current levels but also views the current state of the world as time-invariant. The household determines its flow rates of consumption by solving its maximization problem and lives forever in a steady-state world. If stocks are held, then in this interpretation their levels are constant (i.e., the rate of decumulation through depreciation and consumption is equal to the rate of accumulation through purchases). Thus this steady-state interpretation lends a rudimentary intertemporal flavor to this model, but it is devoid of any dynamic content.

A second intertemporal interpretation of this model is possible if goods at different times are perceived as different goods. By dividing time into a finite number of intervals of equal length and considering each good in each such period as a different good, one can develop a more realistic intertemporal interpretation of the preceding model of household behavior. This approach has been generalized to the case of infinitely many goods, and this allows us to deal with intertemporal problems with continuously varying levels of consumption over time.[4]

The preceding formalization of the household's maximization problem provides sufficient structure for analysis of the existence and uniqueness of equilibria in economies made up of such households (Arrow and Hahn, 1971; Peleg and Yaari, 1970; Stigum, 1973). The difficulty with approaching the formulation of an intertemporal dynamic theory of the household by extending the interpretation of the preceding finite- or infinite-dimensional maximization problem is that it reveals too little of the dynamic structure of the variables that enter the intertemporal decision-making process of the household. For instance, the important questions about households' intertemporal holding, accumulation, and decumulation of consumption goods, money, and debt cannot be analyzed within this framework. Furthermore, it does not allow us to examine the adjustment mechanisms that are present when there is imperfect foresight on the part of the household.

A more fruitful approach to the formulation of an intertemporal theory of the household, useful in deriving propositions about the behavior of dynamic variables, is to introduce such variables explicitly into the decision-making process. As a first step in this direction we shall employ a set of theorems by T.C. Koopmans and derive an appropriate intertemporal utility function.

Koopmans examined the assumptions that a preference ordering defined over infinite horizon streams must satisfy in order to give rise to a utility function of the form

$$J(X) = \sum_{i=1}^{\infty} U(X_i)\alpha^i \tag{II.2.1}$$

where $X \in Y \subset R^\infty$ and X_i is the ith component of X, U has a continuous derivative, and α^i is the discount factor (Koopmans, 1972). Koopmans posited the existence of a complete preference ordering over infinite consumption streams and showed that if

(a)   the preference ordering is continuous,
(b)   consumption in period 1 is preferentially independent of consumption in periods 2, 3, 4, 5 . . . ,
(c)   consumption in period 2 is preferentially independent of consumption in periods 1, 3, 4, 5 . . . ,
(d)   consumption in periods 1 and 2 is pairwise preferentially independent of consumption in periods 3, 4, 5, 6 . . . ,
(e)   the preference ordering is stationary,[5]

then this preference ordering gives rise to a separable multiplicative utility function such as equation II.2.1.

These results can be extended to continuous consumption streams. In this case, $X(t)$ denotes the rate of consumption at time t, and $X(t)\Delta t$ is the actual consumption in the time interval Δt. If we let t range over the closed interval $[0, T]$, divide this interval into n equal parts of length $\Delta t = T/n$, and choose a point t_i from the ith interval, then we can let $n \rightarrow \infty$ and obtain

$$J[X(t)] = \lim_{n \to \infty} \sum_{i=1}^{n} U(X(t_i)) \, \alpha^{t_i} \Delta t = \int_0^T U(X(t)) \, \alpha^t dt$$

which is a separable and multiplicative utility function. Here we have specialized Koopmans's results to a finite-time-horizon problem. This form of the intertemporal utility function excludes Hicksian complementarity over time.[6] The factor α^t will be interpreted as an exponential discount factor (i.e., $\alpha^t = \exp(-\rho t)$, where ρ is the individual's rate of time preference).

We further reinterpret Koopmans's results and allow the household to derive utility from bequests. This is accomplished by attributing to the household a separable utility-of-bequest function $\beta(\overline{X}(T))$, where $\overline{X}(T)$ represents the amount the household could have consumed before T but did not.[7] Bequests can be interpreted as consumption in the $T + 1$ period, and hence the Koopmans theorem can be applied without modification.

Therefore, the representative household solves the following optimization problem:

$$\max_{\{X(t)\}} \int_0^T U(X(t)) \exp(-\rho t)\, dt + \beta \overline{X}(T)) \qquad X(t) \in \Omega \quad \text{(II.2.2)}$$

where Ω is the set of all feasible consumption streams (i.e., it is the household's choice set). Both U and β have first-order derivatives over the relevant domains.

II.3   Definition of commodities, demand, markets, and prices

There exist three commodities in this economy, a physical good, a private debt instrument, and non-interest-bearing government debt. The physical good is a consumption good that is consumed and stored by the household. If stored, it will deteriorate at a constant rate δ. Let $C(t)$ be the amount of the good in physical units that the representative household possesses at time t.

The non-interest-bearing debt of the government, which we shall call money, exists in a fixed amount in the economy and is denominated in units of money. Let $M(t)$ be the amount of money that the representative household holds at time t.

The private debt instruments are perpetuities that return one unit of money's worth of such bonds per time unit. Let $B(t)$ denote the stock of bonds in units of bonds held by the household at time t. If $B(t)$ is positive, then the household is a net lender; if $B(t)$ is negative, the household is a net borrower.

All three commodities are allowed to be used as media of exchange as well as stores of value for carrying forward purchasing power. Hence any commodity can exchange for any other in the three markets (i.e., the market where bonds and money exchange, the market where the consumption good and money exchange, and the market where the consumption good and bonds exchange).

Transactions will initially be modeled as flows (i.e., as piecewise-continuous functions of time). The variable $D_X(t)$ represents the rate at which the commodity D is demanded in exchange for commodity X at time t. It is al-

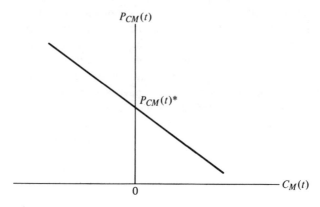

Figure II.1

lowed to assume nonpositive values: if $D_X(t) \leq 0$, then the household desires to supply commodity D in exchange for commodity X at time t. Thus, the individual transaction remains unidentified. This modeling of transactions includes as a special case the traditional instantaneous stock-shift type of discrete transactions in which the transactions variable $D_X(t)$ is zero throughout $[0, T]$ except at a set of points of measure zero.

In an economy with three goods, we can define six demand variables for each household: $C_M(t)$ and $C_B(t)$ represent the rates at which the consumption good is demanded in exchange for money and bonds, respectively; $B_C(t)$ and $B_M(t)$ represent the rates at which bonds are demanded in exchange for the consumption good and money, respectively; $M_C(t)$ and $M_B(t)$ represent the rates at which money is demanded in exchange for the consumption good and bonds. These variables are not constrained to be positive and are denominated in the units of the commodity that is demanded; that is, $C_M(t)$ and $C_B(t)$ are denominated in units of the consumption good, $B_C(t)$ and $B_M(t)$ in units of bonds, and $M_B(t)$ and $M_C(t)$ in units of money.

This information can be summarized in a transactions matrix:

$$D(t) = \begin{bmatrix} 0 & M_C(t) & M_B(t) \\ C_M(t) & 0 & C_B(t) \\ B_M(t) & B_C(t) & 0 \end{bmatrix} \qquad (\text{II.3.1})$$

Let $P_{XY}(t)$ denote the price of commodity X in terms of commodity Y at time t; thus $P_{CM}(t)$ is the price of the consumption good in terms of money. Hence there exist six prices: $P_{CM}(t)$, $P_{CB}(t)$, $P_{MC}(t)$, $P_{MB}(t)$, $P_{BC}(t)$, and $P_{BM}(t)$. However, only three of them are independent, because $P_{CM}(t) = 1/P_{MC}(t)$, $P_{MB}(t) = 1/P_{BM}(t)$, and $P_{CB}(t) = 1/P_{BC}(t)$.

The household's demand curves at any point in time can be represented diagramatically as in Figure II.1. If the market price $P_{CM}(t)$ is below $P_{CM}(t)^*$, then the household will demand $C_M(t)$, as indicated. If the price of consumption goods in terms of money is above $P_{CM}(t)^*$, then the household will supply the consumption good in exchange for money; that is, it will demand money in exchange for the consumption good.

Because the household derives utility from the consumption of the physical good only, it will be desirable to express the rates of demand in terms of this good. Hence $M_C(t)/P_{CM}(t) \equiv m_C(t)$ represents the rate at which the household demands money in exchange for the consumption good, and this demand is denominated in units of the consumption good. Similarly, $B_M(t)/P_{BC}(t) \equiv b_M(t)$ represents the rate, in units of the consumption good, at which the household demands bonds in exchange for money. We define the real transactions matrix by

$$d(t) = \begin{bmatrix} 0 & \dfrac{M_C(t)}{P_{CM}(t)} & \dfrac{M_B(t)}{P_{CM}(t)} \\ C_M(t) & 0 & C_B(t) \\ \dfrac{B_M(t)}{P_{CB}(t)} & \dfrac{B_C(t)}{P_{CB}(t)} & 0 \end{bmatrix} \equiv \begin{bmatrix} 0 & m_C(t) & m_B(t) \\ C_M(t) & 0 & C_B(t) \\ b_M(t) & b_C(t) & 0 \end{bmatrix} \qquad (\text{II.3.2})$$

A price system is consistent if $P_{XY}P_{YZ} = P_{XZ}$, where P_{XY} is the price of X in terms of Y, P_{YZ} is the price of Y in terms of Z, and P_{XZ} is the price of X in terms of Z, for all commodities X, Y, and Z. A necessary and sufficient condition for prices to be consistent in our three-good economy is that $P_{CB}P_{BM} = P_{CM}$ and $P_{CM}P_{MB} = P_{CB}$, because this implies also that $P_{MC}P_{CB} = P_{MB}$. Here we have made use of the fact that $P_{XY} = 1/P_{YX}$.[8] The introduction of costly transactions in the next section admits the possibility of inconsistent price systems.

II.4   Definition of a transactions technology

An essential ingredient in a theory of a monetary economy with explicit accumulation and decumulation asset dynamics is the requirement that transacting use real resources. The cost of transacting originates from two sources. First, there is the direct cost of effecting the exchange of one commodity for another between two traders at a given price. Second, the process of establishing an equilibrium price consumes resources.

We propose to view transactions as a commodity or service, the production of which uses real resources. Demand for this transactions good is comple-

mentary to the market activities of the household, and it is a direct conse-
quence of a technological relationship that dictates the amount of the transactions good needed to carry out a desired level of transactions activities. The
transactions activity of the household is summarized in its transactions matrix $D(t)$ (see equation II.3.1) or $d(t)$ (see equation II.3.2). We shall assume
that the transactions-good demand function has as variables the entries in
$d(t)$. Hence, $T^d: R^6 \rightarrow R^1$; that is $T^d(t) = T^d(d(t))$, where $T^d(t)$ represents
the rate at which the transactions good is demanded. The function T^d is assumed to be differentiable and strictly convex (i.e., this economy is characterized by increasing costs of transacting). (The assumption of strict convexity
will be relaxed in Chapter V.) Also, for now, the function $T^d(t)$ is assumed
to be invariant over time; this means that the existing institutional framework for making transactions is perceived as given and unchanging.[9]

Corresponding to the transactions-good demand function there exists a
supply function with capital and labor as inputs. This supply function represents the amounts of capital and labor that must be relinquished to produce a
given amount of the transactions good. The household may purchase the
transactions good from the transactions-good sector, rather than spend its
time and resources transacting and collecting information about market variables. Each household may generate a different transactions-good demand
function.[10] If $T^{di}d(t)_i$ is the rate at which the ith household demands the
transactions good, then $\sum_{i=1}^{n} T^{di}d(t)_i$ is the economy's aggregate demand for
the transactions good.

In order to maintain the analytical convenience of a single-sector economy,
we assume that the relative price of the transactions good and the consumption good is fixed, and furthermore we calibrate the transactions good so that
this relative price is equal to unity.[11] Viewed in this way, the consumption of
the transactions good is an additional absorption of aggregate supply in the
macroeconomic sense.

Explicit recognition of the fact that transactions cannot be made costlessly
removes the indeterminacy about how transactions take place and about the
role of the medium of exchange by introducing an economic motive for optimizing the arrangement of exchanges. Furthermore, the approach outlined
earlier allows us to introduce costly transactions into a dynamic general-
equilibrium model with intertemporal agents without complicating the structure to an analytically intractable extent.

II.5   Definition of the household's choice set

The first set of constraints that the household faces defines its trading possibilities in each of the three markets. In particular, it is required that the demand for commodity X in exchange for commodity Y be equal to the negative

of the demand for commodity Y in exchange for commodity X times the price of Y in terms of X; that is,

$$M_C(t) = -C_M(t)\,P_{CM}(t) \qquad\qquad (\text{II.5.1})$$

$$M_B(t) = -B_M(t)\,P_{BM}(t) \qquad\qquad (\text{II.5.2})$$

$$B_C(t) = -C_B(t)\,P_{CB}(t) \qquad\qquad (\text{II.5.3})$$

Hence, the household is not allowed to acquire a unit of one commodity without relinquishing an amount of another commodity equal to the exchange rate between the two commodities. Using these constraints and defining $\Pi(t) \equiv P_{CB}(t)/(P_{CM}(t)P_{MB}(t))$ and $\mathrm{III}(t) \equiv P_{CM}(t)/(P_{CB}(t)P_{BM}(t))$, we can rewrite the real transactions demand matrix as

$$d(t) = \begin{bmatrix} 0 & -C_M(t) & -b_M(t)\Pi(t) \\ C_M(t) & 0 & -C_B(t) \\ b_M(t) & C_B(t) & 0 \end{bmatrix} \qquad (\text{II.5.4})$$

Because $P_{CM}(t)P_{MB}(t) = P_{CB}(t)$ implies that $d(t) = -d(t)'$, where the prime denotes the matrix transposition operator, we have shown that $d(t)$ is skew symmetric if the price system is consistent.

In the Arrow-Debreu type of neoclassical general-equilibrium model the household's transactions behavior is constrained by a relationship of the form $p \cdot X \le W$; that is, the inner product of the price vector $p \in R^n$ and quantity vector $X \in R^n$ must be less than or equal to endowments W. In the intertemporal interpretation of this model, commodities are dated and prices are present prices. Wealth is the present value of the household's assets and is required to be positive. (This latter constraint is analogous to the resource constraint that will be developed later.) Thus interpreted, the constraint $p \cdot X \le W$ forces the present value of outlays less the present value of receipts to be smaller than or equal to the present value of the household's wealth. The transactions or budget constraint written in this Walrasian form is a constraint on total demand flows: Total net expenditure must be less than or equal to total wealth.[12]

Corresponding to this type of Walrasian budget constraint, we can define total real demand flows for each commodity by

$$C(t) = C_M(t) + C_B(t)$$

$$M(t)/P_{CM}(t) \equiv m(t) = m_C(t) + m_B(t)$$

$$B(t)/P_{CB}(t) \equiv b(t) = b_C(t) + b_M(t)$$

and form the sum of these demands:

$$C_M(t) + m_C(t) + C_B(t) + b_C(t) + m_B(t) + b_M(t) = 0 \qquad (\text{II.5.5})$$

Substitution of the transactions flow constraints (II.5.1, II.5.2, II.5.3) into equation II.5.5 reveals that equation II.5.5 is satisfied if and only if the price system is consistent.[13] Hence, if the transactions flow constraints are obeyed, and if the price system is consistent, then the corresponding Walrasian budget constraint is also satisfied. If, instead of normalizing $B_M(t)$ by $P_{CB}(t)$, we normalize $B_M(t)$ by $P_{CM}(t) P_{MB}(t)$, then the intertemporal demand functions will always satisfy the Walrasian budget constraint regardless of whether or not the price system is consistent.

The obvious difficulty with formulating a constraint on transactions in terms of total demand flows, as in the work of Walras (1954) and Debreu (1959), is that it implicitly affords the household complete freedom to decide arbitrarily which commodities to exchange when trading. Thus, such a constraint is appropriate only in a barter economy in which transacting is costless. Another important reason that the Walras-Debreu type of general-equilibrium model does not admit a medium of exchange in any meaningful way is the existence of unlimited forward markets that allow all exchanges to be negotiated at the economy's starting point.[14] Similarly, in a world of uncertainty, the assumption that financial markets are complete (i.e., the number of state-contingent claims is equal to the number of possible contingent states of the world) also rules out a useful role for a medium of exchange.

In the Walras-Debreu model a centralized auctioneer is presumed to establish, in a converging tâtonnement process, an equilibrium price vector $\tilde{P}(t) = (\tilde{P}_{CM}(t), \tilde{P}_{CB}(t), \tilde{P}_{BM}(t)) \ \forall \ t \in [0,T]$ that clears all markets on the interval $[0,T]$. Alternatively, it is assumed that households have rational expectations; that is, by the beginning of the interval $[0,T]$ the households have obtained $\tilde{P}(t) \ \forall \ t \in [0,T]$ through a converging learning process. If financial markets are complete, then the introduction of uncertainty in the form of random endowments on the interval $[0,T]$ will not alter the basic model. The uncertainty is contracted away with contingent claims whose prices are established in a complete complement of financial markets. The equilibrium $\tilde{P}(t)$ so obtained is efficient in the sense of Pareto.

This tâtonnement and the learning process that establish $\tilde{P}(t)$ are assumed to be costless and timeless; that is, the households enter the interval $[0,T]$ with full knowledge of $\tilde{P}(t)$. In the tâtonnement or learning process, all contracts are nonbinding until $\tilde{P}(t)$ is established. We shall maintain the assumptions of timelessness in these two types of recontracting processes until Chapter VII. However, we shall dispense with the assumption that the process that at $t = 0$ brings about $\tilde{P}(t) \ \forall \ t \in [0,T]$ is costless. The costs of establishing the equilibrium price vector and equilibrium exchanges are allocated to the potential traders in the form of a tax on transacting that varies according to the sizes and types of their desired trading flows. Furthermore, we assume that the actual exchange of two commodities involves transactions costs.

The two types of costs (i.e., market-clearing costs and transactions costs) are captured in the transactions technology $T^d (C_M(t), C_B(t), b_M(t) \, \Pi \, (t))$ and are payable at the time the transactions take place. In the tâtonnement process of Walras and Debreu the auctioneer determines the equilibrium price vector $\tilde{P}(t) \; \forall \; t \in [0,T]$. The determination of the set of equilibrium trades among the n individuals in the m goods is left unspecified. It is implicitly assumed that the process by which the set of equilibrium trades is determined is costless. The computational complexity of an efficient algorithm that establishes a set of equilibrium trades at each $t \in [0,T]$ is a proxy for the actual cost of finding the set of equilibrium trades in the absence of an auctioneer (i.e., through decentralized exchanges). It can easily be shown that the order of magnitude of the number of steps necessary for an algorithm to produce the equilibrium set of trades decreases with the introduction of a medium of exchange. The requirement that equilibria be Pareto-efficient dictates such an innovation, because these costs are being charged against the trading households. The behaviors of such costs, together with the costs of transacting, determine the properties of the transactions technology. Furthermore, because the process of finding the set of equilibrium trades consumes real resources, it is optimal that the set of equilibrium trades at $t^* \in [0,T]$ be established at $t = t^*$ and not at $t = 0$. Hence the medium of exchange will not be displaced by the household's binding commitment, made at time t, to exchange a stated amount of two goods at a price arrived at in a tâtonnement at $t = 0$. Thus, forward contracts established at $t = 0$ are complete only up to the amounts to be exchanged.[15] Even though transactions occurring on the interval $[0,T]$ are contracted at $t = 0$, the use of a medium of exchange has not been displaced by forward contracts.

If financial markets are incomplete, then a residual of uncertainty remains, and the optimizing behavior of the households will reflect such uncertainty. Unexpected changes in prices or endowments will induce a household to remaximize. In Chapter VII we shall consider economies in which timeless tâtonnement and complete markets are absent.

In order to be able to analyze the household's mode of transacting and, in particular, its use of money within a choice-theoretical framework, it is necessary to decompose the total demand flow so as to identify explicitly the possible types of exchanges. Once these choice variables, together with the transactions flow constraints, have been introduced into the household's intertemporal optimization model, then the transactions technology and the utility maximization hypothesis or cost minimization[16] hypothesis determine the household's optimal exchange behavior, which is summarized in its transactions matrix.

An alternative method of introducing a medium of exchange into a barter economy is by decree (i.e., by assuming that all entries in the transactions matrix are zero except the first row and first column). This method was first adopted by Clower,[17] who introduced the dictum that "money buys goods and goods buy money; but goods do not buy goods," and it has been used more recently by Benassy (1975). But the absence of a choice-theoretical mechanism for deciding on the type of exchange denies any usefulness to money as a medium of exchange or as a store of purchasing power, because a positive rate of return on bond holdings will be a sufficient deterrent against conducting transactions in money or against holding money as a store of purchasing power.

The introduction of a transactions technology in the form of a transactions-good demand function and transactions constraints constitutes one of the reasons the household's intertemporal optimization problem will lead to the existence of nonzero levels of inventories of some or all of the three commodities. Another important motive for stock holding is the need to allocate consumption and endowments optimally over the interval $[0, T]$. If the utility function of the household is such that a smooth consumption path is desired, then the variability in the rate at which the household receives its endowment will mandate the holding of bond and consumption-good inventories. Also, variability in the expected path of prices may lead to speculative stock holding.

Transactions constraints establish interdependencies among the stock-holding decisions of the households. In particular, the accumulation of one stock must lead to the decumulation of the stock of the commodity that was used to purchase it, if all flows remain unchanged. Alternatively, the household could increase the inflow of the commodity used in exchange and thereby increase the outflow of a third commodity and hence decrease its stock if other rates of exchange remain constant.

At any given time, the household's stock of the three commodities is given by the solution to the first-order system of three nonlinear, nonautonomous ordinary differential equations. For example, the money stock that is held by the individual household is characterized by the solution for

$$\frac{dM(t)}{dt} = M_C(t) + M_B(t) \qquad M(0) = M_0$$

The commodity stock held by the household is given by the solution for

$$\frac{dC(t)}{dt} = C_M(t) + C_B(t) - \phi(t) - T^d(t) - \delta C(t) + X(t) \qquad C(0) = C_0$$

where $\phi(t)$ is the rate at which the household consumes out of the consumption-good inventory, and δ is the rate at which this inventory deteriorates. Because we have combined the consumption-good sector and transactions-good sector on the supply side by holding the relative price at unity, the demand for the transactions good, given by $T^d(t)$, will be satisfied from the stock of the consumption good. $X(t)$ is the rate at which the household receives its endowment. Lastly, the equation for the bond stock is

$$\frac{dB(t)}{dt} = B_M(t) + B_C(t) + P_{MB}(t)B(t) \qquad B(0) = B_0$$

Because each bond pays one unit of money per time period in bonds, $P_{MB}(t)B(t)$ is the rate at which interest payment accrues on a bond stock of size $B(t)$. M_0, C_0, and B_0 are the endowments of nominal money, consumption goods, and nominal bonds that the household receives at $t = 0$. If

$$\frac{dP_{CM}}{dt}\frac{1}{P_{CM}} \equiv \hat{P}_{CM} \quad \text{and} \quad \frac{dP_{CB}}{dt}\frac{1}{P_{CB}} \equiv \hat{P}_{CB}$$

(the notation $\hat{}$ denotes proportional change throughout), then the three accumulation equations can be written in terms of the consumption good in the following way:

$$\frac{dm(t)}{dt} = m_C(t) + m_B(t) - \hat{P}_{CM}(t)m(t) \qquad (\text{II.5.6})$$

$$\frac{dC(t)}{dt} = C_M(t) + C_B(t) - \phi(t) - T^d(t) - \delta C(t) + X(t) \qquad (\text{II.5.7})$$

$$\frac{db(t)}{dt} = b_C(t) + b_M(t) - (\hat{P}_{CB}(t) - P_{MB}(t))b(t) \qquad (\text{II.5.8})[18]$$

We can further reduce the number of variables by substituting the transactions flow constraints into the accumulation equations:

$$\frac{dm(t)}{dt} = -C_M(t) - b_M(t)\Pi(t) - \hat{P}_{CM}(t)m(t) \qquad m(0) = M_0 \qquad (\text{II.5.9})$$

$$\frac{dC(t)}{dt} = C_M(t) + C_B(t) - \phi - T^d(t) - \delta C(t) + X(t)$$

$$C(0) = C_0 \quad (\text{II.5.10})$$

$$\frac{db(t)}{dt} = -C_B(t) + b_M(t) - (\hat{P}_{CB}(t) - P_{MB}(t))b(t)$$

$$b(0) = B_0 \quad (\text{II.5.11})[19]$$

The actual real wealth of a household at time t is given by

$$w(t) = C(t) + m(t) + b(t) \qquad (\text{II.5.12})$$

and the household's rate of accumulation of wealth is

$$\frac{dw(t)}{dt} = \frac{dC(t)}{dt} + \frac{dm(t)}{dt} + \frac{db(t)}{dt} \qquad \text{(II.5.13)}$$

(i.e., the sum of the accumulation equations II.5.6, II.5.7, and II.5.8). We can rewrite equation II.5.13 and obtain

$$\frac{dw(t)}{dt} = X(t) - \phi(t) - \hat{P}_{CM}(t)m(t) - \delta C(t) - (\hat{P}_{CB}(t) - P_{MB}(t))b(t)$$
$$- T^d(t) + b_M(t) - b_M(t)\Pi(t) \quad \text{(II.5.14)}$$

which says that the rate of saving, $dw(t)/dt$, equals the rate at which the household receives its endowment minus (a) the rate at which it consumes, (b) the rate at which the three stocks deteriorate, (c) the rate at which it uses the consumption good for transactions purposes, and (d) a valuation gain due to inconsistent prices. If $T^d \equiv 0$ and there is no stock holding, then $dw(t)/dt = X(t) - \phi(t) \ \forall \ t \in [0,T]$; that is, savings equals endowment less consumption.

In order to avoid confusion over the number of constraints, it is important to realize that equations II.5.12, II.5.13, and II.5.14 are implied by the transactions flow constraints and do not constitute independent constraints. We have merely defined a new wealth variable.

In addition to the flow constraints, the household faces a resource stock constraint that restricts its ability to issue bonds in unlimited quantities. If the household is a net issuer of bonds, then it adds negative amounts to its stock of bonds. There are three ways in which to bound the stock of bonds held by a household.[20] First, the household may be constrained to have non-negative total wealth at each point in time:

$$w(t) = m(t) + C(t) + b(t) \geq 0 \qquad \forall \ t \in [0,T] \qquad \text{(II.5.15)}$$

This form of the resource constraint forces household borrowing to be less than or equal to its holding of money and consumption goods. Equation II.5.15 represents an institutional environment in which every loan must be backed in full value by a collateral asset and in which the value of the collateral asset is determined by the current real value of the household's commodity and money stocks rather than by the value of the inventories of these two assets at the date the bond was issued. Therefore, if bonds are issued to finance consumption goods, then these consumption goods themselves can be used as collateral security at the time of purchase. However, any subsequent deterioration, consumption, or decrease in price of the consumption good means that the collateral is losing value. The difficulty with a constraint of this type is that it rules out the use of the capitalized future income stream as collateral security, and hence it does not admit a life-cycle explanation of consumption and saving.

$P_{BC}(t)$	price of bonds in terms of consumption goods
$P_{BM}(t)$	price of bonds in terms of money
$P_{CB}(t)$	price of consumption goods in terms of bonds
$P_{CM}(t)$	price of consumption goods in terms of money
$P_{MB}(t)$	price of money in terms of bonds
$P_{MC}(t)$	price of money in terms of consumption goods
$q(t)$	$\equiv (m(t),C(t),b(t))$
T	length of household's life
$T^d(C_M(t),C_B(t),b_M(t)\Pi(t))$	transactions technology
T_i^d	first-order partial derivative of T^d with respect to the ith variable of T^d
T_{ij}^d	second-order partial derivative of T^d with respect to the ith and jth variables of T^d
$v(t)$	$\equiv (C_M(t),C_B(t),b_M(t),\phi(t))$
$X(t)$	rate at which the household receives consumption-good endowments
$\beta(m(T),C(T),b(T))$	utility-of-bequest function
β_i	first-order partial derivative of β with respect to the ith variable of β
β_{ij}	second-order partial derivative of β with respect to the ith and jth variables of β
$\delta(t)$	rate at which the consumption-good inventory deteriorates
ϵ	effective
$\lambda(t)$	$\equiv (\lambda_M(t),\lambda_C(t),\lambda_B(t))$
$\lambda_B(t)$	present shadow price of an exogenous increase in the real stock of bonds
$\lambda_C(t)$	present shadow price of an exogenous increase in the stock of consumption goods
$\lambda_M(t)$	present shadow price of an exogenous increase in the real stock of money
$\Pi(t)$	$\equiv P_{CB}(t)/(P_{CM}(t)P_{MB}(t))$
ρ	rate of time preference
$\mathrm{III}(t)$	$\equiv P_{CM}(t)/(P_{CB}(t)P_{BM}(t))$
$\char`\^$	proportional rate of change, $(dx/dt)(1/x)$
$\sim$	market-clearing equilibrium value of variable
$\phi(t)$	rate at which the household consumes out of the consumption-good inventory

CHAPTER I

Introduction

In this book we shall describe the dynamic properties and the optimality of movements in prices and quantities in an aggregate economy with an explicitly modelled transactions and market technology. An analysis of the rational dynamic-optimization behavior of the economy's constituent members and of the mechanisms coordinating their plans will provide the basis for our conclusions.

The process of formulation and analysis of optimization models of individual agents for the purpose of constructing a choice-theoretical foundation for macroeconomic models has a long tradition (e.g., Ando and Modigliani, 1963; Baumol, 1952a; Friedman, 1957; Grossman, 1972; Phelps, 1969; Witte, 1963). Yet the existing literature is generally subject to two criticisms.

First, most attempts at providing microeconomic foundations for aggregative economic models have had a partial-equilibrium character.[1] However, because macroeconomic models inherently have a general-equilibrium nature, the appropriateness of such attempts is suspect. For example, it is well understood that many of the prevalent Keynesian specifications of the components of aggregate demand and supply relationships cannot be obtained from individual optimization models within the context of a general-equilibrium framework (Barro and Grossman, 1971; Benassy, 1975; Lucas and Sargent, 1979). In particular, recent literature has brought to light the difficulties of establishing a well-defined demand for money in Walrasian general-equilibrium models.[2] Hence, attempts to incorporate money into macroeconomic models, which are structurally similar to small Walrasian models, have been unsuccessful (Patinkin, 1965).

Second, analyses aimed at providing microeconomic foundations for dynamic macroeconomic models have neglected the importance of intertemporal considerations in the agents' optimization problems. As a result, the importance of expectations formation and of the effects of expectations on the dynamics of prices and quantities in macroeconomies, as well as on the efficacy of government policies, has been underestimated.[3] In particular, the dynamics of properly anticipated prices in assets markets differ radically from the dynamics of prices in markets in which expectations are not rational (Lucas, 1978; Samuelson, 1965). Finally, an analysis of intertemporal accumulation and exchange behavior, together with a model of the formation of price and quantity expectations, is a prerequisite for understanding the inherently dynamic adjustments of prices and quantities in non-Walrasian economies (Leijonhufvud, 1968).

In this book we seek to remedy these shortcomings in two ways. First, we shall model and analyze the agent's intertemporal optimization problem. The model captures both the dynamics of intertemporal asset accumulation and the effect of expectations on current plans. The transactions of the agents are subject to an explicitly modeled transactions technology. Second we shall formulate a dynamic general-equilibrium model of the aggregate economy, which consists of overlapping generations of agents with finite lives (Cass and Yaari, 1966; Samuelson, 1958). The paradigm that all markets clear instantaneously and that agents properly anticipate all future equilibrium prices will be dropped in later chapters by admitting the possibility of incorrect expectations as well as nonzero excess market demands. Because a revision of expectations alters current behavior, spot market equilibria are only temporary when agents incorrectly anticipate future price and quantity variables. Because of price adjustments of finite speed, it is also possible that spot markets do not clear. We shall permit both kinds of disequilibria (i.e., inconsistent plans and nonzero excess demands in spot markets).

Two sets of forces determine the dynamics and optimality of the movements in prices and quantities in this economy: The dynamics of the agents' optimal asset-accumulation activities and trading activities, as determined by their transactions and expectations-formation technologies, define the intertemporal behavior of notional market demands and supplies. The properties of the market-clearing mechanism, which coordinates the agents' plans, determine the dynamics of effective market quantities and prices.

The assumptions employed to characterize the behavior of agents as well as the institutional background of the economy (e.g., curvature and continuity requirements, rational-expectations and optimization hypotheses, and the properties of the market-clearing mechanism) have been chosen so as to be compatible with a substantial body of the existing literature. Hence the properties that are derived are generic to a large class of economies and permit a consolidation of many diverse results obtained in the literature from widely differing models. Furthermore, the aggregation of all commodities into three classes (i.e., monetary, credit, and physical goods) allows for a direct application of the results to dynamic macroeconomic models.

In the first part of this book we shall develop the rational dynamic maximization problem of the finite-life agents. Three aggregate classes of commodities (i.e., money, debt, and physical goods) can be held as assets, and they all can be exchanged for one another subject to a transactions technology. This transactions technology embodies the costs of transacting and con-

Second, the household may be constrained to have nonnegative net worth at any point in time. Here the term "net worth" includes capitalization of future income streams.[21] For a household with life span $[0,T]$, this constraint takes the form

$$w(t) + \int_t^T \left[\frac{dm(t)}{dt} + \frac{dC(t)}{dt} + \frac{db(t)}{dt}\right] \exp\left(-\int_t^\tau P_{MB}(x)\,dx\right) d\tau \geq 0$$

$$\forall\, t \in [0,T] \quad \text{(II.5.16)}$$

Alternatively, constraint II.5.16 can be written as

$$w(t) + \int_t^T \frac{dw(\tau)}{d\tau} \exp\left(-\int_t^\tau P_{MB}(s)\,ds\right) d\tau \geq 0 \qquad \forall\, t \in [0,T] \quad \text{(II.5.17)}$$

that is, current wealth plus the present value of future saving must be nonnegative.

A third way of formulating the resource constraint is to require the household to have nonnegative stock holding at the end of its life:

$$w(t) = m(T) + C(T) + b(T) \geq 0 \quad \text{(II.5.18)}$$

It is easily shown that equations II.5.15 and II.5.16 or II.5.17 imply II.5.18. The converse, however, is not always true.

Lastly, the household must abide by nonnegativity conditions for the money stock, the consumption-good stock, and the rate at which it consumes out of the stock of consumption goods:

$$m(t) \geq 0, \qquad C(t) \geq 0, \qquad \phi(t) \geq 0 \qquad \forall\, t \in [0,T] \quad \text{(II.5.19)}$$

The transaction flow constraints II.5.1, II.5.2, and II.5.3, together with the accumulation equations II.5.6, II.5.7, and II.5.8, the resource constraint in the form of II.5.15 or II.5.16 or II.5.18, and the nonnegativity conditions II.5.19, define the feasible set Ω for the choice variables contained in $\tilde{d}(t)$ and $\phi(t)$ (see equation II.3.1).

The foregoing analysis of the household's feasible set demonstrates (1) that there exists only a flow constraint in the form of transactions flow constraints II.5.1, II.5.2, and II.5.3 and the accumulation equations II.5.6, II.5.7, and II.5.8 or the simpler version

$$\frac{dw(t)}{dt} = \frac{dC(t)}{dt} + \frac{dm(t)}{dt} + \frac{db(t)}{dt}$$

$$= X(t) - \phi(t) - T^d(t) - \hat{P}_{CM}(t)m(t) - \delta C(t)$$

$$- (\hat{P}_{CM}(t) - P_{MB}(t))b(t) + b_M(t) - b_M(t)\Pi(t)$$

and (2) that there exists no stock constraint of the form

$$w(t) = m(t) + C(t) + b(t) \qquad \forall\, t \in [0,T]$$

because the variable $w(t)$ has been arbitrarily introduced and is not a choice variable. Thus the analysis suggests that the use of two constraints, which originated with Sidrauski (1967) and Brainard and Tobin (1968), is redundant. This can be verified by closer examination of the Sidrauski model (Appendix A).

Indeed, analysis of the foregoing choice set of the intertemporal household generates the following general proposition: As long as stocks change continually, a stock constraint is unnecessary. If transactions occur at discrete points in time (see Chapter III), then there still is no need for a stock constraint, provided that exchange possibilities are completely specified.[22] However, if time is arbitrarily divided into discrete periods, such as Hicksian weeks, and the values of variables are determined only at the beginning or end of each of these periods, then a stock constraint may be required. The need for a stock constraint arises only because the mode of exchange during the period is not explicitly specified (Foley, 1975).

The intertemporal maximization problem of the household, as given by equation II.2.2, is now completely specified:[23]

$$\max \int_0^T U(\phi(t)) \exp\left(-\rho t\right) dt + \beta[m(T),C(T),b(T)] \qquad \text{(II.5.20)}$$

subject to

$$\frac{dm(t)}{dt} = m_C(t) + m_B(t) - \hat{P}_{CM}(t)m(t)$$

$$\frac{dC(t)}{dt} = C_M(t) + C_B(t) - \delta C(t) - T^d(t) - \phi(t) + X(t)$$

$$\frac{db(t)}{dt} = b_C(t) + b_M(t) - (\hat{P}_{CB}(t) - P_{MB}(t))b(t)$$

$$m(0) = m_0, \qquad C(0) = C_0, \qquad b(0) = b_0$$

$$m(t) \geq 0, \qquad C(t) \geq 0, \qquad \phi(t) \geq 0 \qquad \forall\, t \in [0,T]$$

$$m(T) + b(T) + C(T) \geq 0$$

Thus, the household's intertemporal optimization problem consists of finding piecewise-continuous arcs $C(t)$, $m(t)$, $b(t)$, $\tilde{d}(t)$, and $\phi(t)$ with $t \in [0,T]$ such that these arcs are contained in the choice set Ω and maximize the stock of present utility. In doing so, the household simultaneously trades present for future consumption flow, selects the form in which to carry forward purchasing power (i.e., money, bonds, or consumption-good stocks), and minimizes the use of real resources when transacting.

Before deriving the first-order conditions for an extremum for problem II.5.20, we shall simplify the problem by eliminating some of the nonnegativity conditions and by substituting the transactions constraints directly into the accumulation equations. The nonnegativity of $\phi(t)$, the rate at which the household consumes the consumption good, is assured by assumption

$$\lim U'(\phi(t)) = 0 \quad \text{as } \phi(t) \to 0^+ \tag{II.5.21}$$

which is due to Cass (1965).[24] Hence the integral of discounted utility diverges to $-\infty$ as $\phi(t) \to 0$. Similarly, we eliminate the resource constraint by requiring that

$$\lim \beta(m(T),C(T),b(T)) \to -\infty \quad \text{as } m(T) + b(T) + C(T) \to 0^+ \tag{II.5.22}$$

Thus the simplified intertemporal maximization problem takes the following form:[25]

$$\max \int_0^T U(\phi(t)) \exp(-\rho t)\, dt + \beta(m(T),C(T),b(T)) \tag{II.5.23}$$

subject to

$$\frac{dm(t)}{dt} = -C_M(t) - b_M(t)\Pi(t) - \hat{P}_{CM}(t)m(t)$$

$$\frac{dC(t)}{dt} = C_M(t) + C_B(t) - \delta C(t) - \delta C(t) - \phi C(t) - T^d(t) + X(t)$$

$$\frac{db(t)}{dt} = -C_B(t) + b_M(t) - (\hat{P}_{CB}(t) - P_{MB}(t))b(t)$$

$$m(0) = m_0, \quad C(0) = C_0, \quad b(0) = b_0$$

$$m(t) \ge 0, \quad C(t) \ge 0, \quad \forall\, t \in [0,T]$$

CHAPTER III

Structure of the intertemporal problem of the household

III.1 Introduction

The purpose of this chapter is to derive and interpret the necessary and sufficient conditions that must be satisfied by optimal solutions to the household's intertemporal maximization problem formulated in equation II.5.23. We shall also analyze the properties of the demand functions that emerge from the maximization problem. In the last section we shall consider nonconvex transactions technologies.

Following Pontryagin and associates (1962), we conceptualize the decision-making process as being divided into two parts. First, the household solves a maximization problem at each point in time. It thereby determines the values of $C_M(t)$, $C_B(t)$, $B_M(t)$, and $\phi(t)$, the endogenous variables that it controls at each instant, as functions of other endogenous and exogenous variables (e.g., its inventories of money bonds and consumption goods and the exogenously given market prices) whose values the household cannot determine at each instant. As time passes, the instantaneous choice variables $C_M(t)$, $C_B(t)$, $B_M(t)$, and $\phi(t)$, determine the values of the evolving dynamic variables through the equations of motion of the latter. The second part of the decision-making process consists in choosing the best path for each of the dynamic variables.

The instantaneous maximization problem yields marginal conditions for the household's exchange and consumption activities at each point in time. Also, it allows us to establish a dual relation between utility maximization and the minimization of resources used in transacting. The dynamic maximization problem yields marginal conditions describing household stock holdings and bequests.

III.2 The instantaneous maximization problem

Let $v(t) = (C_M(t), C_B(t), b_M(t), \phi(t))$ denote an element from the choice set Ω as defined in Section II.5, and let $q(t) = (m(t), C(t), b(t))$ be the corresponding vector of state variables (i.e., of real stock holdings). Following Pontryagin and associates, we define a vector of multiplier functions $\lambda(t) = (\lambda_M(t), \lambda_C(t), \lambda_B(t))$ consisting of one multiplier for each accumulation equa-

22

tion. We form the Lagrangian (also known as the Hamiltonian) of the intertemporal maximization problem as follows:

$$
\begin{aligned}
H(q(t), v(t), \lambda(t), t) = & \; U(\phi(t)) \exp(-\rho t) \\
& + \lambda_M(t) \left(-C_M(t) - b_M(t)\Pi(t) - \hat{P}_{CM}(t)m(t) \right) \\
& + \lambda_C(t) \left(C_M(t) + C_B(t) - \phi(t) - T^d(t) - \delta C(t) + X(t) \right) \\
& + \lambda_B(t) \left(-C_B(t) + b_M(t) - (\hat{P}_{CB}(t) - P_{MB}(t))b(t) \right) \\
& \hspace{5cm} \forall \, t \in [0, T] \qquad \text{(III.2.1)}
\end{aligned}
$$

Next we form the augmented objective function

$$
J[q(t), v(t), \lambda(t)] = \int_0^T H(q(t), v(t), \lambda(t), t) \, dt + \beta(m(T), C(T), b(T))
$$

$$\text{(III.2.2)}$$

As in the finite-dimensional Lagrangian maximization problem, the vectors $q(t)^*$ and $v(t)^*$ will be a solution[1] to problem II.5.23 if and only if there exists a vector $\lambda(t)^*$ such that J has a saddle point at $(q(t)^*, v(t)^*; \lambda(t)^*)$. That is to say, $q(t)^*$ and $v(t)^*$ will be a solution to problem II.5.20 if and only if

$$
J[q(t), v(t); \lambda(t)^*] \le J[q(t)^*, v(t)^*; \lambda(t)^*] \le J[q(t)^*, v(t)^*; \lambda(t)]
$$

for all $v(t) \in \Omega$ and all functions $\lambda(t)$ with at least one piecewise-continuous derivative. Thus, the first-order conditions for a solution to problem II.5.23 can be found by considering all variations in the choice variables that leave $J[\,\cdot\,]$ unchanged.

In particular, it can be shown[2] that if $q(t)^*$ and $v(t)^*$ form a solution to problem II.5.23 or, equivalently, if $J[\,\cdot\,]$ is maximized with respect to $(q(t)^*, v(t)^*)$ and minimized with respect to $\lambda(t)^*$, then

$$
H(q(t)^*, v(t)^*, \lambda(t)^*, t) \ge H(q(t)^*, v(t), \lambda(t)^*, t) \qquad \forall \, v(t) \in \Omega \qquad \text{(III.2.3)}
$$

$$
\frac{\partial H(t)}{\partial \lambda_M(t)} = \frac{dm(t)}{dt} = -C_M(t) - b_M(t)\Pi(t) - \hat{P}_{CM}(t)m(t) \qquad M(0) = M_0
$$

$$
\frac{\partial H(t)}{\partial \lambda_C(t)} = \frac{dC(t)}{dt} = C_M(t) + C_B(t) - \phi(t) - T^d(t) - \delta C(t) + X(t)
$$

$$
C(0) = C_0 \quad \frac{\partial H(t)}{\partial \lambda_B(t)} = \frac{db(t)}{dt}
$$

$$
= -C_B(t) + b_M(t) - (\hat{P}_{CB}(t) - P_{MB}(t))b(t) \qquad B(0) = B_0 \qquad \text{(III.2.4)}
$$

$$
-\frac{\partial H(t)}{\partial m(t)} = \frac{d\lambda_M(t)}{dt} = \hat{P}_{CM}(t)\lambda_M(t)
$$

$$
-\frac{\partial H(t)}{\partial C(t)} = \frac{d\lambda_C(t)}{dt} = \partial\lambda_C(t)
$$

$$-\frac{\partial H(t)}{\partial b(t)} = \frac{d\lambda_B(t)}{dt}$$

$$= (\hat{P}_{CB}(t) - P_{MB}(t))\lambda_B(t) \qquad (III.2.5)$$

$$\lambda_M(t) = \frac{\partial\beta(T)}{\partial m(T)}, \qquad \lambda_C(T) = \frac{\partial\beta(T)}{\partial C(T)}, \qquad \lambda_B(T) = \frac{\partial\beta(T)}{\partial b(T)} \qquad (III.2.6)$$

where all partial derivatives are evaluated along $q(t)^*$, $v(t)^*$, and $\lambda(t)^*$.[3]
Condition III.2.3 is the Maximum Principle. It states that the Hamiltonian
must be maximized with respect to the choice variables at all $t \in [0, T]$.
Equations III.2.4 and III.2.5 are the equations of motion for the system; together with III.2.6 they form a two-point boundary-value problem.

In this section we shall discuss the instantaneous maximization problem
given by the Maximum Principle. The dynamic maximization problem as
given by the two-point boundary-value problem will be discussed in the next
section.

The interpretation of the co-state variable (i.e., $\lambda_M(t)$, $\lambda_C(t)$, and $\lambda_B(t)$) is
similar to the interpretation of Lagrangian multipliers in finite-dimensional
maximization problems. After substituting the equations of motion into the
total differential of $J[\cdot]$ and integrating by parts, we obtain

$$dJ = \lambda_M(0)\frac{dm(0)}{dt} + \lambda_C(0)\,d(C(0)) + \lambda_B(0)\frac{db(0)}{dt} + \int_0^T \frac{\partial H}{\partial v}\,dt$$

According to the Maximum Principle, $\partial H/\partial v = 0$ for all $t \in [0, T]$; therefore

$$\frac{\partial J}{\partial m(0)} = \lambda_M(0), \qquad \frac{\partial J}{\partial C(0)} = \lambda_C(0), \qquad \frac{\partial J}{\partial b(0)} = \lambda_B(0)$$

where all partial derivatives are evaluated at $(q(0)^*, v(0)^*, \lambda(0)^*)$. Hence
$\lambda_M(0)$, $\lambda_C(0)$, and $\lambda_B(0)$ indicate the rate at which the optimal value of J
changes with increases in the initial values of the state variables when the
values of all choice variables are maintained at their optimal levels. Furthermore, Bellman's principle of optimality assures that if any point on the optimal trajectory $(q(t)^*, v(t)^*, \lambda(t)^*)$ is taken as the starting point, then the
path of the choice variables computed from this point will coincide with the
remaining part of the path of the original choice variables (Bellman, 1957).
Hence

$$\frac{\partial J}{\partial m(t)} = \lambda_M(t), \qquad \frac{\partial J}{\partial C(t)} = \lambda_C(t), \qquad \frac{\partial J}{\partial b(t)} = \lambda_B(t) \qquad (III.2.7)$$

for all $t \in [0, T]$, and all partial derivatives are evaluated along $(q(t)^*, v(t)^*,$
$\lambda(t)^*)$. That is, $\lambda_M(t)$, $\lambda_C(t)$, and $\lambda_B(t)$ are the present shadow prices of exogenous increases in the real stock of money, the stock of consumption goods,
and the real stock of bonds, respectively, at time t. These shadow prices are

expressed in units of $J[\cdot]$; they represent the present marginal increase in utility due to exogenous increases in the real stocks of commodities at time t.

The foregoing explanation of the three multiplier functions simplifies the economic interpretation of the Hamiltonian. The first term of the Hamiltonian, $U(\phi(t))\exp(-\rho t)$, represents the present value of the flow of utility from consumption at time t. The second term, $\lambda_M(t)(-C_M(t) - b_M(t)\Pi(t) - \hat{P}_{CM}(t)m(t))$, is the product of the present shadow price of an increase in the real money stock at time t and the rate of increase in the real money stock at the same time t. Therefore, this term represents the present value of the marginal utility due to the increase in the real money stock given by $dm(t)/dt$. The remaining two terms of the Hamiltonian can be interpreted similarly. Thus the Hamiltonian is the present value of the total flow of utility experienced by the household at time t.

The instantaneous maximization problem of the household at time t, which determines the value of the choice variables at that time, consists in maximizing the discounted value of the total flow of utility experienced at time t. When solving this problem, the household takes as given both the market prices and the values of the state and co-state variables. At time t the values of the choice variables determine real rates of change of the state and co-state variables consistent with the equations of motion. The evolving values of the state and co-state variables, in turn, determine the values of the choice variables in the next instant.

The necessary conditions for the Hamiltonian to attain a maximum at all $t \in [0, T]$ are found by setting the first-order partial derivatives of the Hamiltonian with respect to the four choice variables equal to zero.[4] That is,

$$\frac{\partial H(t)}{\partial C_M(t)} = -\lambda_M(t) + \lambda_C(t) - \lambda_C(t)T_1^d(C_M(t), C_B(t), b_M(t)\Pi(t)) = 0$$

$$(\text{III}.2.8)$$

$$\frac{\partial H(t)}{\partial C_B(t)} = \lambda_C(t) - \lambda_B(t) - \lambda_C(t)T_2^d(C_M(t), C_B(t), b_M(t)\Pi(t)) = 0$$

$$(\text{III}.2.9)$$

$$\frac{\partial H(t)}{\partial b_M(t)} = \lambda_B(t) - \lambda_M(t)\Pi(t) - \lambda_C(t)\Pi(t)T_3^d(C_M(t), C_B(t), b_M(t)\Pi(t)) = 0$$

$$(\text{III}.2.10)$$

$$\frac{\partial H(t)}{\partial \phi(t)} = U'(\phi, (t)\exp(-\rho t)\lambda_C(t)) = 0 \qquad (\text{III}.2.11)$$

must hold simultaneously for all $t \in [0, T]$.[5] Hence, we have four equations with which to determine the four choice variables $C_M(t)$, $C_B(t)$, $b_M(t)$, and $\phi(t)$ as functions of $\lambda_M(t)$, $\lambda_C(t)$d $\lambda_B(t)$.

Sufficient conditions for an extremum of the Hamiltonian to be a maximum require that the Hessian of the Hamiltonian be negative definite. A necessary and sufficient condition for this to obtain is that the transactions technology be strictly convex at the extremum of the Hamiltonian.

Equation III.2.11 requires that the household choose its flow rate of consumption so that the discounted marginal utility of an increase in this rate at time t equals the shadow price (discounted marginal utility) of an exogenous increase in its stock of consumption goods at time t. Equations III.2.8, III.2.9, and III.2.10 provide the marginal conditions that determine the market activities of the household at each point in time. On rewriting, we obtain the following three equations:

$$\lambda_M(t) = \lambda_C(t) - \lambda_C(t)T_1^d(t) \tag{III.2.12}$$

$$\lambda_B(t) = \lambda_C(t) - \lambda_C(t)T_2^d(t) \tag{III.2.13}$$

$$\lambda_M(t) = \lambda_B(t)\mathbf{III}(t) - \lambda_C(t)T_3^d(t) \qquad \forall\, t \in [0, T] \tag{III.2.14}$$

Equation III.2.12 requires the household to exchange money for the consumption good at each $t \in [0, T]$ until the loss in present utility due to a unit reduction in the real money stock equals the gain in present utility due to a unit increase in the consumption-good stock less the present utility lost through increased use of the transactions good. Equations III.2.13 and III.2.14 admit a similar explanation of the behavior of the household in the consumption-good-cum-bonds market and the bonds-cum-money market.[6]

Alternatively, equations III.2.11, III.2.12, and III.2.13 can be interpreted together as requiring that the addition of a real unit to the stock of bonds, money, or consumption goods at time t yield the same increase in present utility when converted into the consumption good and consumed at time t.

The two interpretations of the first-order conditions for the instantaneous maximization problem lead to the following proposition.

Market-behavior proposition

The household will conduct its market activities until marginal transfers from one stock to another at time t leave the discounted flow of utility unchanged. Alternatively, unit increases in any real stocks at time t must each generate the same increase in the flow of discounted utility at time t if these increases are converted into consumption goods and consumed at time t.

The implicit or shadow marginal rate of substitution between any pair of the three commodities held as stocks at time t can be defined as the ratio of their shadow prices at time t (i.e., as the ratio of the marginal utilities of adding to the respective inventories). For example, at time t the marginal rate of substitution (MRS) of money for consumption goods is given by

$$\frac{\lambda_M(t)}{\lambda_C(t)} = \frac{\lambda_B(t)[\mathrm{III}(t)] - \lambda_C(t)T_3^d(t)}{\lambda_B(t) + \lambda_C(t)T_2^d(t)} = \frac{\lambda_C(t) - \lambda_C(t)T_1^d(t)}{\lambda_M(t) + \lambda_C(t)T_1^d(t)} \qquad (\mathrm{III}.2.15)$$

where $\mathrm{III}(t) = P_{CM}(t)/(P_{CB}(t)P_{BM}(t))$. The middle term of equation III.2.15 equals the implicit price of substituting an additional unit of money for bonds divided by the implicit price of substituting an additional unit of the consumption good for bonds. Similarly, the right-hand term equals the ratio of the implicit price of obtaining one unit of money in the money-cum-consumption-good market and the implicit price of obtaining an additional unit of the consumption good in the same market. The MRS values at time t of money for bonds and of bonds for the consumption good can be defined as $\lambda_M(t)/\lambda_B(t)$ and $\lambda_B(t)/\lambda_C(t)$, respectively.

From the marginal conditions III.2.12, III.2.13, and III.2.14, which determine the market behavior of the household, and from the properties of the transactions-good demand function, we conclude that[7]

$$\lambda_C(t) - \lambda_M(t) > 0 \quad \text{iff } C_M(t) > 0 \qquad \forall\, t \in [0, T] \qquad (\mathrm{III}.2.16)$$

$$\lambda_C(t) - \lambda_B(t) > 0 \quad \text{iff } C_B(t) > 0 \qquad \forall\, t \in [0, T] \qquad (\mathrm{III}.2.17)$$

$$\lambda_B(t)\mathrm{III}(t) - \lambda_M(t) > 0 \quad \text{iff } B_M(t) > 0 \qquad \forall\, t \in [0, T]$$
$$(\mathrm{III}.2.18)$$

Hence at time $t \in [0, T]$ the household demands the consumption good in exchange for money if and only if the shadow price of addition to the consumption-good stock exceeds the shadow price of addition to the stock of money. Equations III.2.17 and III.2.18 can be interpreted similarly.

Furthermore, equations III.2.12 and III.2.13 allow us to relate differences in the magnitudes of the shadow prices at time t to differences in the magnitudes of the marginal costs of transacting at time t:

$$\lambda_M(t) - \lambda_B(t) > 0 \quad \text{if } T_2^d(t) - T_1^d(t) > 0 \qquad (\mathrm{III}.2.19)$$

$$\lambda_C(t) - \lambda_B(t)\mathrm{III}(t) > 0 \quad \text{if } T_1^d(t) - T_3^d(t) > 0 \qquad (\mathrm{III}.2.20)$$

The Maximum Principle requires that the Hamiltonian be maximized with respect to the choice variables at each point in time. That is, by equation III.2.3,

$$H(q(t)^*, v(t)^*, \lambda(t)^*, t) \geq H(q(t)^*, v(t), \lambda(t)^*, t) \qquad \forall\, v(t) \in \Omega$$

With the aid of this proposition we can establish the duality that exists among subsets of the choice variables. In particular, equation III.2.3 implies

$$(U(\phi(t)^*) - U(\phi(t))) \exp(-\rho t) \geq \lambda_C(t)^*(\phi(t)^* - \phi(t)) \qquad \forall\, t \in [0, T]$$

Hence

$$U(\phi(t)^*) - U(\phi(t)) \geq 0 \quad \text{if } \phi(t)^* - \phi(t) \geq 0 \tag{III.2.21}$$

The inequalities of III.2.21 state that instantaneous utility is maximized along the optimal path. Furthermore, III.2.3 implies that

$$\lambda_C(t)^*(\phi(t) - \phi(t)^*) \geq 0 \quad \text{if } U(\phi(t)) - U(\phi(t)^*) \geq 0 \tag{III.2.22}$$

(i.e., consumption expenditure valued at the shadow price of additions to the consumption-good stock is minimized along the optimal trajectory).

Also, the Maximum Principle implies that

$$(\lambda_C(t)^* - \lambda_M(t)^*)(C_M(t)^* - C_M(t)) \geq \lambda_C(t)^*(T^d(C_M(t)^*, \cdot) - T^d(C_M(t), \cdot))$$
$$\forall\, t \in [0, T]$$

Equivalently,

$$T^d(C_M(t), \cdot) - T^d(C_M(t)^*, \cdot) \geq (\lambda_C(t)^* - \lambda_M(t)^*)(C_M(t) - C_M(t)^*)$$
$$\forall\, t \in [0, T]$$

After considering III.2.16, $\lambda_C(t)^* - \lambda_M(t)^* > 0$ when $C_M(t)^* > 0$, we conclude that

$$T^d(C_M(t), \cdot) - T^d(C_M(t)^*, \cdot) > 0 \quad \text{whenever } C_M(t) - C_M(t)^* > 0$$

That is, $T^d(t)$ is minimized along the optimal trajectory. Similar inequalities can be derived for the remaining choice variables, and in each case we can conclude that $T^d(t)$ is minimized along the optimal trajectory.[8]

Finally, the Maximum Principle allows us to prove that the rate of consumption will be positive at all $t \in [0, T]$. If $\phi(t)^*$ together with $C_M(t)^*$, $C_B(t)^*$, and $b_M(t)^*$ maximize the Hamiltonian and $\phi(\bar{t})^* = 0$ for some $\bar{t} \in [0, T]$, then $\partial H/\partial\phi \leq 0$ at $\bar{t}$. However, $\partial H/\partial\phi = U'(\phi(\bar{t})^* \exp(-\rho t) - \lambda_C(t)^*$ and $U'(0) = \infty$, which contradicts the assumption $\phi(\bar{t})^* = 0$.[9] We can summarize these conclusions in the following proposition.

Duality proposition

The first-order conditions of the instantaneous maximization problem imply that the instantaneous utility is maximized along the optimal path and that consumption expenditure valued at the shadow prices of additions to the consumption-good stock is minimized along the optimal trajectory. Furthermore, the expenditure on transactions cost is minimized along the optimal trajectory. Lastly, the rate of consumption is positive at all $t \in [0, T]$.

III.3   The dynamic maximization problem

In the instantaneous maximization problem the household determines the value of its choice variables $\phi(t)$, $C_M(t)$, $C_B(t)$, and $B_M(t)$ as functions of state and co-state variables and market prices at each $t \in [0, T]$. The choice variables, in turn, determine the rates of change of the state variables through the equations of motion III.2.4. The rate of change of the co-state variables is given in equations III.2.5. As time passes, the changing values of the state and co-state variables determine new values for the choice variables through the household's instantaneous maximization of the Hamiltonian. Given the initial values for the money, bond, and consumption-good stocks, the path of the state variables is completely determined.

Equations III.2.5 indicate that the rate of change of the co-state variables is independent of the choice variables. The position of the path of the co-state variables depends on the final real values of the money, bond, and consumption-good stocks and is determined by the transversality conditions given in equations III.2.6.

Thus the dynamic maximization problem consists in choosing the paths of the co-state variables that satisfy the transversality conditions and the equations of motion III.2.5. For example, if the household chooses a path for the shadow price of additions to the real money stock that satisfies equations III.2.5 but is such that $\lambda_M(T) > \partial\beta(T)/\partial m(T)$, then the money stock marked for bequest will be too large. A transfer of a unit of real money from the bequest stock to the nonbequest stock will increase the present stock of utility due to consumption by $\lambda_M(T)$ and will reduce the present stock of utility due to bequest by $\partial\beta(T)/\partial m(T)$. Hence, the total stock of present utility will be increased by the transfer. A similar argument demonstrates that the household benefits by a transfer into the bequest stock if $\lambda_M(T) < \partial\beta(T)/\partial m(T)$. Therefore, the household maximizes its stock of present utility by choosing paths of the shadow price such that the transversality conditions are satisfied.

In Appendix C the equations of motion have been solved for the paths of the real stocks of money, bonds, and consumption goods, as well as for the paths of the shadow prices. The paths of the shadow prices are positive everywhere and increase exponentially. Underlying the economic interpretation of this exponential increase in the shadow prices is the exponential rate of decay of each real stock. The household has two options: It can augment its real stocks at time t by purchasing commodities in the three markets at time t, or it can acquire the commodities at an earlier time and hold them as inventory stocks. However, while in storage, these commodities decay at an exponential rate. Hence the household is willing to pay an exponentially increasing shadow price for future additions to its real stocks of commodities.

The intertemporal problem of the household has been stated and analyzed in terms of discounted or present variables; that is, the shadow prices were presented in terms of the discounted marginal utility of adding to stocks, and the instantaneous maximization problem consisted of maximizing the discounted flow of utility for all $t \in [0, T]$. In order to be able to examine the role of time preference as a cost of holding stocks, we introduce the undiscounted or current shadow prices of additions to the real money, consumption-good, and bond stocks, respectively, as

$$\eta_M(t) = \lambda_M(t) \exp(\rho t) \qquad \forall\, t \in [0, T] \tag{III.3.1}$$

$$\eta_C(t) = \lambda_C(t) \exp(\rho t) \qquad \forall\, t \in [0, T] \tag{III.3.2}$$

$$\eta_B(t) = \lambda_B(t) \exp(\rho t) \qquad \forall\, t \in [0, T] \tag{III.3.3}$$

The discounted shadow price of adding one unit to the real money stock at time t is $\lambda_M(t)$; therefore, $\hat{\lambda}_M(t)$ represents the percentage rate at which the household gains present utility from holding a unit of real money at time t. The corresponding percentage rates at which the household gains current utility from holding one unit each of real money, consumption goods, and real bonds are given by[10]

$$\hat{\mu}_M(t) = P_{CM}(t) + \rho \tag{III.3.4}$$

$$\hat{\mu}_C(t) = \delta + \rho \tag{III.3.5}$$

$$\hat{\mu}_B(t) = \hat{P}_{CB}(t) - P_{MB}(t) + \rho \tag{III.3.6}$$

Hence, it is possible to distinguish between the gain in present or current utility from an addition to any of the three stocks and the gain in present or current utility that accrues to the household from holding a unit of any of the three stocks for a given period of time.[11]

The costs of holding one additional unit each of real money, consumption goods, and real bonds are given by the right-hand sides of equations III.3.4, III.3.5, and III.3.6, respectively. Thus, the equations of motion for the shadow prices can be interpreted as intertemporal marginal conditions for optimal stock holding. We are thus led to the following proposition.

Asset-accumulation proposition

The household will accumulate each stock until the marginal benefit of holding an additional unit of a stock, as given by the shadow price of additions to this stock, equals the marginal cost of holding an additional unit of a stock, as given by the rate of depreciation and the rate of intertemporal discount.

III.4   Properties of the household's intertemporal demand functions

The first-order necessary conditions that a trajectory $(q(t), v(t), \lambda(t))$ must satisfy in order to be an extremum of the intertemporal problem are sufficient for $(q(t), v(t), \lambda(t))$ to be a maximum, because the augmented objective function $J[q(t), v(t), \lambda(t)]$ (see equation III.2.2) is strictly concave.[12] Furthermore, strict concavity of $J[q(t), v(t), \lambda(t)]$ is a sufficient condition for the optimal trajectory $(q(t)^*, v(t)^*, \lambda(t)^*)$ to be unique.

The existence and the degree of homogeneity of the demand functions as functions of prices and initial endowments of the three stocks can be established by examining equations III.2.4, III.2.5, III.2.6, III.2.8, III.2.9, and III.2.10. In particular, the first-order conditions for a maximum of the Hamiltonian will not be violated if we double $B_M(t)$, $P_{CB}(t)$, and $P_{CM}(t)$, and leave $C_M(t)$ and $C_B(t)$ unchanged at all $t \in [0, T]$. From the equations of motion for the state and co-state variables, as given in equations III.2.4, III.2.5, and III.2.6, we see that doubling $B_M(t)$, $P_{CM}(t)$, and $P_{CB}(t)$ at any $t \in [0, T]$, as well as doubling the initial nominal endowments of money and bonds, will not affect $m(t)$, $b(t)$, and $C(t)$, the paths of real stocks.

Hence, the real demand functions $C_M(t)$, $C_B(t)$, and $b_M(t)\Pi(t)$ are homogeneous of degree zero in $P_{CM}(t)$, $P_{CB}(t)$, $B_M(t)$, M_0, and B_0, and the nominal demand function $B_M(t)$ is homogeneous of degree one in $P_{CM}(t)$, $P_{CB}(t)$, M_0, and B_0 for all $t \in [0, T]$.[13] Thus, the homogeneity property of the real demand functions does not require changes in the interest rate $P_{MB}(t)$ when other prices and nominal initial conditions change. These results are consistent with those obtained in neoclassical models with $T^d(t) \equiv 0$.[14]

In Chapter II, Section 5, it was shown that the intertemporal demand functions satisfy a Walrasian budget constraint of the form

$$C_M(t) + m_C(t) + C_B(t) + b_C(t) + m_B(t) + b_M(t)\Pi(t) = 0$$

$$\forall\, t \in [0, T] \quad (\text{III}.4.1)$$

Equation III.4.1 can also be written as

$$P_{MC}(t)(M_C(t) + M_B(t)) + (C_M(t) + C_B(t)) + P_{BC}(t)(B_C(t) + \Pi(t)B_M(t)) = 0$$

$$\forall\, t \in [0, T]$$

This budget constraint asserts that the net value of trading plans is zero. It will be used in Chapter V to establish Walras's law for the economy.

Differentiability with respect to time of $C_M(t)$, $C_B(t)$, and $B_M(t)$ for all $t \in [0, T]$ is guaranteed by the strict convexity of $T^d(t)$ at all $t \in [0, T]$ and $-U(\phi(t))$ and by the differentiability with respect to time of the shadow prices and market prices (Gale and Nikaido, 1965). To ascertain the direction of change over time of the choice variables, we take time derivatives of the choice, co-state, and parameter variables as they appear in the first-order conditions for a maximum of the Hamiltonian. We then solve for the time derivatives of the choice variables.

The time derivatives of the choice variables are given by the following equations:

$$\frac{dC_M(t)}{dt} = \frac{1}{T_{11}^d(t)}[\delta - \hat{P}_{CM}(t)]\frac{\lambda_M(t)}{\lambda_C(t)} \gtreqless 0 \quad \text{as } \delta - \hat{P}_{CM}(t) \gtreqless 0 \qquad (\text{III}.4.2)$$

$$\frac{dC_B(t)}{dt} = \frac{1}{T_{22}^d(t)} [\delta + P_{MB}(t) - \hat{P}_{CB}(t)] \frac{\lambda_B(t)}{\lambda_C(t)} \gtreqless 0$$

$$\text{as } \delta + P_{MB}(t) - \hat{P}_{CB}(t) \gtreqless 0 \quad \text{(III.4.3)}$$

$$\frac{d[b_M(t)\Pi(t)]}{dt} = \frac{1}{T_{33}^d(t)} \left[(\hat{P}_{CB}(t) - P_{MB}(t) - \delta) \left(\frac{\lambda_B(t)}{\lambda_C(t)} \right) (\Pi(t)) \right.$$

$$\left. + (\delta - P_{CM}(t)) \left(\frac{\lambda_M(t)}{\lambda_C(t)} \right) + \frac{\lambda_B(t)}{\lambda_C(t)} \left(\frac{d(\Pi(t))}{dt} \right) \right]$$

$$\forall\, t \in [0, T] \quad \text{(III.4.4)}$$

The time rate of change of $b_M(t)\Pi(t)$ can be written in terms of the time rate of change of $C_M(t)$ and $C_B(t)$:[15]

$$\frac{d[b_M(t)\Pi(t)]}{dt} = \frac{1}{T_{33}^d(t)} \left[\frac{d(C_B(t)T_{22}^d(t))}{dt\Pi(t)} + \frac{d(C_M(t)T_{11}^d(t))}{dt} + \frac{\lambda_B(t)}{\lambda_C(t)} \frac{d(\Pi(t))}{dt} \right]$$

$$\forall\, t \in [0, T] \quad \text{(III.4.5)}$$

Lastly,

$$\frac{d\phi(t)}{dt} = \frac{U'(\phi(t))}{U''(\phi(t))} (\delta + \rho) < 0 \quad \forall\, t \in [0, T] \quad \text{(III.4.6)}$$

Underlying the economic interpretation of the behavior of these rates of change are the differences in the costs associated with nonzero levels of inventories of the various stocks and the need to meet the transversality conditions for optimal bequest. If the rate of depreciation exceeds the rate of inflation of the price of consumption goods in terms of money, then the rate at which the household acquires consumption goods in exchange for money will rise over time. This increase is due to the difference in the costs of storing money and consumption goods. In particular, the cost of holding wealth in the form of consumption goods rather than money grows over time at a rate of $\delta - \hat{P}_{CM}(t)$. Hence, an optimal policy for the household is to postpone the purchase of consumption goods as long as possible and to attain the desired bequest level of consumption goods through an increasing rate of sale of money.

Equation III.4.3 shows that if the sum of the rate of interest and the rate at which the consumption-good stock depreciates exceeds the rate of inflation of the price of consumption goods in terms of bonds, then the rate at which the household acquires consumption goods in exchange for bonds will increase over time. As before, this secular increase results from the positive difference in the costs of holding inventories of consumption goods and bonds, as given by $\delta - \hat{P}_{CB}(t) + P_{MB}(t)$. Furthermore, $dC_M(t)/dt > 0$ and $dC_B(t)/dt > 0$ for all $t \in [0, T]$. Thus, once the household begins to purchase consumption goods, it will continue to do so.

The direction of the real rate of purchase of bonds in exchange for money is more difficult to establish. However, if $dC_B(t)/dt > dC_M(t)/dt$ for all $t \in [0, T]$,[16] and if the economy is well arbitraged,[17] then the rate at which the household acquires bonds in exchange for money will decline for all $t \in [0, T]$. Again, a positive difference between the cost of holding money stocks and the cost of holding bond stocks underlies the economic interpretation of this rate of change. Hence, the optimizing household postpones acquisition of its optimal bequest level of money stocks as long as possible.

From the transactions flow equations and the preceding results we can establish the rates of change of the remaining three demand functions:

$$\frac{dM_C(t)}{dt} < 0, \qquad \frac{dB_C(t)}{dt} < 0, \qquad \frac{dM_B(t)}{dt} > 0 \qquad \forall\, t \in [0, T] \qquad \text{(III.4.7)}$$

Because both $dB_C(t)/dt$ and $dB_M(t)/dt$ are negative for all $t \in [0, T]$, we know that once the household begins to sell bonds, it will continue to do so.

Equation III.4.6 indicates that the rate of consumption out of the stock of consumption goods decreases over time. This trend results from the fact that the percentage time rate of change of the psychic cost of saving at time t, given by $[U_{11}(\phi(t))/U_1(\phi(t))]\phi(t)$ is negative. This establishes the following proposition.

Intertemporal market-behavior proposition

The household will increase $C_M(t)$, the rate at which it demands consumption goods in exchange for money on $[0, T]$, if

$$\delta - \hat{P}_{CM}(t) > 0$$

that is, if the rate of depreciation exceeds the rate of inflation of the price of consumption goods in terms of money. The household will also increase $C_B(t)$, the rate at which it demands consumption goods in exchange for bonds on $[0, T]$, if

$$\delta + P_{MB}(t) - \hat{P}_{CB}(t) > 0$$

that is, if the rate of depreciation of the consumption-good stock plus the rate of interest exceed the rate of inflation of the price of consumption goods in terms of bonds. The rate of consumption, $\phi(t)$, will decline on $[0, T]$.

III.5   Nonconvex transactions technologies

The analysis of the preceding sections assumes that each household's transactions technology is strictly convex over the entire range of the household's demand functions; that is, the generalized marginal cost in terms of the consumption good of transacting in any of the three markets is increasing. This assumption about the curvature of the transactions technology implies that the demand functions $C_M(t)_i$, $C_B(t)_i$, and $b_M(t)_i\Pi(t)$ ($i = 1, 2, \ldots, n$) are continuous functions of time on the interval $[0, T]$ (see Section III.4) and, hence, that the aggregate market excess-demand functions $C_M(t)$, $C_B(t)$, and $B_M(t)\Pi(t)$ are continuous functions of time on $[0, T]$.[18]

An equilibrium is attained in the three markets at time $t \in [0, T]$ when excess flow demands at time t are zero; then the prices prevailing at time t are equilibrium prices. Each of the three market demand functions has the dimensions of a flow, whereas the household's inventories of the three goods have the dimensions of stocks. Thus the three equilibrium prices $P_{CM}(t)$, $P_{CB}(t)$, and $P_{MB}(t)$ are determined in flow markets.

In this section we shall analyze the effects of nonconvex transactions technologies on the nature of households' market and stock-holding activities within the context of their intertemporal maximization problems defined in Chapter II.

The curvature properties of the transactions technology of the ith ($i = 1, 2, \ldots, n$) household enter its intertemporal maximization problem via the second-order sufficiency conditions for an extremum of the Hamiltonian. These second-order conditions require the Hessian matrix of the ith household's Hamiltonian to be negative definite at each $t \in [0, T]$ when the Hessian is evaluated at the optimal values of the household's demands (see Section III.2). The Hessian matrix of the ith household's Hamiltonian is represented by

$$[H_{lk}^i(t)] = (-1) \begin{bmatrix} T_{11}^{di} & T_{12}^{di} & T_{13}^{di} \\ T_{21}^{di} & T_{22}^{di} & T_{23}^{di} \\ T_{31}^{di} & T_{32}^{di} & T_{33}^{di} \end{bmatrix} \qquad \text{(III.5.1)}$$

where

$$T_{lk}^{di} = T_{lk}^{di}(C_M(t)_i, C_B(t)_i, b_M(t)_i\Pi(t)) \qquad (l, k = 1, 2, 3, \text{ and } i = 1, 2, \ldots, n)$$

is evaluated at the optimal values of $C_M(t)_i$, $C_B(t)_i$, and $b_M(t)_i\Pi(t)$. Hence the requirement that the Hessian of the Hamiltonian be negative definite at the optimal values of the flow demand functions is equivalent to requiring $T^{di}(C_M(t)_i, C_B(t)_i, b_M(t)_i\Pi(t))$ to be strictly convex at the optimal values of $C_B(t)_i$, $C_M(t)_i$, and $b_M(t)_i\Pi(t)$. If the transactions technology is nonconvex, then it is optimal for the ith household to have either unbounded or zero rates of flow demand in the three markets, because a transactions technology that is nonconvex at an extremum of the Hamiltonian implies that the extremum is a minimum rather than a maximum.[19] However, the resource constraint given in equation II.5.18 requires that the amounts of the three commodities held in stock by the household remain finite at each $t \in [0, T]$ when some or all of its three rates of demand are unbounded.

Therefore, if $C_M(t)_i$ is unbounded at the points $t = \tau_s \in [0, T]$ and $s \in I$, then the set I is countable; that is, it consists of a sequence $\{s_1, s_2, \ldots, s_n\}$, and

$$\int_{\tau_s-\epsilon}^{\tau_s+\epsilon} |C_M(t)_i| \, dt < \infty \qquad \forall \, s \in I \quad \text{and} \quad \epsilon > 0 \qquad \text{(III.5.2)}$$

such that $[\tau_s + \epsilon, \tau_s - \epsilon] \subset [0, T] \, \forall \, s \in I$. In particular, this inequality must hold when $C_M(t)$ approaches plus or minus infinity as t approaches τ_s. A class of functions that satisfy this requirement is given by the generalized functions of which the Dirac delta function is a special case.[20] When $|C_M(t)_i|$ $\to \infty$ as $t \to \tau_s$, the change in the consumption-good stock at the singular points τ_s is given by[21]

$$\Delta C(\tau_s \mid C_M) = \lim_{\epsilon \to 0} \int_{\tau_s-\epsilon}^{\tau_s+\epsilon} C_M(t)_i \, dt \qquad \forall \, s \in I \qquad \text{(III.5.3)}$$

This discrete change in the consumption-good stock at the points τ_s, which occurs as a result of $|C_M(t)_i| \to \infty$ as $t \to \tau_s$, is the stock-shift transactions equivalent of the unbounded flow demand at τ_s for all $s \in I$. This, then, is the sense in which the stock-shift mode of transacting is a limiting case of the continuous-flow mode of transacting.

Furthermore, when $C_M(t)_i \to \infty$ as $t \to \tau_s$, with $s \in I$, then define

$$\lim_{\epsilon \to 0} \int_{\tau_s-\epsilon}^{\tau_s+\epsilon} T^{di}(C_M(t)_i, C_B(t)_i, b_M(t)_i\Pi(t)) \, dt = \Gamma^i(\Delta C(\tau_s \mid C_M)) \qquad \text{(III.5.4)}$$

where $\Gamma^i(\Delta C(\tau_s \mid C_M))$ indicates the transactions cost associated with the stock-shift transaction of size $\Delta C(\tau_s \mid C_M)$ at time $t = \tau_s$. If, in addition, the cost of transacting in the stock-shift mode depends on $N(\tau_s \mid C_M(t)_i)$, the number of transactions executed by time $t = \tau_s$ in the consumption-good-cum-money market, then the continuous-time transactions-good demand function $T^{di}(C_M(t)_i, C_B(t)_i, b_M(t)_i\Pi(t))$ approaches a transactions-good demand function of the form[22]

$$\Gamma^i = \Gamma^i(\Delta C(\tau_s \mid C_M(t)_i), \Delta C(\tau_s \mid C_B(t)_i), \Delta B(\tau_s \mid b_M(t)_i\Pi(t)),$$
$$-N(\tau_s \mid C_M(t)_i), -N(\tau_s \mid C_B(t)_i), -N(\tau_s \mid b_M(t)_i\Pi(t))) \qquad \text{(III.5.5)}$$

Thus, in the presence of nonconvex transactions technologies, the intertemporal maximization problem of the ith household can be written as

$$\max \int_0^T U\phi(t)) \exp(-\rho t) \, dt + \beta(m(T), C(T), b(T)) \qquad \text{(III.5.6)}$$

such that

$$C(t) = C_0 + \sum_{\{\tau_s \leq t, s \in I_1\}} \Delta C(\tau_s \mid C_M) + \sum_{\{\tau_s \leq t, s \in I_2\}} \Delta C(\tau_s \mid C_B)$$
$$- \sum_{\{\tau_s \leq t, s \in I_1 \cap I_2 \cap I_3\}} \Gamma(\tau_s) - \int_0^t (\phi(r) + \delta C(r) - X(r)) \, dr \qquad \text{(III.5.7)}$$

$$m(t) = m_0 - \sum_{\{\tau, \leq t, s \in I_1\}} \Delta C(\tau_s \mid C_M) - \sum_{\{\tau, \leq t, s \in I_3\}} \Delta b(\tau_s, b_M(t)\Pi(t))$$

$$- \int_0^t (\Delta P_{CM}/P_{CM}(r))m(r) \, dr \quad \text{(III.5.8)}$$

$$b(t) = b(0) - \sum_{\{\tau, \leq t, s \in I_2\}} \Delta C(\tau_s, C_B) + \sum_{\{\tau, \leq t, s \in I_3\}} \Delta b(\tau_s, b_M(t)\Pi(t))$$

$$+ \int_0^t P_{MB}(t) - (\Delta P_{CB}/P_{CB}(r))b(r) \, dr \quad \text{(III.5.9)}$$

and all further constraints, such as nonnegativity constraints and resource constraints, remain as specified in the continuous-time intertemporal problem.[23] The prices used to deflate B_M at τ_s can be defined at $\tau_s - \epsilon$ or $\tau_s + \epsilon$.

In this mixed discrete-time/continuous-time problem, time is a continuous variable, and the household consumes and receives endowment income at a continuous rate. However, transactions in the three markets occur at discrete points in time. Thus the maximization problem as formulated in equations III.5.6, III.5.7, III.5.8, and III.5.9 provides the household the dates and sizes of transactions in the three markets as well as the rate of consumption. From this information the household infers the sizes of its stock holdings of the three commodities at any $t \in [0, T]$ and the size of its bequest stocks. If the two utility functions are strictly convex and the transactions-good demand function $\Gamma(\cdot)$, as defined in equation III.5.5, is strictly concave, then it can be shown that the maximization problem in equations III.5.6, III.5.7, III.5.8, and III.5.9 has a unique solution (Hadley and Whitin, 1963).

If the transactions technology $\Gamma^i(\cdot)$, as defined in equation III.5.5, is convex, then the marginal cost in terms of the consumption good of increasing the size of a stock-shift transaction at a given transactions datum is increasing, and the marginal cost of increasing the total number of transactions in any one of the three markets is decreasing. Hence, a convex transactions technology $\Gamma^i(\cdot)$ makes optimal for the household a policy of reducing to zero the size of its stock-shift transactions and increasing the number of transactions in each market without bound. In the limiting case, the household trades continuously in the three markets on the interval $[0, T]$. Thus the following general proposition about the market behavior of the household has been established.

Mode-of-trading proposition

If the transactions technology $T^{di}(\cdot)$ or $\Gamma^i(\cdot)$ is strictly convex, then the household possesses flow demand functions that are continuous with respect to time on the interval $[0, T]$, whereas the presence of nonconvexities in $T^{di}(\cdot)$ or $\Gamma^i(\cdot)$ results in stock-shift demand functions that give the sizes of the stock shifts demanded at the various transactions dates $\tau_s \in [0, T]$. Hence, in convex economies (i.e., economies in which households possess convex transactions technologies) the households trade continuously, whereas in nonconvex economies households trade intermittently on the interval $[0, T]$.

Thus the presence of nonconvex transactions technologies poses no difficulty at the microeconomic level, because it has been shown in this section that the household's maximization problem, as defined in Chapter II, can be written alternatively as in equations III.5.6, III.5.7, III.5.8, and III.5.9. This reformulated intertemporal maximization problem has a unique solution in the form of a vector of transactions sizes and times and a flow of consumption defined on $[0, T]$.

The curvature of the household's transactions technology also determines which of the two competing alternative specifications of asset stock adjustment models is appropriate (i.e., the continuous partial stock adjustment model or the discrete stock-shift adjustment model).

We assume that a change in the variables exogenous to the household's maximization has occurred such that the desired composition but not the desired size of the household's asset portfolio has been altered. The mode-of-trading proposition then implies that the presence of a nonconvexity in the household's transactions technology will induce it to achieve the new desired composition of its asset portfolio by a stock-shift transaction in the appropriate markets. Thus the partial adjustment model is not applicable under such circumstances, and for the purpose of empirical specification, the absence of well-defined flow demand functions necessitates the use of asset stock demand functions.

On the other hand, if the household's transactions technology is characterized by a convex curvature, then the portfolio adjustment will be spread over time in a continuous partial stock adjustment mode. Therefore, for the purposes of empirical specification, flow demand functions are appropriate in this regime.[24]

Asset stock adjustment proposition

The partial stock adjustment model is appropriate only when households are faced with a strictly convex transactions technology. In this case, demand functions take the form of continuous flow demands. If the transactions technology exhibits nonconvexities, then the stock-shift portfolio adjustment model is appropriate, and demand functions take the form of asset demands.

CHAPTER IV

Comparative static and dynamic analyses of household behavior

IV.1   Introduction

In this chapter we shall analyze how the household adjusts its choice variables in response to changes in exogenous variables.

Dividing the household's decision-making process into an instantaneous maximization problem and a dynamic maximization problem allows us to dichotomize the analysis of its reactions to changes in exogenous variables. Comparative static analysis of the instantaneous maximization problem reveals the instantaneous adjustments in choice variables that occur at time t as a result of changes at time t in market prices, shadow prices, and parameter variables. Such adjustments in the household's choice variables are prescribed by the marginal conditions for exchange and consumption that must be satisfied at all $t \in [0, T]$.

Changes in the choice variables that occur at time $t \in [0, T]$ affect the paths of the state variables (i.e., the paths of the stocks of consumption goods, real money, and real bonds) through their equations of motion. The new paths of the state variables then no longer satisfy the marginal conditions for optimal bequest given by the transversality conditions in equations III.2.6. Hence the household chooses new paths for the shadow prices such that the transversality conditions are satisfied. However, the new paths of the shadow prices stimulate additional changes in the choice variables at each $t \in [0, T]$. In turn, the paths of the state variables are affected through the equations of motion, thus leading once more to new paths for the shadow prices.

Two features of the model of the intertemporal household presented in Chapter II allow us to obtain determinate answers to comparative-dynamics questions:

(a)   The values of the choice variables at a given $t \in [0, T]$ do not depend on the values of the state variables at any $t \in [0, T]$.

(b)   The values of the shadow prices at a given $t \in [0, T]$ depend only on the values assumed by the state variables at $t = T$.

Hence changes in state variables affect the paths of their shadow prices only through the marginal conditions for optimal bequest, and these changes affect choice variables only through the changes in the paths of the shadow

38

prices. Because the shadow prices at time $t \in [0, T]$ are independent of the state and choice variables at time $t \in [0, T]$, the marginal conditions for stock holding, as given by equations III.2.5, are always satisfied.

IV.2   Comparative static analysis of household behavior

In its instantaneous optimization problem the household maximizes the discounted flow of utility with respect to the vector of choice variables $v(t) = (C_M(t), C_B(t), b_M(t), \phi(t))$ at all $t \in [0, T]$, taking all other variables and parameters as given. The first step in determining the effects of changes in variables exogenous to the household's intertemporal maximization problem on the paths of its endogenous variables is to analyze household behavior at each instant, as the variables regarded as given at that instant change.

The first-order conditions that guarantee that $v(t)^*$ maximizes the Hamiltonian at time t determine a functional relation between $v(t)^*$, shadow prices $\lambda_M(t)$, $\lambda_C(t)$, and $\lambda_B(t)$, market prices $P_{CM}(t)$, $P_{CB}(t)$, and $P_{MB}(t)$, and the discount parameter ρ at time t. Comparative static analysis then reveals the rates of change of the choice variables with respect to changes in shadow prices, market prices, and the discount parameter at each $t \in [0, T]$. For details, see Appendix D.

To simplify the analysis, assume that $T^d(t)$ is additively separable; that is, $T_{ij}^d(t) = 0 \ \forall \ t \in [0, T]$ whenever $i \neq j$ $(i, j = 1, 2, 3)$. Thus the magnitude of the rate of demand for one commodity has no effect on that part of the demand for the transactions good that arises because of a nonzero rate of demand for another commodity.[1]

An increase in the shadow price of additions to the consumption-good stock at time t increases the rate at which the household demands the consumption good in exchange for money and bonds and decreases the rate of consumption at time t. This increase in $\lambda_C(t)$ at time t also reduces the rate of transacting in the market in which bonds exchange for money; that is, $|B_M(t)|$ decreases at time t. The effect of this change is a reduction in the demand for the transactions good. These results suggest that an increase in the shadow price (i.e., an increase in the discounted marginal utility of additions to the consumption-good stock) will cause the household to increase the rate of accumulation of consumption goods, both by increasing the rate of demand for the consumption good and reducing its rate of consumption and by reducing its demand for the transactions good.

The effect of an increase in the shadow price of additions to the real money stock at time t is to decrease the demand for consumption goods and bonds in exchange for money (i.e., to increase the demand for money at time t). Finally, an increase in the shadow price of additions to the real bond stock at time t reduces the rate at which the household demands the consumption good in

Table IV.1. *Comparative static effects of changes in shadow prices at time* t *on choice variables at time* t^a

	dC_M	dC_B	$dB_M{}^b$	$d\phi$
$d\lambda_C$	$\dfrac{1 - T_1}{T_{11}\lambda_C}$	$\dfrac{1 - T_2}{T_{22}\lambda_C}$	$\dfrac{-P_{CM}P_{MB}T_3}{T_{33}\lambda_C}$	$\dfrac{1}{U''(\phi)\exp(-\rho t)}$
$d\lambda_M$	$-\dfrac{1}{T_{11}\lambda_C}$	0	$\dfrac{-P_{CM}P_{MB}T_3}{T_{33}\lambda_C}$	0
$d\lambda_B$	0	$-\dfrac{1}{T_{22}\lambda_C}$	$\dfrac{(P_{CM}P_{BM})^2}{T_{33}\lambda_C P_{CB}}$	0

^{a}This table summarizes how the household adjusts its choice variables at time t with respect to changes in shadow prices at the same time t. If shadow prices change for all $t \in [0, T]$, then the table indicates how the choice variables will change at each $t \in [0, T]$. The marginal conditions III.2.12 and III.2.13, which determine the household's demands for consumption goods in exchange for money and bonds, imply that $\lambda_M(t)/\lambda_C(t) = 1 - T_1^d(C_M(t))$ and $\lambda_B(t)/\lambda_C(t) = 1 - T_2^d(C_B(t))$. Because $\lambda_M(t)$, $\lambda_C(t)$, and $\lambda_B(t)$ are positive for all $t \in [0, T]$ (see Appendix C), $1 - T_1^d(C_M(t))$ and $1 - T_2^d(C_B(t))$ are positive.
^{b}The rates of change in terms of the consumption good of the demand for bonds in exchange for money are given by $d(b_M\Pi)/d\lambda_C = -T_3/T_{33}\lambda_C$, $d(b_M\Pi)/d\lambda_M = -1/T_{33}\lambda_C$, and $d(b_M\Pi)/d\lambda_B = 1/T_{33}\lambda_C\Pi$, where all variables are evaluated at the same time $t \in [0, T]$.

exchange for bonds and increases the rate at which it demands bonds in exchange for money at time t.

In each of the preceding comparative static analyses the effect of an increase in the shadow price of a stock at time t (i.e., the effect of an increase at time t in discounted marginal utility of a stock) is to stimulate adjustments in the choice variables at time t. These adjustments increase the rate of change of the stock at time t. The results are summarized in Table IV.1.

Comparative static analysis of changes in the household's discount factor reveals that when the discount factor is increased at time t, the household does not adjust its demands for the three commodities but decreases its rate of consumption at time t. The comparative static derivative of the rate of consumption with respect to changes in the discount factor of time t is given by

$$\frac{d\phi}{d\rho} = \frac{U'(\phi)}{U''(\phi)} t < 0 \tag{IV.2.1}$$

Changes in any of the exogenously given market prices $P_{CM}(t)$, $P_{CB}(t)$, and $P_{MB}(t)$ at time t do not affect the household's rates of demand for the consumption good in exchange for money or bonds at time t as determined by the instantaneous maximization problem. This implies that the elasticity of the instantaneous demands for money and bonds in exchange for consumption goods at time t with respect to the prices $P_{CM}(t)$ and $P_{CB}(t)$, respectively, is unity.

The influence of changes in any of the market prices on the real rate of demand for bonds in exchange for money, $b_M(t)\,\Pi\,(t)$, depends on the relationship among the market prices established by arbitrage. If $\Pi\,(t)$ remains constant,[2] then no adjustment in $b_M(t)\,\Pi\,(t)$ occurs as $P_{CM}(t)$, $P_{CB}(t)$, or $P_{MB}(t)$ changes, and the elasticity of the instantaneous nominal demand for bonds in exchange for money (i.e., the elasticity of $B_M(t)$ with respect to $P_{CM}(t)$, $P_{CB}(t)$, and $P_{MB}(t)$) is unity. Hence, if $B_M(t)$ is positive (negative), then an increase in $P_{CM}(t)$, $P_{CB}(t)$, or $P_{MB}(t)$ at time t will lead to an equiproportional increase (decrease) in $B_M(t)$ at time t.

The additional effect that occurs because of a decrease in $\Pi(t)$ as $P_{CM}(t)$ or $P_{MB}(t)$ increases is an increase in $b_M(t)\,\Pi\,(t)$, whereas the effect of an increase in this price ratio because of an increase in $P_{CB}(t)$ is a reduction in $b_M(t)\,\Pi(t)$. These additional effects on $b_M(t)\,\Pi(t)$ are implied by the marginal condition that determines $B_M(t)$ at each instant t (see equation III.2.14). In this condition the shadow price of additions to the real bond stock is weighted by the ratio $\mathrm{III}(t) \equiv P_{CM}(t)P_{MB}(t)/P_{CB}(t)$, and we saw previously that an increase in $\lambda_B(t)$ causes an increase in $b_M(t)\,\Pi(t)$. The instantaneous effects at time t on demands due to changes in any of the market prices are summarized in Table IV.2.[3]

Hence, given the restrictions of its instantaneous maximization problem, the household does not adjust its real rates of demand $C_M(t)$, $C_B(t)$, and $b_M(t)\,\Pi(t)$ when changes in market prices are consistent with the arbitrage assumption. This behavior is explained by the fact that the household takes the three shadow prices as exogenously given at the instant when prices change. A change in the household's level or composition of real wealth influences the solution of the instantaneous maximization problem at time t only through a change in the shadow price at time t. However, in the instantaneous maximization problem the shadow prices are invariant as market prices change. Therefore, as the household adjusts its choice variables in response to changes in market prices, it ignores variations in the composition or level of real wealth that result from changes in market prices. Thus, comparative static analysis of the effects of a change in market prices on the instantaneous maximization problem determines the household's compensated instantaneous demand functions. The household behaves as if it had been compensated for changes in the composition or level of real wealth that occurred because of changes in market prices.

If the change in market prices is such that the price ratio $\Pi(t)$ increases, then the marginal cost of acquiring consumption goods in the consumption-

Table IV.2. *Instantaneous effects of changes in market prices on demand*[a]

	dC_M	dC_B	$d(b_M\Pi)$	dM_C	dB_C	dB_M^*	dM_B^*	dB_M	dM_B
$\dfrac{dP_{CM}}{P_{CM}}$	0	0	0	M_C	0	B_M	M_B	$B_M + k$	$M_B - P_{BM}k$
$\dfrac{dP_{CB}}{P_{CB}}$	0	0	0	0	B_C	B_M	M_B	$-k$	$P_{BM}k$
$\dfrac{dP_{MB}}{P_{MB}}$	0	0	0	0	0	B_M	M_B	$B_M + k$	$-P_{BM}k$

[a] The variable k is defined as $k = [(P_{CM}(t)\,P_{MB}(t))^2/P_{CB}(t)]\,(\lambda_B(t)/\lambda_C(t))\,(1/T_{33})$. The values of the differentials marked by asterisks depend on the assumption that $\Pi\,(t)$ does not change as any of the prices change. All of these results can be derived from the matrix equation D.5 in Appendix D.

good-cum-bonds market rises relative to the marginal cost of acquiring consumption goods with bonds by giving through the consumption-good-cum-money and money-cum-bonds markets. The marginal conditions that determine the real demand $b_M(t)\,\Pi(t)$ (see equation III.2.14) then imply that $b_M(t)\,\Pi(t)$ must decrease, while $C_M(t)$ and $C_B(t)$ remain unchanged.

A decrease in the real level of one of the three stocks leads to an increase in its shadow price at each $t \in [0, T]$. The household will react to this increase by changing its choice variables so as to increase the rate of accumulation of the stock at each $t \in [0, T]$. Hence the wealth effect works through the shadow prices of additions to inventories. Thus Table IV.1 represents the income or wealth effects, and Table IV.2 represents the instantaneous substitution effects.

IV.3   An introduction to comparative dynamic analysis of the household's responses to changes in initial endowments of money, bonds, and consumption goods

The previous section contained a comparative static analysis of the effects of changes in market prices, shadow prices, and parameters on the household's solution to its instantaneous maximization problem. It was shown that the instantaneous reactions of the household to changes in market prices represent pure substitution effects, whereas the reactions to changes in shadow prices are the equivalents of income or wealth effects.

In this section we shall investigate the effects of changes in the initial endowments of money, consumption goods, and bonds on the household's demand, consumption, and stock-holding behaviors over its life span $[0, T]$. In the course of this inquiry we shall employ the results from the comparative static analysis of wealth effects together with the marginal conditions for optimal stock holding. Because there does not exist a well-defined mathematical method by which comparative dynamic results can be obtained, it is necessary to make explicit the household's incentives for changing the existing levels of its endogenous variables as the initial endowments change. Hence, after postulating a disturbance in one of the initial endowments, we shall trace how the equilibrium conditions are affected and what the household does to reestablish equilibrium.

The household's initial endowments, together with the equations of motion and its instantaneous optimization problem, determine the level of its real inventories of money, consumption goods, and bonds at each point in time. The instantaneous maximization problem reveals that the household's choice variables at time t depend on the values of the shadow prices, market prices, and parameter variables at time t. Additionally, the position of the paths of the shadow prices are contingent on the final value of the household's real stock holding, and the slopes depend on the various rates of depreciation of the stocks (Appendix C provides solutions to the equations of motion that determine the paths of state and co-state variables). Thus, before analyzing the consequences of changes in the initial endowments for the paths of the household's choice variables $C_M(t)$, $C_B(t)$, $B_M(t)$, and $\phi(t)$ and the paths of the household's state variables $m(t)$, $C(t)$, and $b(t)$, it is necessary to determine how changes in the initial endowments affect the shadow prices at all $t \in [0, T]$. Application of the results from the previous section will then reveal the effects of changes in the shadow prices on the choice variables at each $t \in [0, T]$. Finally, the new paths for the household's stocks of real money, consumption goods, and real bonds are determined by the equations of motion for the state variables. The assumption that the utility-of-bequest function is separable (i.e., $\beta_{ij}(m(T), C(T), b(T)) = 0$ whenever $i \neq j$ ($i, j = 1, 2, 3$)), is employed to simplify the following analysis.

IV.4   A comparative dynamic analysis of the household's response to changes in initial endowments of money

The comparative dynamic analysis of the household's response to an increase in its initial endowments of money has been divided into two stages.

Stage I begins with an analysis of the effect that an increase in the initial money stock has on λ_M, the shadow price of additions to the money stock. The comparative statics results of Section IV.2 are then employed to determine the effects of the change in λ_M on the household's choice variables $C_M(t)$, $C_B(t)$, $B_M(t)$, and $\phi(t)$. These changes in the rates of demand and consumption affect $M(t)$, $C(t)$, and $B(t)$, the stocks of money, consumption goods, and bonds, through the equations of motion. Lastly, this change in the household's stocks induces changes in the shadow prices of additions to these stocks.

In stage II we explore the effects of the stage I changes in the shadow prices of additions to the bond and consumption-good stocks on the household's choice variables as well as the subsequent effects on the stocks of bonds, money, and consumption goods. Hence, at the end of stages I and II of the household's adjustment process, it has established new rates of demand and consumption and new levels for its three stocks. In stage II we do not analyze the effects of the change in the stock of money brought about with the changes in the choice variables in stages I and II. However, it will be shown that the household's money stock at the end of stage II, namely, $m(t)^{**}$, lies strictly between the original money stock, $\overline{m}(t)$, and the original money stock plus the postulated increase, $\overline{m}(t) + \Delta m_0(t)$; that is,

$$\overline{m}(t) < m(t)^{**} < \overline{m}(t) + \Delta m_0(t) \qquad \forall \, t \in [0, T]$$

We then proceed to a second iteration by repeating the stage I and stage II adjustment processes, with the disturbance in the money stock equal to $M(T)^{**} - \overline{M}(T)$. In each subsequent iteration the disturbance in the stock of money is set equal to the difference between the money stock at the end of the last iteration and the money stock at the beginning of the last iteration. We shall prove that the disturbance in the stock of money gets smaller and that the iterations converge to an equilibrium. We shall then have established the following proposition.

Comparative dynamics proposition 1

An increase in the initial endowment of money results in an increase in the demand for consumption goods and bonds in exchange for money and an increase in the demand for consumption goods in exchange for bonds at all $t \in [0, T]$. The household's stocks of money, bonds, and consumption goods will exceed their original levels at all $t \in [0, T]$, and the rate of consumption will increase everywhere on $[0, T]$.

Figure IV.1 is a schematic representation of one iteration of the household's adjustment process and its dichotomization into two stages. The subscript i denotes the ith iteration, and an arrow indicates an implication; t varies over all of $[0, T]$. The $(i+1)$st iteration begins with $\overline{q}(0)_{i+1} = (m(0)_i^{**}, C(0)_i^{**}, b(0)_i^{**})$ as initial endowment vector and $\overline{v}(t)_{i+1} = (C_M(t)_i^{**}, C_B(t)_i^{**}, b_M(t_i^{**}, \phi(t)_i^{**})$ as vector of choice variables and $(\Delta M_0)_{i+1} = (M(T)_i^{**} - \overline{M}(T)_i) < (\Delta M_0)_i$.

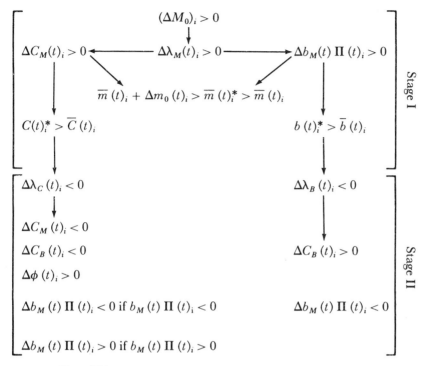

Figure IV.1

We shall now proceed to establish the preceding proposition by following the line of reasoning outlined at the beginning of this section.

An increase in the initial endowment of nominal money by ΔM_0, ceteris paribus, raises the real stock of money at time T by $\Delta m_0(T)$. Because of the strict concavity and separability of the utility-of-bequest function $\beta(\cdot)$, this increase in final real money holdings implies that $\beta_1(\overline{m}(T) + \Delta m_0(T)) < \overline{\lambda}_M(T)$, where $\overline{\lambda}_M(T)$ and $\overline{M}(T)$ denote the values of the shadow price and the money stock, respectively, before any change in initial endowments. In order to satisfy the transversality conditions, the household must choose a new path for $\lambda_M(t)$ such that $\lambda_M(T) = \beta_1(\overline{m}(T) + \Delta m_0(T))$. The fact that this new path $\lambda_M(t)$ is everywhere below the old path $\overline{\lambda}_M(t)$,[4] together with the results from the comparative static analysis summarized in Table IV.1, implies that the choice variables $C_M(t)$ and $b_M(t)\Pi(t)$ must be higher at all $t \in [0, T]$.[5] Thus the rate of change of the real money stock, given by the accumulation equation II.5.9., decreases at each $t \in [0, T]$, and the real money stock falls below $\overline{M}(t) + \Delta M_0$ everywhere. The enlarged demands for consumption goods and real bonds in exchange for money cause the rates at which the household accumulates consumption goods and real bonds to increase, thereby augmenting the stocks of consumption goods and bonds at each $t \in [0, T]$. These aspects of the household's adjustment process are called stage I. Hence, in stage I the household is able to adjust all variables, but in so doing it ignores the effects of the increases in $C(t)$ and $b(t)$ on $\lambda_C(t)$ and $\lambda_B(t)$.[6] During stage II of its adjustment process the household reacts to the changes in $\lambda_C(t)$ and $\lambda_B(t)$.

The function $\beta_1(m(T))$ is continuous and decreasing in the variable $m(T)$; $\lambda_M(t)$ is a continuous and increasing function of $\beta_1(m(T))$ at each $t \in [0, T]$; $C_M(t)$ and $b_M(t)\Pi(t)$ are continuous and decreasing in the variable $\lambda_M(t)$ at each $t \in [0, T]$. We have thus proved the following proposition.

Comparative dynamics proposition 1.1

After all stage I adjustments have been completed, the household will have a greater demand for consumption goods and bonds in exchange for money at each $t \in [0, T]$, and it will have higher bond, money, and consumption-good stocks throughout the interval $[0, T]$; that is,[7]

$$C_M(t)^* > \overline{C}_M(t), \qquad b_M(t)^*\Pi(t) > \overline{b}_M(t)\Pi(t) \qquad \forall\, t \in [0, T] \qquad \text{(IV.4.1)}$$

$$C(t)^* > \overline{C}(t), \qquad b(t)^* > \overline{b}(t) \qquad \forall\, t \in [0, T] \qquad \text{(IV.4.2)}$$

$$\overline{m}(t) + \Delta\, m_0(t) > m(t)^* > \overline{m}(t) \qquad \forall\, t \in [0, T] \qquad \text{(IV.4.3)}$$

The increases in the real stock of bonds and in the stock of consumption goods at each $t \in [0, T]$ stimulate a decline in the shadow prices of additions to these stocks at each $t \in [0, T]$.[8] In the preceding section, comparative static analysis of the effects of changes in the shadow prices on the choice variables showed that a decrease in $\lambda_C(t)$ at each $t \in [0, T)$ causes reductions in $C_M(t)$ and $C_B(t)$, an increase in $\phi(t)$, an increase in $B_M(t)$ if $B_M(t) > 0$; and a decrease in $B_M(t)$ if $B_M(t) < 0$ at each $t \in [0, T]$. The diminution in $\lambda_B(t)$ at each $t \in [0, T]$ induces a decline in $B_M(t)$ and an increase in $C_B(t)$ at each $t \in [0, T]$.[9] These changes constitute stage II in the household's adjustment process.

During stage II the reduction in $\lambda_C(t)$ causes the household to increase its rate of consumption and to reduce its demand for consumption goods, thus diminishing at each $t \in [0, T]$ the stock of consumption goods, $C(t)^*$, accumulated during stage I. However, considerations of continuity suggest that the reduction in total demand for the consumption good together with the increased rate of consumption cannot reduce $C(T)$ below $\overline{C}(T)$. That is, after stage I and stage II choice-variable adjustments, the final stock of the consumption good remains above its original level $\overline{C}(T)$. Similarly, the reduction in $\lambda_B(t)$ resulting from the increase in $b(t)$ at each $t \in [0, T]$ causes the total demand for bonds in exchange for money and consumption goods to decline everywhere on the interval $[0, T]$. However, continuity again implies that the real bond stock at $t = T$ cannot fall below $\overline{b}(T)$ after stage I and stage II adjustments in the choice variables have been made. Hence,

$$C(T)^{**} > \overline{C}(T) \tag{IV.4.4}$$

and

$$b(T)^{**} > \overline{b}(T) \tag{IV.4.5}$$

where double asterisks indicate that stage I and stage II adjustments have been completed.

So far in stage II of its adjustment process, the household has disregarded the cross-effects of the decrease in $\lambda_C(t)$ on the real bond stock (i.e., $(dC_B(t)/d\lambda_C(t)) \Delta\lambda_C(t)$ and $(d(b_M(t)\Pi(t))/d\lambda_C(t)) \Delta\lambda_C(t)$ and on the real money stock (i.e., $(dC_M(t)/d\lambda_C(t)) \Delta\lambda_C(t)$ and $(d(b_M(t)\Pi(t))/d\lambda_C(t)) \Delta\lambda_C(t)$). It has also ignored the cross-effects of the decrease in $\lambda_B(t)$ on the consumption-good stock (i.e., $(dC_B(t)/d\lambda_B(t)) \Delta\lambda_B(t)$ and on the real money stock (i.e., $(d(b_M(t)\Pi(t))/d\lambda_B(t)) \Delta\lambda_B(t)$). However, we shall show next that these changes in the household's stocks, induced by the cross-effects, are not strong enough to invalidate inequality IV.4.4 or IV.4.5.

Because $C(T)^{**} > \overline{C}(T)$ when cross-effects are ignored (see inequality IV.4.4), and $(dC_B(t)/d\lambda_B(t)) \Delta\lambda_B(t) > 0$, $C(T)^{**} > \overline{C}(T)$ remains valid after the household completes all adjustments, including those stimulated by cross-effects. Also, $(dC_B(t)/d\lambda_C(t)) \Delta\lambda_C(t) < 0$; thus the only cross-effect that might reduce $B(T)^{**}$ occurs when $(dB_M(t)/d\lambda_C(t)) \Delta\lambda_C(t) < 0$. If $C_B(T)$ increases on $[0, T]$ during stage II, then the right-hand side of equation III.2.13, namely, $\lambda_B(t) = \lambda_C(t) (1 - T_2^d(C_B(t)))$, must decrease, because $\lambda_C(t)$ is lower on $[0, T]$. However, a reduction in $\lambda_B(t)$ on $[0, T]$ implies that $B(T)^{**} > \overline{B}(T)$.[10] If $C_B(t)$ decreases and $C_M(t)$ increases on $[0, T]$,[11] then equation IV.4.5 indicates that $B_M(t)$ must increase everywhere on $[0, T]$. However, if $B_M(t)$ increases everywhere on $[0, T]$ during stage II, then, after the household executes all adjustments, $b(T)^{**} > \overline{b}(T)$. The completion of stage I adjustments results in $m(T)^{*} > \overline{m}(T)$ (see inequality IV.4.3). All stage II changes in the choice variables further increase $m(T)^{*}$ unless $(dB_M(t)/d\lambda_C(t)) \Delta\lambda_C(t) > 0$. However, the equation $\lambda_M(t) = \lambda_C(t) (1 - T_1^d(C_M(t)))$ (see equation III.2.12), together with a lower $\lambda_C(t)$ and higher $C_M(t)$ on $[0, T]$, implies that $\lambda_M(t)$ must be lower on $[0, T]$. Therefore, $m(T)$ must increase even when $(dB_M(t)/d\lambda_C(t)) \Delta\lambda_C(t) > 0$. We have thus established the following proposition.

Comparative dynamics proposition 1.2

After all stage II adjustments have been executed, the household will have higher bond, money, and consumption-good stocks at time T:

$$m(T)^{**} > \overline{m}(T), \quad C(T)^{**} > \overline{C}(T), \quad b(T)^{**} > \overline{b}(T)$$

where double asterisks indicate that the variable has attained its stage II equilibrium value.

Now we must show that the stage II changes in $C_M(t)$ and $b_M(t)\Pi(t)$ are not strong enough to upset the changes in these choice variables that occurred in stage I. We shall also investigate the change in $C_B(t)$ in stage II.

The equations of motion for the consumption-good stock and for the real bond stock (see equations II.5.10 and II.5.11), together with inequalities IV.4.4 and IV.4.5, imply

$$\int_0^T \left[\frac{dC_M(t)}{d\lambda_M(t)} \Delta\lambda_M(t) + \frac{dC_M(t)}{d\lambda_C(t)} \Delta\lambda_C(t) \right.$$
$$\left. + \frac{dC_B(t)}{d\lambda_C(t)} \Delta\lambda_C(t) - \frac{d\phi(t)}{d\lambda_C(t)} \Delta\lambda_C(t) \right] d\tau > 0 \quad \text{(IV.4.6)}$$

$$\int_0^T \left[\frac{d(b_M(t)\Pi(t))}{d\lambda_M(t)} \Delta\lambda_M(t) + \frac{d(b_M(t)\Pi(t))}{d\lambda_B(t)} \Delta\lambda_B(t) \right.$$
$$\left. - \frac{dC_B(t)}{d\lambda_B(t)} \Delta\lambda_B(t) \right] d\tau > 0 \quad \text{(IV.4.7)}$$

where $\Delta\lambda_M(t) < 0$, $\Delta\lambda_B(t) < 0$, and $\Delta\lambda_C(t) < 0$ for all $t \in [0, T]$ denote the changes in the shadow prices in stages I and II. Because $(dC_B(t)/d\lambda_C(t)) \Delta\lambda_C(t) < 0$, $(d\phi(t)/d\lambda_C(t)) \Delta\lambda_C(t) > 0$, and $(dC_B(t)/d\lambda_B(t)) \Delta\lambda_B(t) > 0$ for all $t \in [0, T]$, inequalities IV.4.6 and IV.4.7 imply

$$\int_0^T \left[\frac{dC_M(t)}{d\lambda_M(t)} \Delta\lambda_M(t) + \frac{dC_M(t)}{d\lambda_C(t)} \Delta\lambda_C(t) \right] dt > 0 \quad \text{(IV.4.8)}$$

$$\int_0^T \left[\frac{d(b_M(t)\Pi(t))}{d\lambda_M(t)} \Delta\lambda_M(t) + \frac{d(b_M(t)\Pi(t))}{d\lambda_B(t)} \Delta\lambda_B(t) \right] dt > 0 \quad \text{(IV.4.9)}$$

Hence, the stage I decrease in $\lambda_M(t)$ on the interval $[0, T]$ causes an increase in the integral of the increases in $C_M(t)$ over the same interval that exceeds in magnitude the integral of the decreases in $C_M(t)$ caused by a stage II reduction in $\lambda_C(t)$. A similar statement is true for the changes in the choice variable $b_M(t)\Pi(t)$.

However, the percentage rate of change $(dC_M(t)/d\lambda_M(t)) \Delta\lambda_M(t)$ equals the percentage rate of change $(dC_M(t)/d\lambda_C(t)) \Delta\lambda_C(t)$.[12] Thus, $(dC_M(t)/d\lambda_M(t)) \Delta\lambda_M(t) + (dC_M(t)/d\lambda_C(t)) \Delta\lambda_C(t)$ cannot change signs on $[0, T]$.

This fact, together with inequality IV.4.8, implies

$$\frac{dC_M(t)}{d\lambda_M(t)}\Delta\lambda_M(t) + \frac{dC_M(t)}{d\lambda_C(t)}\Delta\lambda_C(t) > 0 \qquad \forall\, t \in [0,\,T] \qquad \text{(IV.4.10)}$$

The difference between the percentage rate of change $(d(b_M(t)\,\Pi(t))/d\lambda_M(t))\,\Delta\lambda_M(t)$ and the percentage rate of change $(d(b_M(t)\,\Pi(t))/d\lambda_B(t))\,\Delta\lambda_B(t)$ equals $P_{MB}(t) - \hat{P}_{MB}(t).$[13] If $P_{MB}(t) - \hat{P}_{MB}(t) < 0$ for all $t \in [0,\,T]$, then inequality IV.4.9 implies

$$\frac{d(b_M(t)\Pi(t))}{d\lambda_M(t)}\Delta\lambda_M(t) + \frac{d(b_M(t)\Pi(t))}{d\lambda_B(t)}\Delta\lambda_B(t) \lesseqqgtr 0 \qquad \text{as } t \lesseqqgtr t^* \qquad \text{(IV.4.11)}$$

where $t \in [0,\,T]$ and $0 < t^* \le T$. However, if $(P_{MB}(t) - \hat{P}_{MB}(t)) > 0$ for all $t \in [0,\,T]$, then inequality IV.4.9 implies

$$\frac{d(b_M(t)\Pi(t))}{d\lambda_M(t)}\Delta\lambda_M(t) + \frac{d(b_M(t)\Pi(t))}{d\lambda_B(t)}\Delta\lambda_B(t) \gtreqqless 0 \qquad \text{as } t \lesseqqgtr t^* \qquad \text{(IV.4.12)}$$

where $t \in [0,\,T]$ and $0 \le t^* < T$.

Therefore, although the integral of the changes in $b_M(t)\,\Pi(t)$ is positive over the interval $[0,\,T]$,

$$\int_0^T \left[\frac{d(b_M(t)\Pi(t))}{d\lambda_M(t)}\Delta\lambda_M(t) + \frac{d(b_M(t)\Pi(t))}{d\lambda_B(t)}\Delta\lambda_B(t)\right] dt > 0 \qquad \text{(IV.4.13)}$$

the household may reduce its real demand for bonds in exchange for money over some subinterval of $[0,\,T]$. Particularly, if the interest rate (i.e., $P_{MB}(t)$) rises fast enough, then initially the change in the demand for bonds in exchange for money is greater than zero, but this change declines over $[0,\,T]$ and may become negative after some point t^*, where $0 < t^* \le T$. In this scenario the household adds to its stock of bonds early in the interval $[0,\,T]$ in order to maximize its benefits from increased interest income. However, if the interest rate declines or does not rise fast enough, then the change in the demand for bonds in exchange for money is negative on $[0,\,t^*)$, with $t^* < T$, increases on all of $[0,\,T]$, and is positive on $(t^*,\,T]$. Hence, the relationship between the rate of increase of the interest rate and the interest rate itself determines the rate at which the household adds to its stock of bonds.

The choice-variable change that remains to be investigated is the stage II adjustment in $C_B(t)$. The marginal conditions determining the household's demands at each $t \in [0,\,T]$ (see equations III.2.12, III.2.13, and III.2.14) imply

$$(1 - \Pi(t)) + \Pi(t)T_1^d(C_M(t)) - T_2^d(C_B(t)) = \Pi(t)T_3^d(b_M(t)\Pi(t)) \qquad \text{(IV.4.14)}$$

Total differentiation of equation IV.4.14 establishes

$$\Pi(t)T_{11}^d(C_M(t))\, dC_M(t) = \Pi(t)T_{33}^d(b_M(t)\Pi(t))\, d(b_M(t)\Pi(t))$$
$$+ T_{12}^d(C_B(t))\, dC_B(t) \quad (IV.4.15)$$

Hence, $dC_B(t) = (dC_B(t)/d\lambda_C(t))\,\Delta\lambda_C(t) + (dC_B(t)/d\lambda_B(t))\,\Delta\lambda_B(t) \gtrless 0$ if $T_{11}^d(C_M(t))\, dC_M(t) \gtrless T_{33}^d(b_M(t)\,\Pi(t))\, d(b_M(t)\,\Pi(t))$. The changes in $C_M(t)$ and $B_M(t)$ resulting from the stage I adjustment of $\lambda_M(t)$ are such that $T_{11}^d(C_M(t))\,(dC_M(t)/d\lambda_M(t))\,\Delta\lambda_M(t) = T_{33}^d(b_M(t)\,\Pi(t))\,(d(b_M(t)\,\Pi(t))/d\lambda_M(t))\,\Delta\lambda_M(t)$. Therefore, it suffices to examine the changes in $C_M(t)$ and $B_M(t)$ that occur in stage II. The changes in $C_M(t)$ and $b_M(t)\,\Pi(t)$ due to the decrease in $\lambda_C(t)$ are given in note 9 for this chapter.

$$T_{11}^d(C_M(t))\, \frac{dC_M(t)}{d\lambda_C(t)}\, d\lambda_C(t)$$

$$= (1 - T_1^d(C_M(t)))\, \frac{\beta_{22}(C(T))}{\beta_2(C(T))}\, (C(T)^{**} - C(T)^{*}) \quad (IV.4.16)$$

$$T_{33}^d(b_M(t)\Pi(t))\, \frac{d(b_M(t)\Pi(t))}{d\lambda_C(t)}\, \Delta\lambda_C(t)$$

$$= - T_3^d(b_M(t)\Pi(t))\, \frac{\beta_{22}(C(T))}{\beta_2(C(T))}\, (C(T)^{**} - C(T)^{*}) \quad (IV.4.17)$$

The change in $B_M(t)$ caused by the change in $\lambda_B(t)$ is

$$T_{33}^d(b_M(t)\Pi(t))\, \frac{d(b_M(t)\Pi(t))}{d\lambda_B(t)}\, \Delta\lambda_B(t)$$

$$= \frac{1}{\Pi(t)}\, \frac{\beta_{33}b(T)\exp\left(-\int_t^T (\hat{P}_{CB} - P_{MB} - \delta)\, d\tau\right)}{\beta_2(C(T))}$$
$$\cdot (b(T)^{**} - b(T)^{*}) \quad (IV.4.18)$$

Thus, a necessary and sufficient condition for $dC_B(t) > 0$ is

$$(1 - T_1^d(C_M(t)) + T_3^d(b_M(t)\Pi(t))\, \frac{\beta_{22}(C(T))}{\beta_2(C(T))}\, (C(T))^{**} - C(T)^{*})$$

$$> \frac{1}{\Pi(t)}\, \frac{\beta_{33}b(T)\exp\left(-\int_t^T (\hat{P}_{CB} - P_{MB} - \delta)\, d\tau\right)}{\beta_2(C(T))}$$
$$\cdot (b(T)^{**} - b(T)^{*}) \quad (IV.4.19)$$

The percentage rates of change of $(dC_B(t)/d\lambda_C(t))\,\Delta\lambda_C(t)$ and $(dC_B(t)/d\lambda_B(t))\,\Delta\lambda_B(t)$ are equal;[14] hence, $dC_B(t) > 0$ for all $t \in [0, T]$, or $dC_B(t) < 0$

for all $t \in [0, T]$. Furthermore, there always exists a value of T large enough to guarantee that inequality IV.4.19 holds at $t = 0$. That is, for every ΔM_0 there exists a T such that $dC_B(t) > 0$ for all $t \in [0, T]$.

The last question that remains concerns the cross-effects of the change in $C_B(t)$ on $C_M(t)$ and $b_M(t) \Pi(t)$. A large increase in $C_B(t)$ on $[0, T]$ will result in a large increase in $C(t)$. It is thus necessary to show that the resulting large decrease in $\lambda_C(t)$ will not produce a lower $C_M(t)$ or $b_M(t) \Pi(t)$ everywhere on $[0, T]$. Similarly, a large decrease in $C_B(t)$ will result in a large increase in $b(t)$, and we must show that the necessary reduction in $\lambda_B(t)$ is not so large as to reduce $b_M(t) \Pi(t)$ and $C_M(t)$ on $[0, T]$. If the choice variable $C_B(t)$ increases everywhere on $[0, T]$, then inequality IV.4.11 or IV.4.12 will remain valid, because otherwise $b(T)^{**} < \overline{b}(T)$, thus contradicting inequality IV.4.5. If $C_B(t)$ decreases everywhere on $[0, T]$, then by equation IV.4.15 $b_M(t) \Pi(t)$ must increase everywhere on $[0, T]$ provided that $C_M(t)$ increases also. Hence, following all adjustments, inequalities IV.4.11 and IV.4.12 remain valid descriptions of the change in $B_M(t)$.

If $C_B(t)$ is higher in stage II, then equation IV.4.15, together with the fact that $B_M(t)$ is higher on some subinterval of $[0, T]$ (as shown by inequalities IV.4.11 and IV.4.12), implies that $dC_M(t) = (dC_M(t)/d\lambda_M(t)) \Delta\lambda_M(t) + (dC_M(t)/d\lambda_C(t)) \Delta\lambda_C(t) > 0$ for all $t \in [0, T]$. If $C_B(t)$ decreases on $[0, T]$, then $C_M(t)$ must increase on $[0, T]$ in stage II, because otherwise $C(T)^{**} < \overline{C}(T)$, which contradicts inequality IV.4.4. Hence $C_M(t)$ is higher after all adjustments have been made in stage.II.

Thus far the comparative dynamic analysis has ignored the income effects of changes in demand for the transactions good due to changes in $C_M(t)$, $C_B(t)$, and $b_M(t) \Pi(t)$. If these income effects are such that $C(T)$ decreases but $C(T)^* > \overline{C}(T)$ remains, then none of the qualitative conclusions of the foregoing analysis will change. However, if the income effects increase the demand for the transactions good such that $C(T)^*$ falls below $\overline{C}(T)$, then $C_M(t)$ and $C_B(t)$ must increase in stage II, whereas $\phi(t)$ declines, and $B_M(T)$ increases if $B_M(t) > 0$ or decreases if $B_M(t) < 0$. Because these changes must be such that $B(T)^* > B(T)$,[15] none of the qualitative results concerning the changes in the choice variables and state variables will change, except that $C(T)^*$ may be below $C(T)$.[16] Hence we have proved the following proposition.

Comparative dynamics proposition 1.3

After all stage II adjustments have been made, the household will demand more consumption goods in exchange for money and bonds at each $t \in [0, T]$ and will demand more bonds for money at some $t \in [0, T]$; that is;

$$C_M(t)^{**} > \overline{C}_M(t) \qquad \forall\, t \in [0, T]$$

$$C_B(t)^{**} > \overline{C}_B(t) \qquad \forall\, t \in [0, T]$$

$$b_M(t)\,\Pi(t) > \overline{b}_M(t)\,\Pi(t) \qquad t^* < t \le T$$

$$b_M(t)^{**}\,\Pi(t) < \overline{b}_M(t)\,\Pi(t) \qquad 0 \le t \le t^* < T$$

where double asterisks indicate that the variable has attained its stage II equilibrium value. The rate of comparison $\phi(t)$ increases everywhere on $[0, T]$.

Hence, the analysis of all possible adjustments that could occur in stages I and II is complete, but it ignores changes in $\lambda_M(t)^*$ caused by stage II adjustments of $m(T)^*$. However, any change in the final real money stock must be less than $\Delta m_0(t)$, because $b(T)$ and $C(T)$ increase. Therefore, the adjustment process can be repeated with an initial change in endowments equal to $(\Delta M_0)_1 = M(T)^{**} - \overline{M}(T)$.

With each iteration the change in endowments shrinks. Thus the adjustment process is stable in the following sense: When $q(T) = (C(T), m(T), b(T))$ and $v(t) = (C_M(t), C_B(t), b_M(t)\,\Pi(t), \phi(t))$, then $\exists$ an $\epsilon > 0$ and a positive integer N such that[17]

$$|q(T)_i^{**} - q(T)_i| < \epsilon \quad \text{whenever } i > N, \text{ and also } \forall\, t \in [0, T]$$

$$|v(t)_i^{**} - \overline{v}(t)_i| < \epsilon \quad \text{whenever } i > N$$

That is, iterations tend toward the unique and globally stable equilibrium associated with the new endowment vector.[18]

Because the initial trajectories for the choice and state variables with the endowment vector $(\overline{C}(0), \overline{m}(0), \overline{b}(0))$ are optimal, and $C(T)^{**} > \overline{C}(T)$, $m(T)^{**} > m(T)$, and $b(T)^{**} > \overline{b}(T)$, it must be that[19]

$$C(t)^{**} > \overline{C}(t) \qquad \forall\, t \in [0, T] \tag{IV.4.20}$$

$$m(T)^{**} > \overline{m}(T) \qquad \forall\, t \in [0, T] \tag{IV.4.21}$$

$$b(t)^{**} > \overline{b}(t) \qquad \forall\, t \in [0, T] \tag{IV.4.22}$$

Inequality IV.4.22 restricts the household's pattern of demands for bonds to the extent that the household cannot reduce its demand for bonds in exchange for money and subsequently increase its demands for bonds (i.e., $t^* \le 0$ in equation IV.4.12).

In summary, the equilibrium values of the choice and state variables associated with the initial endowment vector $(\overline{C}(0), m(0)+\Delta m_0(0), b(0))$ are such that the state variables exceed their original values everywhere and that $C_M(t)$ increases everywhere, whereas $C_B(t)$ increases everywhere if T is large enough. The choice variable $B_M(t)$ increases initially and may decrease as t approaches T; however, the integral of the changes in $b_M(t)\,\Pi(t)$ over $[0, T]$ is positive. The rate of consumption $\phi(t)$ increases everywhere on $[0, T]$.

IV.5   A comparative dynamic analysis of the household's response to changes in initial endowments of bonds

The comparative dynamic analysis of the effect of a change in the initial endowments of bonds on the trajectories of the household's state and choice variables parallels the preceding investigation into the effects of changes in the initial money stock.

In stage I of the household's adjustment process we analyze the effect of the increase in the initial bond stock on the shadow price of additions to this stock (i.e., λ_M). The comparative statics results of Section IV.2 are then used to determine the effects of the change in λ_M on the choice variables $C_M(t)$, $C_B(t)$, $B_M(t)$, and $\phi(t)$. The changes in these rates of demand and consumption affect the money, bond, and consumption-good stocks through the equations of motion. This change in the household's stocks in turn induces changes in the shadow prices of additions to these stocks.

In stage II of the household's adjustment process we explore the effects of the stage I changes in the shadow prices of additions to the consumption-good and money stocks on the household's choice variables, and further we analyze the effects of these changes in the choice variables on the household's stocks of money, bonds, and consumption goods. Thus, at the end of stages I and II of the household's adjustment process, it has established new rates for its demand and consumption and new levels for its three stocks.

However, in stage II we have not analyzed the effects on the bond stock of changes in the choice variables in stages I and II. But, as in the previous section, it will be shown that the household's bond stock at the end of stage II, $b(t)^{**}$, lies strictly between the original bond stock, $\bar{b}(t)$, and the original bond stock augmented by the increase in endowments, $\bar{b}(t) + \Delta b_0(t)$; that is,

$$\bar{b}(t) < b(t)^{**} < \bar{b}(t) + \Delta b_0(t) \qquad \forall\, t \in [0, T]$$

We then start a new iteration, with the disturbance in the initial stock of bonds equal to $b(T)^{**} - b(T)$ and the initial bond stock equal to $b(0)^{**}$. In each subsequent iteration the disturbance in the initial endowment is set equal to the difference between the bond stocks at the end and the beginning of the last iteration. We will then have established the following proposition.

Comparative dynamics proposition 2

An increase in the initial endowment of bonds results in a demand for consumption goods in exchange for money and bonds everywhere on $[0, T]$. The demand for bonds in exchange for money must be lower for at least a first part of $[0, T]$, but it may be higher as t approaches T. The household's stocks of bonds, money, and consumption goods all will be higher on $[0, T]$. The rate of consumption will also be higher everywhere on $[0, T]$.

The proof for the preceding proposition is similar to the proof for compar-

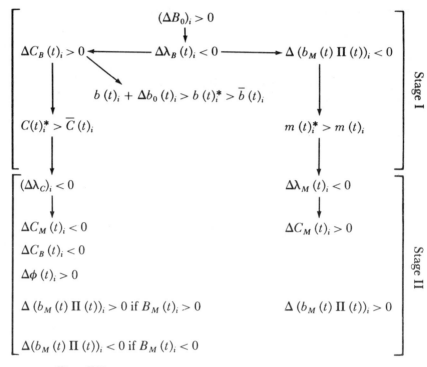

Figure IV.2

ative dynamics proposition 1 in that the analysis of the effects of changes in the initial endowment of bonds on the trajectories of the state and choice variables parallels the preceding investigation of the effects of changes in the initial money endowment. In particular, an increase in the initial nominal bond stock, ΔB_0, ceteris paribus, leads to an increase in the final real bond stock, $\Delta B_0(T)$, and thus to a decrease in $\lambda_B(t)$ at each $t \in [0, T]$.[20]

Figure IV.2 shows a schematic representation of the household's adjustment process. The $(i + 1)$st iteration begins with $(m(0)_i^{**}, C(0)_i^{**}, b(0)_i^{**})$ as initial endowment vector and $(C_M(t)_i^{**}, C_B(t)_i^{**}, b_M(t)_i \Pi(t)^{**}, \phi(t)_i^{**})$ as vector of choice variables, and $(\Delta B_0)_{i+1} = B(T)_i^{**} - \overline{B}(T)_i < (\Delta B_0)_i$. Then the change in the shadow price of real bonds causes an increase in the demand for consumption goods in exchange for bonds and a decrease in the demand for bonds in exchange for money at each $t \in [0, T]$.[21] These changes in the two choice variables result in a larger consumption-good stock and a larger real money stock at each $t \in [0, T]$. The increases in the stocks of consumption goods and real money are financed with the increment in the initial bond endowment, but the bond stock remains above its original level at all $t \in [0, T]$.[22] The changes in the state and choice variables described earlier constitute stage I of the household's adjustment process, and its outcome is summarized by the following proposition.

Comparative dynamics proposition 2.1

After all stage I adjustments have been completed, the household will have a larger demand for consumption goods in exchange for bonds and a smaller demand for bonds in exchange for money everywhere on $[0, T]$. The household also will have higher stocks of bonds, money, and consumption goods everywhere on $[0, T]$; that is,[23]

$$C_B(t)^* > \overline{C}_B(t), \qquad b_M(t)^* \, \Pi\,(t) < \overline{b}_M(t) \, \Pi\,(t) \qquad \forall\, t \in [0, T] \quad \text{(IV.5.1)}$$

$$C(t)^* > \overline{C}(t), \qquad m(t)^* > \overline{m}(t) \qquad\qquad\qquad \forall\, t \in [0, T] \quad \text{(IV.5.2)}$$

$$\overline{b}(t) + \Delta b_0(t) > b(t)^* > \overline{b}(t) \qquad\qquad\qquad\qquad \forall\, t \in [0, T] \quad \text{(IV.5.3)}$$

The review of stage I ignores the decreases in $\lambda_C(t)$ and $\lambda_M(t)$ caused by increases in $C(T)$ and $M(T)$. The household considers the effects of the decreases in $\lambda_C(t)$ and $\lambda_M(t)$ on the choice and state variables in stage II of the adjustment process.[24]

The decrease in $\lambda_C(t)$ at each $t \in [0, T]$ induces decreases in $C_M(t)$ and $C_B(t)$ at each $t \in [0, T]$ and a decrease in $B_M(t)$ if $B_M(t) < 0$ or an increase in $B_M(t)$ if $B_M(t) > 0$. The rate of consumption $\phi(t)$ is higher everywhere. Furthermore, the decrease in $\lambda_M(t)$ at each $t \in [0, T]$ impels the household to increase $C_M(t)$ and $B_M(t)$ at all $t \in [0, T]$.[25] The decreases in $C_M(t)$ and $C_B(t)$ and the increase in $\phi(t)$ cause $C(T)^*$ to decline; however, continuity ensures that $C(T)^*$ cannot fall below $\overline{C}(T)$. Similarly, although $M(T)^*$ declines because of the increases in $C_M(t)$ and $B_M(t)$, $M(T)^*$ cannot fall below $\overline{M}(T)$.

The analysis of stage II of the household's adjustment process ignores the cross-effects of the decrease in $\lambda_C(t)$ on the real money stock (i.e., $(dC_M(t)/d\lambda_C(t))\,\Delta\lambda_C(t)$ and $(d(b_M(t)\,\Pi\,(t))/d\lambda_C(t))\,\Delta\lambda_C(t))$ and on the real bond stock (i.e., $(dC_B(t)/d\lambda_C(t))\,\Delta\lambda_C(t)$ and $(d(b_M(t)\,\Pi\,(t))/d\lambda_C(t))\,\Delta\lambda_C(t))$. Also, it disregards the cross-effects of the decrease in $\lambda_M(t)$ on the consumption-good stock (i.e., $(dC_M(t)/D\lambda_C(t))\,\Delta\lambda_C(t))$ and on the stock of real bonds (i.e., $(d(b_M(t)\,\Pi\,(t))/d\lambda_M(t))\,\Delta\lambda_M(t))$.

Without considering cross-effects, it was established that $C(T)^{**} > \overline{C}(T)$, and because $(dC_M(t)/d\lambda_M(t))\,\Delta\lambda_M(t) > 0$, this inequality holds even after completion of all adjustments arising from cross-effects.

It was also shown that $m(T)^{**} > \overline{m}(T)$, without considering cross-effects. If $dC_M(t) > 0$ (see equation IV.5.18), then the right-hand side of the marginal condition that determines $C_M(t)$ (i.e., $\lambda_M(t) = \lambda_C(t)\,(1 - T_1^d\,(C_M(t)))$) (see equation III.2.12) decreases. Hence $\lambda_M(t)$ decreases everywhere on $[0, T]$, implying that $m(T)$ has increased. If $dC_M(t) < 0$, then $dC_B(t) > 0$ for all $t \in [0, T]$, because otherwise $C(T)^{**} < \overline{C}(T)$, and then equation IV.4.15 implies that $b_M(t) \, \Pi \, (t)$ decreases everywhere on $[0, T]$, and $m(T)$ increases. Therefore, $m(T)^{**} > \overline{m}(T)$ after all adjustments have been made. The marginal condition that determines $C_B(t)$ (i.e., $\lambda_B(t) = \lambda_C(t) \, (1 - T_2^d(C_B(t)))$) (see equation III.2.13), together with the facts that $\lambda_C(t)$ decreases everywhere on $[0, T]$ (because $C(T)^{**} > \overline{C}(T)$) and $dC_B(t) > 0$ when $dC_M(t) < 0$, implies that $\lambda_B(t)$ decreases, and hence $\overline{b}(t)^{**}$ must exceed $\overline{b}(T)$. We have thus established the following proposition.

Comparative dynamics proposition 2.2

After all adjustments have been made in stage II, the household will have higher consumption-good and money stocks; that is,

$$C(T)^{**} > \overline{C}(T) \tag{IV.5.4}$$

$$m(T)^{**} > \overline{m}(T) \tag{IV.5.5}$$

We shall now investigate whether the effects of the changes in $\lambda_C(t)$ and $\lambda_M(t)$ on $C_B(t)$ and $b_M(t) \, \Pi \, (t)$ in stage II are such as to reinforce or reverse the effects on $C_B(t)$ and $b_M(t) \, \Pi \, (t)$ due to the decrease in $\lambda_B(t)$ in stage I.

The equations of motion for the consumption-good stock and the real money stock, together with inequalities IV.5.4 and IV.5.5, imply that

$$\int_0^T \left[\frac{dC_B(t)}{d\lambda_B(t)} \Delta\lambda_B(t) + \frac{dC_B(t)}{d\lambda_C(t)} \Delta\lambda_C(t) \right.$$

$$\left. + \frac{dC_M(t)}{d\lambda_C(t)} \Delta\lambda_C(t) - \frac{d\phi(t)}{d\lambda_C(t)} \Delta\lambda_C(t) \right] dt > 0 \quad \text{(IV.5.6)}$$

$$- \int_0^T \left[\frac{d(b_M(t)\Pi(t))}{d\lambda_B(t)} \Delta\lambda_B(t) + \frac{d(b_M(t)\Pi(t))}{d\lambda_M(t)} \Delta\lambda_M(t) \right.$$

$$\left. + \frac{dC_M(t)}{d\lambda_M(t)} \Delta\lambda_M(t) \right] dt > 0 \quad \text{(IV.5.7)}$$

where $\Delta\lambda_B(t) < 0$, $\Delta\lambda_C(t) < 0$, and $\Delta\lambda_M(t) < 0$ denote changes in the shadow prices that occurred during stages I and II. Because

$$\frac{dC_M(t)}{d\lambda_C(t)} \Delta\lambda_C(t) < 0, \qquad \frac{d\phi(t)}{d\lambda_C(t)} \Delta\lambda_C(t) > 0,$$

$$\frac{dC_M(t)}{d\lambda_M(t)} \Delta\lambda_M(t) > 0 \qquad \forall \, t \in [0, T]$$

inequalities IV.5.6 and IV.5.7 imply that

$$\int_0^T \left[\frac{dC_B(t)}{d\lambda_B(t)} \Delta\lambda_B(t) + \frac{dC_B(t)}{d\lambda_C(t)} \Delta\lambda_C(t) \right] dt > 0 \tag{IV.5.8}$$

$$\int_0^T \left[\frac{d(b_M(t)\Pi(t))}{d\lambda_B(t)} \Delta\lambda_B(t) - \frac{d(b_M(t)\Pi(t))}{d\lambda_M(t)} \Delta\lambda_M(t) \right] dt > 0 \qquad \text{(IV.5.9)}$$

The percentage rate of change of $(dC_B(t)/d\lambda_B(t)) \Delta\lambda_B(t)$ over time equals the percentage rate of change of $(dC_B(t)/d\lambda_C(t)) \Delta\lambda_C(t)$.[26] Therefore, $(dC_B(t)/d\lambda_B(t)) \Delta\lambda_B(t) + (dC_B(t)/d\lambda_C(t)) \Delta\lambda_C(t)$ cannot change signs on $[0, T]$, which implies, by inequality IV.5.8, that

$$dC_B(t) = \frac{dC_B(t)}{d\lambda_B(t)} \Delta\lambda_B(t) + \frac{dC_B(t)}{d\lambda_C(t)} \Delta\lambda_C(t) > 0 \qquad \forall\, t \in [0, T] \qquad \text{(IV.5.10)}$$

The percentage rate of change of $(d(b_M(t)\,\Pi\,(t))/d\lambda_B(t)) \Delta\lambda_B(t)$ is given by $\hat{P}_{CM} - \delta + \hat{P}_{MB} - P_{MB}$, and the percentage rate of change over time of $(d(b_M(t)\,\Pi\,(t))/d\lambda_M(t)) \Delta\lambda_M(t)$ is given by $\hat{P}_{CM} - \delta$ (see note 13 for this chapter). If the difference between these two rates is negative (i.e., $\hat{P}_{MB} - P_{MB} < 0$), then

$$d(b_M(t)\Pi(t)) = \frac{d(b_M(t)\Pi(t))}{d\lambda_B(t)} \Delta\lambda_B(t)$$
$$+ \frac{d(b_M(t)\Pi(t))}{d\lambda_M(t)} \Delta\lambda_M(t) \lesseqgtr 0 \qquad \text{as } t \lesseqgtr t^* \qquad \text{(IV.5.11)}$$

where $t \in [0,T]$ and $0 < t^*$ by inequality IV.5.9. That is, if the percentage increase in the interest rate over time is less than the interest rate itself, then initially the household buys more money, and its rate of acquisition of money in exchange for bonds declines over time. If $\hat{P}_{MB} - P_{MB} > 0$, then

$$d(b_M(t)\,\Pi\,(t)) \gtreqless 0 \qquad \text{as } t \lesseqgtr t^* \qquad \text{(IV.5.12)}$$

where $t \in [0, T]$ and $t^* < T$ by inequality IV.5.9. In this case the increase in the rate of interest is high enough to induce the household to buy more bonds initially and thus to decrease its rate of acquisition of bonds over time. However, the pattern of change in $b_M(t)\,\Pi\,(t)$ described by inequality IV.5.12 implies that at the outset of the adjustment process the stock of money decreases to a level below its original value $\overline{m}(t)$. A subsequent section of this chapter will show that such a reduction in the money stock implies that the original money stock was not optimal. Hence, equation IV.5.11 provides an exhaustive description of the behavior of the changes in $b_M(t)\,\Pi\,(t)$.

It remains to investigate the stage II changes in the choice variable $C_M(t)$. Equation IV.4.15 implies that a necessary and sufficient condition for $C_M(t)$ to increase at $t \in [0, T]$ is given by

$$\Pi\,(t)\, T_{33}^d\, (b_M(t)\,\Pi\,(t)) d(b_M(t)\,\Pi\,(t))$$
$$+ T_{22}^d\, (C_B(t)) dC_B(t) > 0 \qquad \forall\, t \in [0, T] \qquad \text{(IV.5.13)}$$

where the two differentials are defined by

$$d(b_M(t)\Pi(t)) = \frac{d(b_M(t)\Pi(t))}{d\lambda_B(t)}\,\Delta\lambda_B(t) + \frac{d(b_M(t)\Pi(t))}{d\lambda_M(t)}\,\Delta\lambda_M(t)$$

$$+ \frac{d(b_M(t)\Pi(t))}{d\lambda_C(t)}\Delta\lambda_C(t) \qquad\qquad (IV.5.14)$$

$$dC_B(t) = \frac{dC_B(t)}{d\lambda_B(t)}\,\Delta\lambda_B(t) = \frac{dC_B(t)}{d\lambda_C(t)}\,\Delta\lambda_C(t) \qquad (IV.5.15)$$

The stage I changes in the two choice variables $b_M(t)\,\Pi(t)$ and $C_B(t)$ are such that

$$\Pi(t)\,T_{33}\frac{d(b_M(t)\Pi(t))}{d\lambda_B(t)}\,\Delta\lambda_B(t) + T_{22}\frac{dC_B(t)}{d\lambda_B(t)}\,\Delta\lambda_B(t) = 0$$

$$\forall\, t \in [0,\,T] \quad (IV.5.16)$$

Hence, for $C_M(t)$ to increase, inequality IV.5.13 must hold when the differentials are defined by

$$d(b_M(t)\Pi(t)) = \frac{d(b_M(t)\Pi(t))}{d\lambda_C(t)}\,\Delta\lambda_C(t) + \frac{d(b_M(t)\Pi(t))}{d\lambda_M(t)}\,\Delta\lambda_M(t)$$

$$dC_B(t) = \frac{dC_B(t)}{d\lambda_C(t)}\,\Delta\lambda_C(t)$$

Because

$$T_{33}^d\frac{d(b_M(t)\Pi(t))}{d\lambda_C(t)}\,\Delta\lambda_C(t) = -\,T_3^d\frac{\beta_{22}(\overline{C}(T))}{\beta_2(\overline{C}(T))}\,(C(T)^* - \overline{C}(T))$$

$$T_{33}^d\frac{d(b_M(t)\Pi(t))}{d\lambda_M(t)}\,\Delta\lambda_M(t)$$

$$= -\,\frac{\beta_{11}\overline{m}(T)}{\beta_2(\overline{C}(T))}\exp\left(-\int_t^T (\hat{P}_{CM} - \delta)\,d\tau\right)m(T)^* - \overline{m}(T)$$

$$T_{22}^d\frac{dC_B(t)}{d\lambda_C(t)}\,\Delta\lambda_C(t) = (1 - T_2^d)\frac{\beta_{22}(\overline{C}(T))}{\beta_2(\overline{C}(T))}\,(C(T)^* - \overline{C}(T))$$

equation IV.5.13 can be rewritten as

$$[1 - T_2^d - \Pi T_3^d]\frac{\beta_{22}(\overline{C}(T))}{\beta_2(\overline{C}(T))}\,(C(T)^* - \overline{C}(T)) - \Pi\,\frac{\beta_{11}\overline{m}(T)}{\beta_2(\overline{C}(T))}$$

$$\cdot\exp\left(-\int_t^T (\hat{P}_{CM} - \delta)\,d\tau\right)(m(T)^* - \overline{m}(T)) > 0 \quad (IV.5.17)$$

By substituting equation III.2.13 into equation III.2.14, it can be shown that $1 - T_2^d - \Pi\,T_3^d > 0$; thus the first term in inequality IV.5.17 is negative, and the second term is positive. Hence, the expression in IV.5.17 is larger the lower the value of t and the higher the value of T. Furthermore, there always exists a T large enough so that IV.5.17 is satisfied. From note 12 for this chapter we know that the percentage rates of change of $(dC_M(t)/d\lambda_M(t))$ $\Delta\lambda_M(t)$ and $(dC_M(t)/d\lambda_C(t))$ $\Delta\lambda_C(t)$ are both equal to $(\hat{P}_{CM}(t) - \delta)$; therefore the change in $C_M(t)$,

$$dC_M(t) = \frac{dC_M(t)}{d\lambda_C(t)} \Delta\lambda_C(t) + \frac{dC_M(t)}{d\lambda_M(t)} \Delta\lambda_M(t) \qquad \text{(IV.5.18)}$$

is such that $dC_M(t) > 0 \ \forall \ t \in [0, T]$, or $dC_M(t) < 0 \ \forall \ t \in [0, T]$. Hence

$$dC_M(t) > 0 \qquad \forall \ t \in [0, T] \qquad \text{(IV.5.19)}$$

if T is large enough.

The changes in the state variables that are due to the cross-effects produce changes in the choice variables; thus it is necessary to establish the validity of the qualitative results presented in equations IV.5.10, IV.5.11, and IV.5.19, given these further adjustments. If $dC_M(t) > 0 \ \forall \ t \in [0, T]$ (see equation IV.5.18), then $d(b_M(t) \ \Pi \ (t)) < 0$ on some subinterval of $[0, T]$ (see equation IV.5.14), because $dC_M(t) > 0$ and $d(b_M(t) \ \Pi \ (t)) > 0 \ \forall \ t \in [0, T]$ implies that $\overline{M}(T)^{**} < \overline{M}(T)$, which contradicts inequality IV.5.5. Furthermore, by equation IV.4.15, $dC_B(t) > 0 \ \forall \ t \in [0, T]$ (see equation IV.5.15) if $dC_M(t) > 0$ and $d(b_M(t) \ \Pi \ (t)) < 0$ for some $t \in [0, T]$. If $dC_M(t) < 0 \ \forall \ t \in [0, T]$ (see equation IV.5.18), then $dC_B(t) > 0 \ \forall \ t \in [0, T]$ (see equation IV.5.15), because $dC_M(t) < 0$ and $dC_B(t) < 0 \ \forall \ t \in [0, T]$ implies that $C(T)^{**} < \overline{C}(T)$, which contradicts inequality IV.5.4. Additionally, by equation IV.4.15, $d(b_M(t) \ \Pi \ (t)) < 0 \ \forall \ t \in [0, T]$ if $dC_M(t) < 0$ and $dC_B(t) > 0 \ \forall \ t \in [0, T]$. The foregoing arguments demonstrate that the cross-effects cannot invalidate the qualitative results established earlier concerning the changes in the choice variables. We have thus established the following proposition.

Comparative dynamics proposition 2.3

After all adjustments have been completed in stage II, the household will demand more consumption goods in exchange for money as well as bonds. The household will demand fewer bonds in exchange for money on the initial part of $[0, T]$ and may demand more bonds in exchange for money as t approaches T. The rate of consumption increases everywhere on $[0, T]$; that is,

$$C_B(t)^{**} > \overline{C}_B(t) \qquad \forall \ t \in [0, T]$$
$$C_M(t)^{**} > \overline{C}_M(t) \qquad \forall \ t \in [0, T]$$
$$b_M(t) \ \Pi \ (t)^{**} < \overline{b}_M(t) \ \Pi \ (t) \qquad 0 \le t \le t^* \le T$$
$$b_M(t) \ \Pi \ (t)^{**} > \overline{b}_M(t) \ \Pi \ (t) \qquad 0 < t^* \le t \le T$$
$$\phi(t)^{**} > \overline{\phi}(t) \qquad \forall \ t \in [0, T]$$

Hence, all possible adjustments that can occur in stage I and stage II have been analyzed, but the analysis ignores the change in $\lambda_B(t)^*$ brought about by the change in $b(T)^*$ resulting from stage II adjustments. After all adjustments of stages I and II, the change in $b(T)$ must be less than $\Delta b_0(T)$ (i.e., $b(T)^{**} - \bar{b}(T) < \Delta b_0(T)$), because $C(T)$ and $m(T)$ increase. A reexamination of the adjustment process with the initial changes in endowments defined by $(B_0)_1 = B(T)^{**} - \bar{B}(T)$ reveals that as in the case of an increase in the initial money stock, the process is stable, because the initial changes in endowments become smaller with each iteration. If the initial trajectories for the choice and state variables, given the endowment vector $(\bar{C}(0), \bar{m}(0), b(0))$, are optimal, and because $C(T)^{**} > \bar{C}(T), m(T)^{**} > \bar{m}(T)^{**}$, $b(T)^{**} > \bar{b}(T)$, one can conclude that

$$C(t)^{**} > \bar{C}(t) \quad \forall\, t \in [0, T] \tag{IV.5.20}$$

$$m(t)^{**} > \bar{m}(t) \quad \forall\, t \in [0, T] \tag{IV.5.21}$$

$$b(t)^{**} > \bar{b}(t) \quad \forall\, t \in [0, T] \tag{IV.5.22}$$

(see note 19 for this chapter).

In summary, the preceding analysis demonstrates that the equilibrium values of the choice and state variables associated with the endowment vector $(\bar{C}(0), \bar{m}(0), \bar{b}(0) + \Delta b_0(0))$ are such that the state variables exceed their original values everywhere and that $C_B(t)$ increases everywhere on $[0, T]$ and $C_M(t)$ increases everywhere if T is large enough. The demand for bonds in exchange for money (i.e., $b_M(t)\,\Pi\,(t)$) must decrease initially and may increase as t approaches T, and the integral of the changes in $b_M(t)\,\Pi\,(t)$ over $[0, T]$ is negative. The rate of consumption $\phi(t)$ increases everywhere on $[0, T]$.

IV.6   A comparative dynamic analysis of the household's response to changes in initial endowments of consumption goods

Following the method of analysis in the previous two sections, the comparative dynamic analysis of the household's response to an increase in its initial endowments of consumption goods has been divided into two stages.

In stage I we analyze the effects of the increase in the consumption-good stock on the shadow price of additions to this stock, $\lambda_C(t)$. This is followed by an investigation of the effects of the decrease in $\lambda_C(t)$ on the household's demands and consumption, and then the effects of the changes in these choice variables on the household's stock holding through the equations of motion are analyzed.

The stage I changes in the household's stocks induce changes in the shadow prices of additions to these stocks. The effects of these changes on the household's choice and state variables are analyzed in stage II of the household's adjustment process.

In stage II we do not analyze the effects of the change in the consumption-good stock brought about by changes in the choice variables in stages I and II. However, it will be shown that the household's consumption-good stock at the end of stage II, $C(t)^{**}$, lies strictly between the original level of this stock, $\overline{C}(t)$, and the original level augmented by the postulated increase, $\overline{C}(t) + \Delta C_0$; that is,

$$\overline{C}(t) < C(t)^{**} < \overline{C}(t) + \Delta C_0 \qquad \forall\, t \in [0, T]$$

We then proceed to a second iteration by repeating stages I and II with the values of the state variables at the end of stage II as initial values and with $C(T)^{**} - \overline{C}(T)$ as the disturbance in the consumption-good stock. We shall prove that this disturbance gets smaller with each iteration, and thus this process converges. We shall establish the following proposition.

Comparative dynamics proposition 3

An initial increase in the household's stock of consumption goods results in increased demand for money and bonds in exchange for consumption goods as well as an increase in trading in the market whose bonds exchange for money. The rate of consumption also increases everywhere on $[0, T]$. All three stocks will be higher on $[0, T]$.

In proving comparative dynamics proposition 3 we first notice that an increase in the initial endowment of consumption goods of ΔC_0, ceteris paribus, leads to an increase of ΔC_0 in the stock of consumption goods at time T and thus to a decrease in the shadow price of the consumption-good stock (i.e., $\lambda_C(t))^{27}$ at all $t \in [0, T]$. This reduction in $\lambda_C(t)$ causes a diminution in the demand for consumption goods in exchange for money and bonds and an increase in the rate of consumption. The demand for bonds in exchange for money increases if $B_M(t) > 0$ and decreases if $B_M(t) < 0$.[28] The contraction in $C_M(t)$ at all $t \in [0, T]$ causes an increase in the real stock of money, and the downward shift of $C_B(t)$ at all $t \in [0, T]$ results in an increase in the real stock of bonds at each $t \in [0, T]$. The choice variable $B_M(t)$ is adjusted because the scarcity of the transactions good has decreased; $b_M(t)\, \mathrm{II}\,(t)$ changes so as to increase usage of the transactions good. It is assumed that the change in $b_M(t)\, \mathrm{II}\,(t)$ is not large enough to cause a decrease in $m(t)$ or $b(t)$ in stage I. Hence the stage I adjustments in demand and stock holding can be summarized in the following proposition.

Comparative dynamics proposition 3.1

After the household completed all stage I adjustments in its choice and state variables that follow the increase in its initial endowment of consumption goods, it will demand more money and bonds in exchange for consumption goods, and it will increase its rate of demand in the market in which bonds and money trade. All three of its stocks will increase everywhere on $[0, T]$ as will its rate of consumption. Hence,

$$C_M(t)^* < \overline{C}_M(t) \qquad \forall\, t \in [0, T] \tag{IV.6.1}$$

$$C_B(t)^* < \overline{C}_B(t) \qquad \forall\, t \in [0, T] \tag{IV.6.2}$$

$$m(t)^* > \overline{m}(t) \qquad \forall\, t \in [0, T] \tag{IV.6.3}$$

$$b(t)^* > \overline{b}(t) \qquad \forall\, t \in [0, T] \tag{IV.6.4}$$

$$\overline{C}(t) + \Delta C > C(t)^* > \overline{C}(t) \qquad \forall\, t \in [0, T] \tag{IV.6.5}$$

$$B_M(t)^* \gtrless \overline{B}_M(t) \quad \text{if } \overline{B}_M(t) \gtrless 0 \qquad \forall\, t \in [0, T] \tag{IV.6.6}$$

The increases in the real stocks of money and bonds cause decreases in the shadow prices of money and bonds; that is, $\lambda_M(t)$ and $\lambda_B(t)$ decline everywhere on $[0, T]$.[29] The decrease in $\lambda_M(t)$ at each $t \in [0, T]$ results in an increase in $C_M(t)$ and $b_M(t)\,\Pi(t)$ at each $t \in [0, T]$,[30] and the decrease in $\lambda_B(t)$ at each $t \in [0, T]$ leads to a decrease in $b_M(t)\,\Pi(t)$ and an increase in $C_B(t)$ at each $t \in [0, T]$.[31] These changes in demands constitute stage II in the household's adjustment process.

The stage II increases in $C_M(t)$ and $b_M(t)\,\Pi(t)$ caused by the decrease in $\lambda_M(t)$ diminish the real stock of money below $m(t)^*$. However, the continuity properties cited earlier ensure that the real money stock cannot fall below $\overline{m}(t)$. The increase in $C_B(t)$ and the decrease in $b_M(t)\,\Pi(t)$ induced by the decrease in $\lambda_B(t)$ reduce the real bond stock below $b(t)^*$, but again continuity ensures that the real bond stock cannot fall below $\overline{b}(t)$. The cross-effects (i.e., the effect of $(d(b_M(t)\,\Pi(t))/d\lambda_M(t))\,\Delta\lambda_M(t)$ on $b(t)^*$ and the effect of $(d(b_M(t)\,\Pi(t))/d\lambda_B(t))\,\Delta\lambda_B(t)$ on $m(t)^*$) tend to increase $b(t)^*$ and $m(t)^*$. Furthermore, $(dC_M(t)/d\lambda_M(t))\,\Delta\lambda_M(t) > 0$ and $(dC_B(t)/d\lambda_B(t))\,\Delta\lambda_B(t) > 0$ imply that the consumption-good stock is higher everywhere on $[0, T]$. Hence, after all effects have been considered, we have the following proposition.

Comparative dynamics proposition 3.2

After all stage II adjustments in the household's plans have been made, it will have higher bond, money, and consumption-good stocks; that is,

$$m(t)^{**} > \overline{m}(t) \qquad \forall\, t \in [0, T] \tag{IV.6.7}$$

$$b(t)^{**} > \overline{b}(t) \qquad \forall\, t \in [0, T] \tag{IV.6.8}$$

$$C(t)^{**} > \overline{C}(t) \qquad \forall\, t \in [0, T] \tag{IV.6.9}$$

Next we must show that the stage II effects of the decreases in λ_M and λ_C on the household's choice variables will not reverse the stage I effects of the decrease in λ_C on the household's choice variables.

The percentage rate of change of $(dC_M(t)/d\lambda_M(t))\,\Delta\lambda_M(t)$ over time equals the percentage rate of change of $(dC_M(t)/d\lambda_C(t))\,\Delta\lambda_C(t)$.[32] Thus, if the differential $dC_M(t)$ is defined by

$$dC_M(t) = \frac{dC_M(t)}{d\lambda_C(t)}\,\Delta\lambda_C(t) + \frac{dC_M(t)}{d\lambda_M(t)}\,\Delta\lambda_M(t) \qquad \text{(IV.6.10)}$$

then $dC_M(t)$ cannot change sign on $[0,\ T]$. Similarly, the percentage rates of change over time of $(dC_B(t)/d\lambda_C(t))\,\Delta\lambda_C(t)$ and $(dC_B(t)/d\lambda_B(t))\,\Delta\lambda_B(t)$ are equal.[33] Hence, if the differential $dC_B(t)$ is defined by

$$dC_B(t) = \frac{dC_B(t)}{d\lambda_C(t)}\,\Delta\lambda_C(t) + \frac{dC_B(t)}{d\lambda_B(t)}\,\Delta\lambda_B(t) \qquad \text{(IV.6.11)}$$

then $dC_B(t)$ cannot change signs on $[0,\ T]$.

The effect of the decrease in $\lambda_C(t)$ on $b_M(t)\,\Pi(t)$ depends on the sign of $B_M(t)$; therefore, it is not possible to determine unambiguously the direction of the change in $b_M(t)\,\Pi(t)$ when the endowment of the consumption good changes. However, one can distinguish two possibilities, depending on the sign of the integral of the following differential:

$$d(b_M(t)\,\Pi(t)) = \frac{d(b_M(t)\,\Pi(t))}{d\lambda_C(t)}\,\Delta\lambda_C(t)$$
$$+ \frac{d(b_M(t)\,\Pi(t))}{d\lambda_M(t)}\,\Delta\lambda_M(t) + \frac{d(b_M(t)\,\Pi(t))}{d\lambda_B(t)}\Delta\lambda_B(t) \qquad \text{(IV.6.12)}$$

If $\int_0^T d(b_M(t)\Pi(t))\,dt > 0$, then $dC_M(t) < 0$ for all $t \in [0,\ T]$, because otherwise $m(t)^{**} > \overline{m}(t)$, contradicting inequality IV.6.7, and $dC_B(t) < 0$ $\forall\ t \in [0,\ T]$, by equation IV.4.15. If $\int_0^T d(b_M(t)\Pi(t))\,dt < 0$, then $dC_B(t) < 0$ $\forall\ t \in [0,\ T]$; otherwise $b(t)^{**} < \overline{b}(t)$, contradicting inequality IV.6.8, and $dC_M(t) < 0$ $\forall\ t \in [0,\ T]$, by equation IV.4.15. Thus, on completion of all stage II adjustments, the qualitative results concerning the changes in the state and choice variables given in equations IV.5.22 through IV.6.5 remain valid. We have thus proved the following proposition.

Comparative dynamics proposition 3.3

After all stage II adjustments that arise because of an increase in the initial endowment of consumption goods have been made, the household will have a higher demand for money and bonds in exchange for consumption goods, and it will increase its activities in the market where bonds exchange for money. The household's stocks of money, bonds, and consumption goods will be higher everywhere, as will be its rate of consumption. Hence,

$$C_M(t)^{**} < \overline{C}_M(t) \qquad \forall\ t \in [0,\ T]$$
$$C_B(t)^{**} < \overline{C}_B(t) \qquad \forall\ t \in [0,\ T]$$

$$b_M(t)^{**}\Pi(t) \gtreqless \overline{b}_M(t)\Pi(t) \quad \text{as } B_M(t) \gtreqless 0 \qquad \forall\, t \in [0, T]$$

$$m(t)^{**} > \overline{m}(t) \qquad \forall\, t \in [0, T]$$

$$b(t)^{**} > \overline{b}(t) \qquad \forall\, t \in [0, T]$$

$$C(t)^{**} > \overline{C}(t) \qquad \forall\, t \in [0, T]$$

Further reexamination of the adjustment process with the initial change in endowment given by $(\Delta C_0)_1 = C(T)^{**} - \overline{C}(T)$, where, according to inequality IV.6.5, $(\Delta C_0)_1 < \Delta C_0$, reveals that, as in the case of an increase in the endowment of bonds or money, this adjustment process is stable. The changes in endowment $(\Delta C_0)_i$ become smaller with each iteration.

The diminutions in $C_M(t)$ and $C_B(t)$ induced by the decrease in $\lambda_C(t)$ cause increases in $m(t)$ and $b(t)$ at all $t \in [0, T]$. Dropping the assumption that the stage I change in $B_M(t)$ does not reduce $m(t)$ below $\overline{m}(t)$ or reduce $b(t)$ below $\overline{b}(t)$ leaves invalid inequality IV.6.3 or IV.6.4. However, all other results in inequalities IV.6.1, IV.6.2, and IV.6.5 remain valid.[34]

This chapter so far has dealt with the effects of changes in the vector of initial endowments $(C(0), m(0), b(0))$ on the trajectory of the state variables $(C(t), m(t), b(t))$ and on the choice-variable trajectory $(C_M(t), C_B(t), b_M(t)\Pi(t), \phi(t))$, which are completely determined. To summarize the results, an increase in the initial money stock by ΔM_0 causes increases in $C(t)$, $m(t)$, and $b(t)$ at all $t \in (0, T]$. Also, the choice variables $C_M(t)$ and $C_B(t)$ increase everywhere on $[0, T]$, and $b_M(t)\Pi(t)$ increases initially and may decrease as t approaches T. The rate of consumption increases everywhere on $[0, T]$. An increase in the initial stock of bonds by ΔB_0 induces increases in $C(t)$, $m(t)$, and $b(t)$ at all $t \in [0, T]$. The demands for consumption goods in exchange for money and bonds (i.e., $C_M(t)$ and $C_B(t)$) increase everywhere on $[0, T]$, and $b_M(t)\Pi(t)$ decreases initially and may increase as t approaches T. The rate of consumption out of the inventory of consumption goods increases at all $t \in [0, T]$. An increase in the consumption-good endowment results in decreases in $C_B(t)$ and $C_M(t)$ and increases in $C(t)$ and $\phi(t)$ at each $t \in [0, T]$. The effect of this increase in $C(t)$ on the demand for bonds in exchange for money depends on the sign of $B_M(t)$. The state variables $m(t)$ and $b(t)$ increase everywhere on $[0, T]$ if the change in $B_M(t)$ is not strong enough to negate the increases in $m(t)$ and $b(t)$ due to the decreases in $C_M(t)$ and $C_B(t)$.

IV.7   An analysis of changes in the household's endowment vector at time $t > 0$

Thus far we have considered the effects of exogenous changes in the household's initial endowments of money, bonds, and consumption goods on the choice and state variables. Now this analysis must be extended to include exogenous anticipated changes in the household's stocks of money, bonds, and consumption goods that occur at $t = t_1 \in (0, T]$.

Exogenous changes in any of the household's real stocks induce changes in the shadow prices. It is through these alterations in shadow prices that exogenous changes in endowments influence the choice variables. However, shadow prices at any $t \in [0, T]$ change only when the values of the household's real stocks at $t = T$ change. Hence, an exogenous change in the money stock of ΔM that occurs at $t_1 \in (0, T]$ induces adjustments in the choice variables and the stocks of bonds and consumption goods identical with those induced by an equal-size change in $M(t)$ at $t = 0$.

The apparent invariance of the adjustments of choice variables and stocks of bonds and consumption goods with respect to the timing of the change in the money stock is due to the fact that the resulting change in the real value of the final money stock is the same regardless of when the exogenous changes occur. The path of the real money stock over $[0, t_1)$ is lower when the change in $M(t)$ occurs at t_1 than the optimal path when the change occurs at $t = 0$. However, from t_1 onward, the two paths coincide. Economic interpretation of the preceding proposition can be found in the household's desire to accumulate an optimal bequest stock of real money. The real value at $t = T$ of a change in the nominal money stock is the same irrespective of when the change occurs. Hence the resulting changes in choice and state variables are also independent of the timing of the change in the nominal money stock. If the household experiences more than one exogenous change during its lifetime, it adjusts its choice variables and state variables as though the change in the initial endowment of nominal money were equal to the sum of all the changes in the nominal stock that occurred over $[0, T]$.[35]

Similarly, the comparative dynamic analysis of the effects of changes in the initial stocks of bonds or consumption goods can be extended to situations in which the change occurs at $t_1 \in (0, T]$ rather than at $t = 0$. As in the case of a change in the money stock, an alteration in the bond stock or consumption-good stock at any $t_1 \in (0, T]$ has the same effect as a change of equal magnitude at $t = 0$. Hence, as long as all changes are fully anticipated, the household reacts identically to changes in the stocks of money, bonds, or consumption goods over all of the interval $[0, T]$, even though the changes occur only on some subinterval of $[0, T]$.

According to Bellman's principle of optimality (Bellman, 1957), an optimal policy has the property that if at any $t_1 \in (0, T]$ the household remaximizes given $M(t_1)$, $B(t_1)$, and $C(t_1)$[36] as initial conditions for the state variables, then the resulting trajectories over $[t_1, T]$ of the choice and state variables must coincide on $[t_1, T]$ with the trajectories of the original maximization problem the household solved at $t = 0$ with M_0, B_0, and C_0 as initial conditions. Thus, an unanticipated increase in the stock of money, bonds, or consumption goods at $t = t_1 \in (0, T]$ can be analyzed by taking t_1 as the starting point for the maximization problem, with $M(t_1)$, $B(t_1)$, and $C(t_1)$ as initial conditions for the three state variables. Then the results obtained earlier concerning the effects of changes in the initial endowments of money, bonds, or consumption goods on the paths of the choice and state variables apply directly.

IV.8   An introduction to comparative dynamic analysis of the household's response to changes in market prices

In the second section of this chapter, the method of comparative statics was applied to an investigation of the effects of changes in any of the exogenously given market prices at time $t \in [0, T]$ on the behavior of the household at the same time t within the context of its instantaneous maximization problem. It was shown that all real rates of demand (i.e., $C_M(t)$, $C_B(t)$, and $b_M(t)\Pi(t)$) remain unchanged when price adjustments are consistent with the arbitrage assumption (i.e., when the price ratio $\Pi(t)$ remains constant). However, if the household is confronted with arbitrary price changes, then $b_M(t)\Pi(t)$ increases as $\Pi(t)$ decreases, but $C_M(t)$ and $C_B(t)$ remain unchanged (see Table IV.2). The next three sections concern the comparative dynamic effects on the household's choice variables of arbitrary displacements of any of the three exogenously given market prices.

The comparative static adjustment in $b_M(t)\Pi(t)$ at $t \in [0, T]$ that occurs in the instantaneous maximization problem as a result of an arbitrary change in a market price at time t causes changes in the real bond and money stocks at the same time. The changes in $b(t)$ and $m(t)$ at $t = T$ due to the change in $b_M(t)\Pi(t)$ at $t \in [0, T]$ induce shifts in the paths of the shadow prices $\lambda_B(t)$ and $\lambda_M(t)$, which in turn cause further changes in $b_M(t)\Pi(t)$, $C_B(t)$, and $C_M(t)$ at each $t \in [0, T]$. Therefore, within the confines of the instantaneous maximization problem, any market price change generates an instantaneous adjustment in $b_M(t)\Pi(t)$ only at the time the price change occurs. However, the resulting shifts in the paths of the shadow prices due to the changes in $m(T)$ and $b(T)$ affect all of the choice variables at all $t \in [0, T]$. Thus, an anticipated change in a market price at $t \in [0, T]$ leads to a change in demand on $[0, T]$ rather than at t only, as long as the change in market prices resulted in changes in the real stocks of bonds and money at $t = T$.

The total effect of any change in one of the three market prices on the household's choice variables can be divided into three separate effects: a substitution effect, a wealth effect, and an intertemporal substitution effect.

The comparative statics change in $b_M(t)\Pi(t)$ that is concurrent with the price change, together with the adjustments in $b_M(t)\Pi(t)$, $C_B(t)$, and $C_M(t)$

on $[0, T]$ resulting from changes in the shadow prices, constitute the substitution effect of an arbitrary displacement of a market price on $[0, T]$. Properly interpreted, this substitution effect represents the replacement of one method of acquiring a commodity by another, rather than the substitution of one commodity for another in consumption. For example, if $P_{CB}(t)$ rises everywhere, the household decreases its demand for $C_B(t)$ and increases its demand for $C_M(t)$ and $M_B(t)$ at each $t \in [0, T]$; that is, the household intensifies its use of the third market.

In addition to the substitution effect, a displacement in $P_{CB}(t)$ or $P_{CM}(t)$ on $[0, T]$ causes further direct changes in $b(t)$ and $m(t)$, because $P_{CB}(t)$ and $P_{CM}(t)$ deflate the nominal bond and money stocks, respectively. The adjustments in $b(T)$ and $m(T)$ resulting from changes in $P_{CB}(t)$ and $P_{CM}(t)$ on $[0, T]$ induce further shifts in $\lambda_B(t)$ and $\lambda_M(t)$ at all $t \in [0, T]$. The adjustments in the real rates of demand on $[0, T]$ induced by such movements in shadow prices are the dynamic analogues of the income or wealth effects of arbitrary displacements in $P_{CB}(t)$ and $P_{CM}(t)$.

When analyzing the effects of a change in market prices on the household's choice variables, the additional adjustments that occur as a result of changes in the rates of inflation and deflation or the interest rate must also be analyzed. The substitution and wealth effects of changes in market prices are induced by variations in the levels of the shadow prices that leave the percentage rates of change over time of the shadow prices unchanged. The equations of motion for the shadow prices (equations III.2.5) demonstrate that changes in $\hat{P}_{CM}(t)$, $\hat{P}_{CB}(t)$, or $P_{MB}(t)$ have additional effects on the paths of the shadow prices. In particular, a rise in $\hat{P}_{CM}(t)$ or $\hat{P}_{CB}(t)$ or a diminution in $P_{MB}(t)$, the rate of interest on $S \in [0, T]$, increases $\hat{\lambda}_M(t)$ and $\hat{\lambda}_B(t)$ at each $t \in S$. Because the levels of the shadow prices at time $t = T$ are not affected by these changes in the slopes of $\lambda_B(t)$ and $\lambda_M(t)$, the increases in $\hat{\lambda}_B(t)$ and $\hat{\lambda}_M(t)$ at each $t \in S$ must result in reductions in $\lambda_M(t)$ and $\lambda_B(t)$ at all $t \in [0, s')$, where s' is the largest element in S. The smaller the value of t, the larger are these decreases in $\lambda_M(t)$ and $\lambda_B(t)$. The adjustments in demands induced by these changes in the shadow prices constitute the intertemporal substitution effects of changes in market prices.

In the next chapter we shall consider price changes that leave $\Pi(t)$ unchanged on $[0, T]$. This type of price change causes wealth effects and intertemporal substitution effects only.

IV.9   A comparative dynamic analysis of the household's response to changes in the price of consumption goods in terms of money

In this section we shall analyze the adjustment in plans that the household undertakes in response to an increase in $P_{CM}(t)$. We shall do so by isolating first the substitution effect, then the wealth effect, and finally the intertemporal substitution effect. This section will thus establish the following proposition.

Comparative dynamics proposition 4

In the standard case in which the static substitution effect dominates both the wealth effect and the intertemporal substitution effect, an increase in $P_{CM}(t)$ on $S \subseteq [0, T]$ induces the household to decrease $C_M(t)$ and increase $C_B(t)$ at each $t \in [0, T]$ and to increase $b_M(t)\Pi(t)$ on the nonempty interval $R''' \subseteq [0, T]$. The real stock of money is higher, and the real stock of bonds is lower, at each $t \leq t'''$, where t''' is the least element in R'''. However, $m(t)$ is lower and $b(t)$ is higher for some $t > t'''$, so that in the final analysis $m(t)$ decreases unambiguously and $b(t)$ increases unambiguously.[37] The consumption good stock and thus the rate of consumption are lower at each $t \in [0, T]$.

If the wealth effect dominates both substitution effects, then the set R''' is empty,[38] and $b_M(t)\Pi(t)$ as well as $C_M(t)$ shift downward at each $t \in [0, T]$. The real money stock, the real bond stock, and the consumption-good stock are smaller at each $t \in [0, T]$. The change in $C_B(t)$ cannot be determined unambiguously. Hence, the only qualitative differences between the case of a dominant wealth effect and the standard case are that $b_M(t)\Pi(t)$ and $b(t)$ are lower everywhere and that the direction of change in $C_B(t)$ is ambiguous.

Finally, if the intertemporal substitution effect dominates, then $C_M(t)$ is higher at $t < t^*$, thus raising the possibility that $C(t)$ might be higher on $[0, T]$ and that the rate of consumption might shift upward at each $t \in [0, T]$.

In the following discussion of the effects of changes in any one of the three exogenously given prices of $P_{CM}(t)$, $P_{CB}(t)$, and $P_{MB}(t)$, let $S \subseteq [0,T]$ be the set of t at which the price has changed, and let s' be the largest element in S.

In the context of the household's instantaneous maximization problem, an increase in the price of consumption goods in terms of money at time $t \in S$ leaves the demand for consumption goods in exchange for money and bonds unchanged. However, the concurrent change in the instantaneous demand for bonds in exchange for money at time t is given by (see Table IV.2)

$$\frac{dB_M(t)P_{CM}(t)}{dP_{CM}(t)} = B_M(t) + \Pi(t)^2 P_{CB}(t)\frac{\lambda_B(t)}{\lambda_C(t)T_{33}^d} \qquad \forall\, t \in S \qquad (IV.9.1)$$

If $B_M(t) > 0$ (i.e., if the household demands rather than supplies bonds in exchange for money), then the percentage increase in $B_M(t)$ exceeds the percentage increase in $P_{CM}(t)$, and $b_M(t)\Pi(t)$ shifts upward. If the household supplies bonds in exchange for money (i.e., if $B_M(t) < 0$ and $dB_M(t)P_{CM}/dP_{CM} > 0$), then the supply of bonds diminishes as $P_{CM}(t)$ increases. In this case the percentage change in the supply of bonds is smaller than the percentage change in $P_{CM}(t)$, but $b_M(t)\Pi(t)$ will nevertheless increase. However, if $B_M(t) < 0$ and $dB_M(t)P_{CM}(t)/dP_{CM}(t) < 0$, then the supply of bonds increases as $P_{CM}(t)$ increases. Because $P_{CM}(t)P_{MB}(t)$ is the price of consumption goods in terms of bonds, an increase in $P_{CM}(t)$, with $P_{MB}(t)$ constant means that the price of bonds in terms of consumption goods has decreased. Hence, the possibility of an increase in the supply of bonds as $P_{CM}(t)$ increases corresponds to the perverse case of a backward-bending supply of nominal bonds.

The increase in the instantaneous demand for bonds in exchange for money resulting from an increase in $P_{CM}(t)$ at $t \in S$ leads to an increase in the real bond stock $b(t)$ at $t \in S$ and a simultaneous decrease in real money stock $m(t)$.[39] The changes in the real stocks of bonds and money at time $t = T$ that are due to the instantaneous increase in $b_M(t)\Pi(t)$ at $t \in S$ (i.e., at those t where $P_{CM}(t)$ increases) generate a decrease in the shadow price of bonds and an increase in the shadow price of money at all $t \in [0,T]$.[40] The decrease in the shadow price of bonds causes a reduction in the household's demand for bonds in exchange for money and an increase in its demand for consumption goods in exchange for bonds (see Table IV.1) at each $t \in [0,T]$.[41] The increase in the shadow price of money causes reductions in the household's demand for bonds in exchange for money and in its demand for consumption goods in exchange for money at each $t \in [0,T]$ (see Table IV.1).[42]

If we look at the substitution effect of the change in $P_{CM}(t)$ at each $t \in S$ only and ignore the wealth effect and the intertemporal substitution effect, then,

$$\int_S \frac{d(b_M(t)\Pi(t))}{dP_{CM}(t)} \Delta P_{CM}(t)\, dt$$
$$+ \int_0^T \left[\frac{d(b_M(t)\Pi(t))}{d\lambda_M(t)} \Delta\lambda_M(t) + \frac{d(b_M(t)\Pi(t))}{d\lambda_B(t)} \Delta\lambda_B(t) \right] dt > 0 \quad \text{(IV.9.2)}$$

That is, the instantaneous increases in $b_M(t)\Pi(t)$ on S due to the increase in $P_{CM}(t)$ on S outweighs the reduction in $b_M(t)\Pi(t)$ on $[0,T]$ due to the changes in the shadow prices of money and bonds on $[0,T]$.[43] Thus the household increases its total purchase of bonds in exchange for money on $[0,T]$ but rearranges its flow demand so that $b_M(t)\Pi(t)$ increases on some nonempty set $R' \subset S$ and decreases at $t \in [0,T]$ such that $t \notin R'$. Therefore, as the marginal cost of acquiring consumption goods in exchange for money in the consumption-good-cum-money market increases, the household decreases $C_M(t)$ at all $t \in [0,T]$. However, the household increases $C_B(t)$, the demand for consumption goods in the consumption-good-cum-bonds market, at all $t \in [0,T]$ and increases its total purchases of bonds on $[0,T]$ in the bonds-cum-money market. Thus, the net effect of these adjustments in demands is to increase the real bond stock at $t = T$ and decrease the real money stock at $t = T$.

If the set S on which $P_{CM}(t)$ increases is connected, then the set R' on which $b_M(t)\Pi(t)$ increases is connected. Let t' be the least element in R'. We can then summarize the foregoing results in the following proposition.

Comparative dynamics proposition 4.1

The substitution effect of an increase in $P_{CM}(t)$ on the nonempty set $S \subset [0,T]$, when considered by itself, results in an increase in $C_B(t)$ and a decrease in $C_M(t)$ at each $t \in [0,T]$; $b_M(t)\Pi(t)$ will be higher on some nonempty set $R' \subset S$ and lower at each $t \notin R'$. These adjustments in demand imply that the real bond stock must be smaller at $t \leq t'$ and larger at some t such that $t' < t \leq T$, and the money stock must be larger for all $t \leq t'$ and smaller for some t such that $t' < t \leq T$. Because $C_M(t)$ has been reduced and $C_B(t)$ has been increased at each $t \in [0,T]$, the net effect of the increase in $P_{CM}(t)$ on the consumption-good stock appears to be ambiguous. However, the increase in $C_B(t)$ is less than the diminution in $C_M(t)$ at each $t \in [0,T]$, because the rising marginal cost of transacting prevents the household from enlarging its net acquisition of consumption goods in exchange for money as $P_{CM}(t)$ increases. Hence the consumption-good stock is diminished at each $t \in [0,T]$, and its shadow price increases everywhere. The only interesting effect induced by the increase in $\lambda_C(t)$ is the decrease in the rate of consumption at each $t \in [0,T]$.[44]

The wealth effect of the increase in $P_{CM}(t)$ prompts a further decline in the real money stock, $m(t)$, because the price used to deflate the nominal stock of money has increased.[45] The decrease in $m(t)$ at $t = T$ results in an increase in the shadow price of money at each $t \in [0,T]$. Thus the household is impelled to decrease its demand for consumption goods and bonds in exchange for money; that is, the household reduces $C_M(t)$ and $b_M(t)\Pi(t)$ at each $t \in [0,T]$.[46] The decrease in $C_M(t)$ at each $t \in [0,T]$ results in a diminished stock of consumption goods and a higher shadow price of consumption goods.[47] This rise in $\lambda_C(t)$ at each $t \in [0,T]$ induces the household to increase $C_B(t)$ and decrease $\phi(t)$ at each $t \in [0,T]$.[48] The decrease in $b_M(t)\Pi(t)$ at each $t \in [0,T]$ causes a reduction in the real stock of bonds; hence, $\lambda_B(t)$ increases at each $t \in [0,T]$.[49] The increase in the shadow price of bonds results in a decrease in $C_B(t)$ at $t \in [0,T]$.[50] Thus we have the following proposition.

Comparative dynamics proposition 4.2

The wealth effect due to the increase in $P_{CM}(t)$ brings about declines in $C_M(t)$, $b_M(t)\Pi(t)$, and $\phi(t)$ at each $t \in [0, T]$, whereas its effect on $C_B(t)$ is ambiguous. The contraction in the real money stock due to the increase in $P_{CM}(t)$ thus spills over onto the other stocks and causes the household to reduce $C(t)$ and $b(t)$ at each $t \in [0, T]$.

A comparison of the substitution and wealth effects reveals that both effects induce reductions in $C_M(t)$ and $\phi(t)$ at each $t \in [0, T]$, and both effects prompt reductions in the stocks of real money and consumption goods. However, the wealth effect evokes a reduction in $b_M(t) \, \Pi \, (t)$ at each $t \in [0, T]$, and the substitution effect causes $b_M(t) \, \Pi \, (t)$ to increase at each $t \in R'$ and to decrease at all $t \notin R'$. Hence, the wealth effect tends to shrink the set R', heightening the possibility that the reduction in $b_M(t) \, \Pi \, (t)$ due the wealth effect might dominate the increase in $b_M(t) \, \Pi \, (t)$ on R' due to the substitution effect. Thus the integral inequality of IV.9.2 may be invalidated, resulting in a reduction in the real stock of bonds. In turn, the reduction in $b(t)$ will then lead the household to reduce $C_B(t)$ on all $t \in [0, T]$.

Therefore, if the substitution effect of the increase in $P_{CM}(t)$ on S dominates the wealth effect, then the household decreases $C_M(t)$ and increases $C_B(t)$ at each $t \in [0, T]$; $b_M(t) \, \Pi \, (t)$ increases at all $t \in R'' \subset R$; and the rate of consumption decreases everywhere on $[0, T]$. The real stock of money increases and the real bond stock decreases at each $t \leq t''$; however, the real stock of money will decrease and the real bond stock will increase for some $t > t''$, where t'' is the smallest element in R''. The total acquisition of real bonds on $[0, T]$ increases, whereas that of money decreases; that is, $b(T)$ increases and $m(T)$ decreases.

On the other hand, if the wealth effect dominates the substitution effect, then the household reduces $b_M(t) \, \Pi \, (t)$ at each $t \in [0, T]$; that is, the set R'' is empty. In this case the real stock of bonds as well as the real stock of money and the consumption-good stock are lower at each $t \in [0, T]$. Also, the demand for consumption goods in the consumption-good-cum-money market is diminished at each $t \in [0, T]$. Because the change in $C_B(t)$ due to the wealth effect only is ambiguous, it is impossible to ascertain the change in $C_B(t)$ when the wealth effect dominates the substitution effect.

Finally, the analysis turns to the intertemporal substitution effect that arises if the adjustment in $P_{CM}(t)$ on S is such that $\hat{P}_{CM}(t)$ changes on S. If the rate of inflation of $P_{CM}(t)$ increases; then $\lambda_M(t)$ must increase everywhere on S, because $d\lambda_M(t)/dt = \hat{P}_{CM}(t)\lambda_M(t)$ (see equation III.2.5). However, the absolute level of $\lambda_M(t)$ at $t = T$ is identical with the level it assumed following the adjustments induced by the substitution and wealth effects.[51] Hence $\lambda_M(t)$ must decrease everywhere on $[0, s')$, and its decrease is larger the smaller the value of t. The reduction in $\lambda_M(t)$ leads the household to augment its demands for consumption goods and bonds in exchange for money at all $t \in [0, s')$, and the increases in $C_M(t)$ and $b_M(t) \, \Pi \, (t)$ are larger the smaller the value of t.

Hence, an increase in the cost of holding money induces the household to decrease its money stock everywhere on $[0, s')$, which in turn has the effect of increasing the level of $\lambda_M(t)$ on $[0, T]$. The combined effect of the reduction in $\lambda_M(t)$ due to the increase in $\hat{\lambda}_M(t)$ and the increase in $\lambda_M(t)$ due to the decrease in the real money stock is to tilt $\lambda_M(t)$ on $[0, T]$. That is, the slope of $\lambda_M(t)$ with respect to t increases on S, and $\lambda_M(t)$ decreases on $[0, t^*)$ and increases on $(t^*, T]$, where $0 < t^* < T$. Thus, on the interval $[0, t^*)$ the household raises $C_M(t)$ and $b_M(t)\,\Pi\,(t)$, whereas it reduces $C_M(t)$ and $b_M(t)\,\Pi\,(t)$ on $(t^*, T]$. The real stock of money is lower everywhere, but $b(t)$ and $C(t)$ are higher on $[0, T]$; hence, $\lambda_B(t)$ and $\lambda_C(t)$ decrease at each $t \in [0, T]$.[52] The effect on $C_B(t)$ of the decreases in $\lambda_B(t)$ and $\lambda_C(t)$ at each $t \in [0, T]$ is ambiguous, but the decrease in $\lambda_C(t)$ induces an increase in $\phi(t)$ at each $t \in [0, T]$.[53] Therefore, the effects of an increase in $\hat{P}_{CM}(t)$, the rate at which the real money stock deteriorates, is summarized by the tilting of the demand schedules $C_M(t)$ and $b_M(t)\,\Pi\,(t)$ on $[0, T]$. That is, these schedules are higher at small values of t and lower at larger values of t, so as to decrease $m(T)$ and increase $C(T)$ and $b(T)$. We thus have proved the following proposition.

Comparative dynamics proposition 4.3

The intertemporal substitution effect of an increase in $\hat{P}_{CM}(t)$ on $S \subseteq [0, T]$ is to raise $C_M(t)$ and $b_M(t)\,\Pi\,(t)$ on $[0, t^*)$ and to reduce $C_M(t)$ and $b_M(t)\,\Pi\,(t)$ on $(t^*, T]$. The real stock of money is lower and the real stocks of bonds and consumption goods are higher everywhere on $[0, T]$.

Lastly, we shall consider what changes occur in the household's choice and state variables when all three effects are combined.

Let $R' \subseteq [0, T]$, $R'' \subseteq [0, T]$, and $R''' \subseteq [0, T]$ be the sets of all t on which the household increases $b_M(t)\,\Pi\,(t)$ when it considers the substitution effect by itself, the substitution and wealth effects, and all three effects, respectively. Let $t' \in R'$, $t'' \in R''$, and $t''' \in R'''$ be the least elements in these sets. Combining the intertemporal substitution effect with the substitution and wealth effects, the increase (decrease) in $b_M(t)\,\Pi\,(t)$ at each $t < t^*$ $(t > t^*)$ due to the intertemporal substitution effect will force $t''' \leq t''$. Furthermore, the combination of all three effects increases $m(t)$ and decreases $b(t)$ at all $t \leq t'''$, whereas it decreases $m(t)$ and increases $b(t)$ for some $t > t'''$. The intertemporal substitution effect reinforces the increase in $b(t)$ and the decrease in $m(t)$ due to the substitution effect (see inequality IV.4.2). However, the intertemporal substitution effect causes the household to increase $C_M(t)$ at each $t < t^*$, thus inducing an increase in $C(t)$ at each $t \in [0, T]$, whereas the substitution and wealth effects result in reductions in $C_M(t)$ and $C(t)$ at each $t \in [0, T]$. Hence, there exists the possibility of a dominant intertemporal substitution effect that causes an increase in $C_M(t)$ on $[0, t^*)$ and an increase in $C(t)$ on $[0, T]$ when the three effects are considered in concert. In this case the rate of consumption increases for each $t \in [0, T]$. This establishes the validity of comparative dynamics proposition 4.

IV.10 A comparative dynamic analysis of the household's response to changes in the price of consumption goods in terms of bonds

In this section we shall analyze the effects of an increase in $P_{CB}(t)$ on the household's market and consumption behavior. In doing so we will prove the following proposition.

Comparative dynamics proposition 5

In the standard case in which the static substitution effect dominates both the intertemporal substitution effect and the wealth effect, an increase in $P_{CB}(t)$ on $S \subseteq [0, T]$ induces the household to decrease $C_B(t)$ and increase $C_M(t)$ at each $t \in [0, T]$ and to decrease $b_M(t) \, \Pi \, (t)$ on the nonempty interval $R''' \subseteq [0, T]$. The real stock of money decreases and the real stock of bonds increases at each $t \leq t'''$, where t''' is the least element in R'''. However, $m(t)$ increases and $b(t)$ decreases for some $t > t'''$, so that in the final analysis $m(t)$ increases unambiguously and $b(t)$ decreases unambiguously. The consumption-good stock and thus the rate of consumption will be lower at each $t \in [0, T]$.

If the wealth effect dominates both substitution effects, then the set R''' is empty, and $b_M(t) \, \Pi \, (t)$ increases at each $t \in [0, T]$. The real money stock, the real bond stock, and the consumption-good stock are diminished at each $t \in [0, T]$. Also, the household reduces $C_B(t)$ and $\phi(t)$ at each $t \in [0, T]$. The change in $C_M(t)$ is ambiguous when the wealth effect dominates the substitution effects. Hence the only qualitative differences between the case of a dominant wealth effect and the standard case are that $b_M(t) \, \Pi \, (t)$ increases everywhere on $[0, T]$ and the real money stock is lower on $[0, T]$.

If the intertemporal substitution effect dominates, then $C_B(t)$ increases at $t < t^* \in [0, T]$, raising the possibility that $C(t)$ might increase on $[0, T]$ and thus that the rate of consumption might increase at each $t \in [0, T]$.

In the context of the instantaneous maximization problem, an increase in the price of the consumption good in terms of bonds on $S \subseteq [0, T]$ leaves the demand for the consumption good in exchange for money or bonds unchanged. However, a change in $P_{CB}(t)$ on S induces adjustments in the demand for bonds in exchange for money on S. The change in $B_M(t)$ is given by (see Table IV.2)

$$\frac{dB_M(t)P_{CB}(t)}{dP_{CB}(t)} = -\Pi(t)^2 \, P_{CB}(t) \frac{\lambda_B(t)}{\lambda_C(t)T_{33}^d} \qquad \forall \, t \in S \qquad \text{(IV.10.1)}$$

Hence, an increase in $b(t)$ on S leads to a reduction in the instantaneous demand for bonds in exchange for money on S. This decrease in $b_M(t) \Pi(t)$ on S increases the real money stock $m(t)$ and decreases the real bond stock $b(t)$ at all $t \in S$.[54]

Considering only the substitution effect of the change in $P_{CB}(t)$ on S, and ignoring both the wealth and intertemporal substitution effects, implies

$$\int_S \frac{d(b_M(t)\Pi(t))}{dP_{CB}(t)} P_{CB}(t)\, dt$$

$$+ \int_0^T \left(\frac{d(b_M(t)\Pi(t))^{\cdot}}{d\lambda_M(t)} \Delta\lambda_M(t) + \frac{d(b_M(t)\Pi(t))}{d\lambda_B(t)} \Delta\lambda_B(t) \right) dt < 0 \quad \text{(IV.10.2)}$$

That is, the instantaneous decrease in $b_M(t) \Pi(t)$ on S due to the increase in $P_{CB}(t)$ on S outweighs the increase in $b_M(t) \Pi(t)$ in $[0, T]$ due to the change in the shadow prices of money and bonds in $[0, T]$. Hence, the household decreases its total purchases of bonds in exchange for money on $[0, T]$ but rearranges its flow demand so that $b_M(t) \Pi(t)$ is lower on some nonempty set $R' \subset S$ and higher at all $t \notin R'$.

Let t' be the least element in R'. Then the real stock of bonds is larger and the real stock of money is smaller at each $0 \leq t \leq t'$, whereas the real bond stock is smaller and the real money stock is larger at some $t > t'$. However, inequality IV.4.4 implies that $m(T)$ is larger and $b(T)$ is smaller after all adjustments in demands have been made. Therefore, as the marginal cost of obtaining consumption goods in the consumption-good-cum-bonds market increases, the household decreases $C_B(t)$, its demand in that market, at each $t \in [0, T]$ and increases $C_M(t)$, its demand for consumption goods in exchange for money, at each $t \in [0, T]$. Also, by reducing $b_M(t) \Pi(t)$ on R', the household decreases its total purchases of bonds in the bonds-cum-money market. We have thus established the following proposition.

Comparative dynamics proposition 5.1

The substitution effect of the increase in $P_{CB}(t)$ leads to an increase in $C_M(t)$ and a decrease in $C_B(t)$ everywhere on $[0, T]$; $b_M(t) \Pi(t)$ is lower on some nonempty set $R' \subset S$ and higher at all $t \notin R'$. If t' is the least element in R', then the real stock of bonds is larger and the real stock of money is smaller at each $0 \leq t \leq t'$, whereas the reverse is true for some $t > t'$, and $b(T)$ is smaller and $m(T)$ is larger.

In addition to the foregoing decrease in the real stock of bonds, the increase in $P_{CB}(t)$ also causes a direct decrease in $b(t)$, because $P_{CB}(t)$ is used to deflate the nominal bond stock. The changes in the real stocks of money and bonds at $t = T$, which are due to the instantaneous decrease in $b_M(t)\Pi(t)$ at each $t \in S$, lead to a decrease in the shadow price of money and to an increase in the shadow price of bonds at all $t \in [0, T]$. The increase in the shadow price of bonds causes the household to reduce its demand for the consumption good in exchange for bonds and to increase its demand for bonds in exchange for money at each $t \in [0, T]$. The decrease in the shadow price of money brings about an increase in demand for consumption goods in exchange for money and an increase in demand for bonds in exchange for money at each $t \in [0, T]$ (see Table IV.1).

Hence, the wealth effect of the increase in $P_{CB}(t)$ originates with the decrease in $b(t)$ due to the deflation of the nominal bond stock by $P_{CB}(t)$. The decrease in $b(t)$ at $t = T$ results in a further increase in $\lambda_B(t)$ at each $t \in [0, T]$, thus causing $b_M(t)\Pi(t)$ to increase and $C_B(t)$ to decrease at each $t \in [0, T]$. The diminution in $C_B(t)$ induces a decrease in $C(t)$ at each $t \in [0, T]$; hence, $\lambda_C(t)$ increases at each $t \in [0, T]$. The increase in $b_M(t)\Pi(t)$ causes a reduction in $m(t)$ at each $t \in [0, T]$ and thus increases $\lambda_M(t)$ at each $t \in [0, T]$. The increase in $\lambda_C(t)$ causes the household to increase $C_M(t)$ and to decrease $\phi(t)$ everywhere. Also, the increase in $\lambda_M(t)$ leads to a decrease in $C_M(t)$ at each $t \in [0, T]$.[55] We have thus established the following proposition.

Comparative dynamics proposition 5.2

The wealth effect due to an increase in $P_{CB}(t)$ on S brings about a decrease in $C_B(t)$ and an increase in $b_M(t)\Pi(t)$ at each $t \in [0, T]$. The effect on $C_M(t)$ is ambiguous, but the rate of consumption will decline everywhere on $[0, T]$. As a result of the wealth effect, all real stocks will be smaller at each $t \in [0, T]$.

A comparison of the substitution and wealth effects reveals that both cause reductions in $C_B(t)$, $\phi(t)$, and $C(t)$ at each $t \in [0, T]$, and both induce the household to decrease its real bond stock. However, the wealth effect results in an increase in $b_M(t)\Pi(t)$ at each $t \in [0, T]$, whereas the substitution effect causes $b_M(t)\Pi(t)$ to decrease at each $t \in R'$ and increase at all $t \in R'$. Hence, the wealth effect tends to shrink the set R' and creates the possibility that the increase in $b_M(t)\Pi(t)$ due to the wealth effect might dominate the decrease in $b_M(t)\Pi(t)$ on R' due to the substitution effect, thus invalidating the integral inequality IV.10.2 and causing the real money stock to be lower everywhere. Therefore, the wealth effect tends to reinforce changes induced by the substitution effect, except in the case of $b_M(t)\Pi(t)$.

If the substitution effect of the increase in $P_{CB}(t)$ on S dominates the wealth effect, then the household decreases $C_B(t)$ and increases $C_M(t)$ at each $t \in [0, T]$; $b_M(t)\Pi(t)$ is lower at each $t \in R'' \subset R$, and the rate of consumption is lower everywhere on $[0, T]$. The real stock of money is lower and the real bond stock is higher at each $t \leq t''$, and the real stock of money is higher and the real stock of bonds is lower for some $t > t''$ when t'' is the least element in R''. The total acquisitions on $[0, T]$ of real bonds and real money decrease and increase, respectively; that is, $b(T)$ decreases and $m(T)$ increases.

On the other hand, if the wealth effect dominates, then the household increases $b_M(t)\Pi(t)$ at each $t \in [0, T]$, and the stocks of real money, real bonds, and consumption goods are smaller on $[0, T]$. Also, the household reduces $C_B(t)$ and $\phi(t)$ at each $t \in [0, T]$. But when the wealth effect dominates the substitution effect, the change in $C_M(t)$ is ambiguous.

Finally, it remains to consider the intertemporal substitution effect that arises if $P_{CB}(t)$ changes on S so as to change $\hat{P}_{CB}(t)$ on S. An increase in $\hat{P}_{CB}(t)$ implies an increase in $\hat{\lambda}_B(t)$ on S, because $d\lambda_B(t)/dt = (\hat{P}_{CB}(t) - P_{MB}(t))\lambda_B(t)$ (see equations III.2.5). However, the level of $\lambda_B(t)$ at $t = T$ remains identical with the level it assumed following the adjustments induced by the substitution and wealth effects. Hence, $\lambda_B(t)$ must decrease everywhere on $[0, s')$, and the decrease is larger the smaller the value of t. The decrease in $\lambda_B(t)$ at each $t \in [0, s')$ leads the household to increase its demand for consumption goods and money in exchange for bonds at each $t \in [0, s')$, and the decrease in $C_B(t)$ and the increase in $b_M(t)\Pi(t)$ are larger the smaller the value of t. Hence, an increase in the cost of holding bonds results in a reduction in the real bond stock everywhere on $[0, T]$. This, in turn, has the effect of increasing the level of $\lambda_B(t)$ everywhere on $[0, T]$. The combined effect of the reduction in $\lambda_B(t)$ due to the increase in $\hat{\lambda}_B(t)$ and the increase in $\lambda_B(t)$ due to the decrease in the real bond stock is to tilt $\lambda_B(t)$ on $[0, T]$. That is, the slope of $\lambda_B(t)$ increases with respect to t on S, and $\lambda_B(t)$ decreases on $[0, t^*)$ and increases on $(t^*, T]$, where $0 < t^* < T$. Hence, an increase in $\hat{P}_{CB}(t)$ increases $C_B(t)$ and decreases $b_M(t)\Pi(t)$ on the interval $[0, t^*)$, and it reduces $C_B(t)$ and increases $b_M(t)\Pi(t)$ on $(t^*, T]$. The real bond stock is lower everywhere on $[0, T]$, and $C(t)$ and $m(t)$ are higher on $[0, T]$. Thus, $\lambda_C(t)$ and $\lambda_M(t)$ decrease. The effect of the decreases in $\lambda_C(t)$ and $\lambda_M(t)$ on $C_M(t)$ is ambiguous, but the decrease in $\lambda_C(t)$ will result in an increase in the rate of consumption at each $t \in [0, T]$. This gives rise to the following proposition.

Comparative dynamics proposition 5.3

The intertemporal substitution effect of an increase in $P_{CB}(t)$ results in a higher $C_B(t)$ and lower $b_M(t)\Pi(t)$ on the interval $[0, t^*)$, whereas on the interval $(t^*, T]$, $C_B(t)$ is lower and $b_M(t)\Pi(t)$ is higher. The real stock of bonds is lower everywhere on $[0, T]$, and the real stocks of money and consumption goods are higher on $[0, T]$.

Lastly, we combine all three effects in order to prove comparative dynamics proposition 5.

Let $R' \subseteq [0, T]$, $R'' \subseteq [0, T]$, and $R''' \subseteq [0, T]$ be the sets of all t on which the household lowers $b_M(t)\Pi(t)$ when it considers the substitution effect alone, the substitution and wealth effects, and all three effects, respectively. Let $t' \in R'$, $t'' \in R''$, and $t''' \in R'''$ be the least elements in these sets. Combining the intertemporal substitution effect with the substitution and wealth effects, the decrease (increase) in $b_M(t)\Pi(t)$ at each $t < t^*$ $(t > t^*)$ due to the intertemporal substitution effect will force $t''' \leq t''$. Furthermore, the combination of all three effects decreases $m(t)$ and increases $b(t)$ at each $t \leq t'''$, and it increases $m(t)$ and decreases $b(t)$ at some $t > t'''$. The intertemporal substitution effect reinforces the increase in $m(T)$ and the decrease in $b(T)$ due to the substitution effect (see inequality IV.10.2). However, the intertemporal substitution effect causes the household to increase $C_B(t)$ at each $t < t^*$, thus inducing an increase in $C(t)$ at each $t \in [0, T]$, whereas the substitution and wealth effects result in reductions in $C_B(t)$ and $C(t)$ at each $t \in [0, T]$. Hence, there exists the possibility of a dominant intertemporal substitution effect that causes an increase in $C_B(t)$ on $[0, t^*)$ and an increase in $C(t)$ on $[0, T]$ when the three effects are considered in concert. In this case the rate of consumption is larger at each $t \in [0, T]$.

IV.11   A comparative dynamic analysis of the household's response to changes in the interest rate

In this section we shall analzye the effects of an increase in $P_{MB}(t)$ on the household's choice variables. The results can be summarized in the following proposition.

Comparative dynamics proposition 6

In the standard case in which the static substitution effect dominates the intertemporal substitution effect, an increase in $P_{MB}(t)$ on $S \subseteq [0, T]$ induces the household to increase $b_M(t)\Pi(t)$ on the nonempty interval $R''' \subseteq [0, T]$ and to decrease $C_M(t)$ and increase $C_B(t)$ on $[0, T]$. The real stock of money increases and the real stock of bonds decreases on $[0, t''']$, where t''' is the least element in R'''. However, the real stock of money is lower and the real stock of bonds is higher at some $t > t'''$, so that in the final analysis $m(T)$ and $b(T)$ unambiguously decrease and increase, respectively. Changes in the consumption-good stock and hence in the rate of consumption are indeterminate. If the intertemporal substitution effect dominates the static substitution effect, then $C_B(t)$ is lower on $[0, t^*)$ and $C(t)$ and $\phi(t)$ are smaller on $[0, T]$.

    In the context of the instantaneous maximization problem, an increase in the price of money in terms of bonds on $S \subseteq [0, T]$ leaves unchanged the demand for consumption goods in exchange for money or bonds on $[0, T]$. The change in the household's demand for bonds in exchange for money on S is given by

$$\frac{dB_M(t)P_{MB}(t)}{dP_{MB}(t)} = B_M(t) + \mathrm{III}(t)^2 P_{CB}(t) \frac{\lambda_B(t)}{\lambda_C(t)T_{33}^d} \qquad \forall\, t \in S \qquad (IV.11.1)$$

where the right-hand side of the equation is the same as the right-hand side of equation IV.9.1. If $B_M > 0$ (i.e., the household demands bonds), then the percentage increase in $B_M(t)$ exceeds the percentage increase in $P_{MB}(t)$. If the household supplies bonds (i.e., $B_M(t) < 0$) and $dB_M(t)P_{MB}(t)/dP_{MB}(t) > 0$, then the supply of bonds in exchange for money decreases as $P_{MB}(t)$ increases. However, if $B_M(t) < 0$ and $dB_M(t)P_{MB}(t)/dP_{MB}(t) < 0$, then the supply of bonds increases as $P_{MB}(t)$ increases. This represents the perverse case of a backward-bending supply curve for bonds, which occurs when $P_{BM}(t)$ is large relative to $B_M(t)$ (Hicks, 1946).

No wealth effects result from the increase in $P_{MB}(t)$ on S, but substitution effects originate with the increase in $b(t)$ and the decrease in $m(t)$ on S due to the instantaneous increase in $b_M(t)\Pi(t)$ on S. The changes in the choice variables due to the substitution effects are identical with those resulting when $P_{CM}(t)$ increases on S. Hence we have the following proposition.

Comparative dynamics proposition 6.1

The substitution effects of an increase in $P_{MB}(t)$ lead to an increase in $b_M(t)\Pi(t)$ on R' and a decrease in $b_M(t)\Pi(t)$ at each $t \notin R' \subset [0, T]$. The choice variables $C_M(t)$ and $C_B(t)$ are lower and higher, respectively, on $[0, T]$. The real money stock is higher and the real bond stock is lower at $t \le t'$, but the real money stock is lower and the real bond stock is higher at some $t > t'$. The changes in the real stocks of money and bonds are such that $m(T)$ decreases and $b(T)$ increases. The effects of the increase in $P_{MB}(t)$ on the consumption-good stock and hence on the rate of consumption are ambiguous.

Because $P_{MB}(t)$ determines the slope of the intertemporal path of the shadow price of bonds, that is,

$$\frac{d\lambda_B(t)}{dt} = (\hat{P}_{CB}(t) - P_{MB}(t))\lambda_B(t)$$

(see equations III.2.5), there exists an additional intertemporal substitution effect of a change in $P_{MB}(t)$ on S. An increase in $P_{MB}(t)$ on S implies a decrease in $\hat{\lambda}_B(t)$ on S. However, the level of $\lambda_B(t)$ at $t = T$ is identical with the level it assumed following the adjustments due to the substitution effects. Hence, $\lambda_B(t)$ increases everywhere on $[0, s')$, and the increase is larger the smaller the value of t. The increase in $\lambda_B(t)$ induces the household to decrease its demand for consumption goods in exchange for bonds and to increase its demand for bonds in exchange for money at each $t \in [0, s')$. The decrease in $C_B(t)$ and the increase in $b_M(t)\Pi(t)$ will be larger the smaller the value of t.

Thus, a decrease in the cost of holding bonds results in an increase in the real bond stock everywhere on $[0, T]$. This, in turn, has the effect of decreasing the level of $\lambda_B(t)$ everywhere on $[0, T]$. The combination of the increase in $\lambda_B(t)$ on $[0, s')$ due to the decrease in $\hat{\lambda}_B(t)$ and the decrease in $\lambda_B(t)$ on $[0, T]$ due to the increase in $b(t)$ tilts $\lambda_B(t)$ on $[0, T]$. That is, $\hat{\lambda}_B(t)$ decreases on S and $\lambda_B(t)$ is lower for values of t such that $t^* < t < T$ and higher for values of t such that $0 < t < t^*$. Thus the increase in $P_{MB}(t)$ decreases $C_B(t)$ and increases $b_M(t)\Pi(t)$ on $(t^*, T]$. These changes in $C_B(t)$ and $b_M(t)\Pi(t)$ on $[0, T]$ are such that both the consumption-good stock and the real money stock decrease at all $t \in [0, T]$. The decline in the consumption-good stock will lead to a decline in the rate of consumption at each $t \in [0, T]$. We have therefore established the following proposition.

Comparative dynamics proposition 6.2

The intertemporal substitution effect of an increase in $P_{MB}(t)$ on $S \subseteq [0, T]$ leads to a higher $b_M(t)\Pi(t)$ and a lower $C_B(t)$ on $[0, s')$, whereas $b_M(t)\Pi(t)$ decreases and $C_B(t)$ increases on $(s', T]$, where s' is the largest element in S. The real bond stock increases everywhere on $[0, T]$, and the real money and consumption-good stocks decrease at all $t \in [0, T]$.

Let $R' \subseteq [0, T]$ and $R''' \subseteq [0, T]$ be the sets of t on which the household increases $b_M(t)\Pi(t)$ when it considers the substitution effect alone and when it considers both the substitution and intertemporal substitution effects, respectively. Let $t' \in R'$ and $t''' \in R'''$ be the least elements of R' and R'''. Combining the intertemporal substitution effect of an increase in $P_{MB}(t)$ with the static substitution effect, the increase in $b_M(t)\Pi(t)$ on $[0, t^*)$ and the decrease in the same variable on $(t^*, T]$ forces $t''' < t'$. Hence, $m(t)$ is higher and $b(t)$ is lower at $t \leq t'''$, whereas $m(t)$ and $b(t)$ are smaller and larger, respectively, at some $t > t'''$. The changes in the real stocks of money and bonds due to the intertemporal substitution effect reinforce the increase in $b(T)$ and the decrease in $m(T)$ due to the substitution effect. However, the intertemporal substitution effect causes the household to reduce $C_B(t)$ on $[0, t^*)$ and thus leads to a reduction in $C(t)$ on $[0, t^*)$, whereas the substitution effect results in an increase in $C_B(t)$ on all of $[0, T]$. Hence, there exists the possibility that the intertemporal substitution effect dominates and causes a decrease in $C_B(t)$ on $[0, t^*)$ and a decrease in $C(t)$ on $[0, T]$ when both substitution effects are considered. In this case the rate of consumption diminishes at each $t \in [0, T]$. This establishes the validity of comparative statics proposition 6.

In the special case in which the consumption-good-cum-bonds market is not in use, the substitution effect produces an increase in $b_M(t)\Pi(t)$ at each $t \in R'$ and a decrease in $b_M(t)\Pi(t)$ at each $t \notin R'$, and $C_M(t)$ decreases everywhere on $[0, T]$. The real bond stock is lower and the real money stock is higher at each $t \leq t'$. However, the real bond and money stocks are higher and lower, respectively, at some $t > t'$ such that in the final analysis $m(T)$ decreases and $b(T)$ increases. The consumption-good stock and the rate of consumption are lower at each $t \in [0, T]$. The combination of the intertemporal substitution effect and the substitution effect forces $t''' < t'$.

This completes the analysis of the household's adjustments of its intertemporal market and stock-holding behavior in response to exogenous changes in market prices. The investigation reveals that the substitution effect of a price change induces the household to diminish its demand in the market in which the price rises and to increase its demand in the other two markets. Hence, an increase in $P_{CB}(t)$ on $S \subseteq [0,T]$ results in a decrease in $C_M(t)$ at each $t \in [0, T]$, an increase in $C_B(t)$ at each $t \in [0, T]$, and an increase in $B_M(t)\Pi(t)$ at each $t \in R' \subseteq [0, T]$. An increase in $P_{CB}(t)$ on $S \subseteq [0, T]$ leads to a decrease in $C_B(t)$ at each $t \in [0, T]$, an increase in $C_M(t)$ at each $t \in [0, T]$, and a decrease in $B_M(t)\Pi(t)$ on $R' \subseteq [0, T]$. Finally, an increase in $P_{MB}(t)$ on $S \subseteq [0,T]$ impels the household to increase $B_M(t)\Pi(t)$ on $R' \subseteq [0, T]$, to increase $C_B(t)$ at each $t \in [0, T]$, and to decrease $C_M(t)$ at each $t \in [0, T]$. The wealth effect further reduces demand for the good whose price has risen. The intertemporal substitution effect of a price change initially induces a decrease in demand for the good whose rate of depreciation has increased and an increase in demand for the other two goods. However, as t approaches T, the first of these changes reverses itself, decreasing demand for the good whose rate of depreciation has increased. The combined effect over $[0, T]$ of these two changes is to decrease the stock that has become relatively more costly to hold and to increase the remaining two stocks.

IV.12 A comparative dynamic analysis of the household's responses to changes in δ, ρ, $X(t)$, and $T^d(t)$

In this section we examine the comparative dynamics of the household's market and stock-holding activities with respect to changes in δ (the rate of depreciation of the consumption-good stock), ρ (the household's personal rate of discount), $X(t)$ (the flow of consumption-good endowment), and $T^d(t)$ (the household's transactions technology).

An anticipated decrease in δ or an anticipated increase in $X(t)$ at each $t \in S \subseteq [0, T]$ does not immediately influence the household's solution to its instantaneous maximization problem $t \in S$. However, a decrease in δ or an increase in $X(t)$ at each $t \in S$ results in an increase in $C(t)$ at each $t \in S$. Hence, the consumption-good stock at $t = T$ will be higher. If ρ increases at $t \in S \subseteq [0, T]$, the household decreases the rate at which it consumes at each $t \in S$. This decrease in $\phi(t)$ at each $t \in S$ results in an increase in $C(t)$ at each $t \in S$

and hence an increase in the final consumption-good stock, $C(T)$. Thus, the results from the analysis of the effects of an increase in the initial endowment of the consumption good on the market and stock-holding activities of the household can be extended to this analysis. Hence, we have the following proposition.

Comparative dynamics proposition 7

A decrease in δ or an increase in ρ or $X(t)$ at each $t \in S$ will, through the resulting increase in $C(T)$, lead the household to reduce $C_M(t)$ and $C_B(t)$ at each $t \in [0, T]$ and lead to increases in $m(t)$ and $b(t)$ at each $t \in [0, T]$. Also, the household reduces $C(t)$ at each $t \le \bar{s}$ and increases $C(t)$ at some $t > \bar{s}$ such that $C(T)$ increases, where $\bar{s}$ is the least element in S. When δ decreases or when $X(t)$ increases on S, then the rate of consumption increases at each $t \in [0, T]$. If ρ increases at each $t \in S$, then $\phi(t)$ decreases at each $T \in M \subset S$, and it increases at each $t \notin M$ such that[56]

$$\int_M \frac{d\phi(t)}{d\rho} \Delta\rho \, dt + \int_0^T \frac{d\phi(t)}{d\lambda_C(t)} \Delta\lambda_C(t) \, dt < 0 \qquad \text{(IV.12.1)}$$

The effects of changes δ, ρ, and $X(t)$ on $b_M(t)\Pi(t)$ are ambiguous.

Section IV.4 provides the requisite results for determining the effects of changes in the transactions technology on the household's market and stock-holding activities. A change in $T^d(\cdot)$ can be dichotomized conceptually into a change in the slope of $T^d(\cdot)$ in the $T^d(t)$, $C_M(t)$, $C_B(t)$, and $b_M(t)\Pi(t)$ space when the level of $T^d(\cdot)$ is held constant and a change in the level of $T^d(\cdot)$ when the slope of $T^d(\cdot)$ is held constant. This method of decomposing changes in $T^d(\cdot)$ into shifts in $T_i^d(\cdot)$ $(i = 1, 2, 3)$ and dislocations in the level of $T^d(\cdot)$ allows distinction between those choice-variable adjustments that are induced by changes in marginal transactions costs and those that emanate from changes in the total cost of transacting when marginal costs are constant.

A decrease in the level of $T^d(\cdot)$ at each $t \in S \subset [0, T]$ that leaves the slopes $T_i^d(\cdot)$ $(i = 1, 2, 3,)$ unchanged has no direct effect on the household's instantaneous maximization problem at any $t \in [0, T]$. However, the decrease $T^d(\cdot)$ at each $t \in S$ results in an increase in $C(t)$ at each $t \in S$ and thus an increase in $C(T)$. The increase in $C(T)$ induces the household to diminish $C_M(t)$ and $C_B(t)$ at each $t \in [0, T]$ and to increase $\phi(t)$ at each $t \in [0, T]$. Hence we obtain the following proposition.

Comparative dynamics proposition 8

A decrease in the level of $T^d(\cdot)$ at each $t \in S \subset [0, T]$ that leaves the slopes $T_i^d(\cdot)$ $(i = 1, 2, 3)$ unchanged will induce the household to hold larger stocks of real money, bonds, and consumption goods at each $t \in [0, T]$. $C_B(t)$ and $C_M(t)$ will be lower and $\phi(t)$ will be higher everywhere on $[0, T]$.

Within the context of the instantaneous maximization problem, a decrease in the marginal cost of acquiring consumption goods in exchange for money in the consumption-good-cum-money market (i.e., a decrease in $T_1^d(C_M(t))$) at each $t \in S \subseteq [0, T]$ with $C_M(t)$ unchanged at $t \in S$) results in an increase in $\dot{C}_M(t)$ at each $t \in S$. The first-order condition that determines the value of $C_M(t)$ at each $t \in [0, T]$ is

$$T_1^d(C_M(t)) = 1 - \frac{\lambda_M(t)}{\lambda_C(t)} \qquad \forall\, t \in [0, T] \qquad \text{(IV.12.2)}$$

(see equation III.2.12). Because $\lambda_M(t)$ and $\lambda_C(t)$ are exogenously given in the instantaneous maximization problem, a decrease in $T_1^d(C_M(t))$ at $t \in S$ must result in an instantaneous increase in $C_M(t)$ at $t \in S$. The increase in $C_M(t)$ at each $t \in S$ results in an increase in $C(t)$ and a decrease in $m(t)$ at each $t \in S$. Therefore, $C(T)$ increases and $m(T)$ decreases. The increase in $C(T)$ causes a decrease in $\lambda_C(t)$ at each $t \in [0, T]$ that, in turn, induces the household to decrease $C_M(t)$ and $C_B(t)$ and to increase $\phi(t)$ at each $t \in [0, T]$. Also, the decrease in $\lambda_C(t)$ causes an increase (decrease) in $b_M(t)\Pi(t)$ if $B_M(t)$ is positive (negative). The increase in $\lambda_M(t)$ results in upward shifts in $C_M(t)$ and $b_M(t)\Pi(t)$ at each $t \in [0, T]$.

After all adjustments in demands are complete, $C_M(t)$ is higher on a nonempty subset $M \subseteq S$, and $C_M(t)$ is lower at each $t \notin M$.[57] The demand for consumption goods in exchange for bonds declines at each $t \in [0, T]$. The variable $b_M(t)\Pi(t)$ is lower at each $t \in [0, T]$ unless $B_M(t) > 0$, and the decrease in $\lambda_C(t)$ causes an increase in $b_M(t)\Pi(t)$ large enough to dominate the decrease in the same variable due to the increase in $\lambda_M(t)$.[58] This situation arises when the marginal transactions cost of increasing $b_M(t)\Pi(t)$ is high (see Table IV.1).

Hence, as the marginal cost of acquiring consumption goods in the consumption-good-cum-money market decreases, the household increases its demand for consumption goods in this market and decreases its rate of acquisition of consumption goods in the consumption-good-cum-bonds market and its purchases of bonds in the bonds-cum-money market. If $\overline{m}$ is the least element in M, then $C(t)$ is lower and $m(t)$ is higher at each $t \leq \overline{m}$, whereas $C(t)$ is higher and $m(t)$ is lower at some $t > \overline{m}$ such that $C(T)$ increases and $m(T)$ decreases. The effect of the change in $T_1^d(C_M(t))$ on the bond stock is ambiguous. We summarize these results in the following proposition.

Comparative dynamics proposition 9

A decrease in the marginal cost of acquiring consumption goods in the consumption-good-cum-money market (i.e., a decrease in $T_1^d(C_M(t))$) at each $t \in S \subseteq [0, T]$ with

$C_M(t)$ unchanged) results in a higher $C_M(t)$ on a nonempty subset $M \subset S$ and a lower $C_M(t)$ at each $t \notin M$. $C_B(t)$ will be lower everywhere on $[0, T]$. If $\overline{m}$ is the least element in M, then $C(t)$ is lower and $m(t)$ is higher at each $t \leq \overline{m}$, whereas $C(t)$ is higher and $m(t)$ is lower at some $t > \overline{m}$ such that $m(T)$ is lower and $C(T)$ is higher.

In the context of the instantaneous maximization problem, a decrease in the marginal cost of acquiring consumption goods in exchange for bonds in the consumption-good-cum-bonds market (i.e., a decrease in $T_2^d(C_B(t))$ at each $t \in S \subseteq [0, T]$ with $C_B(t)$ unchanged at $t \in S$) results in an increase in $C_B(t)$ at each $t \in S$. The first-order condition that determines $C_B(t)$ at each instant $t \in [0, T]$ is

$$T_2^d(C_B(t)) = 1 - \frac{\lambda_B(t)}{\lambda_C(t)} \qquad \forall\, t \in [0, T] \qquad \text{(IV.12.3)}$$

(see equation III.2.13). The shadow prices $\lambda_B(t)$ and $\lambda_C(t)$ are exogenously given in the instantaneous maximization problem; hence, $C_B(t)$ must increase at $t \in S$ when $T_2^d(C_B(t))$ decreases at $t \in S$. The increase in $C_B(t)$ at $t \in S$ results in an increase in $C(t)$ and a decrease in $b(t)$ at each $t \in S$. Thus, $C(T)$ increases and $b(T)$ decreases.

The increase in $C(T)$ brings about a decrease in $\lambda_C(t)$ at each $t \in [0, T]$ that induces the household to diminish $C_M(t)$ and $C_B(t)$ and to increase $\phi(t)$ at each $t \in [0, T]$. The household increases (decreases) $b_M(t)\Pi(t)$ at each $t \in [0, T]$ if $B_M(t) > 0$ $(B_M(t) < 0)$. The decrease in $b(T)$ results in an increase in $\lambda_B(t)$ and leads the household to decrease $C_B(t)$ and increase $b_M(t)\Pi(t)$ at each $T \in [0, T]$. The fact the $b(T)$ must decline implies that

$$\int_S \Delta C_B(t)\, dt + \int_0^T \frac{dC_B(t)}{d\lambda_B(t)}\, \Delta\lambda_B(t)\, dt > 0 \qquad \text{(IV.12.4)}$$

where $\Delta C_B(t)$ is the instantaneous change in $C_B(t)$ due to the decrease in $T_2^d(C_B(t))$. We therefore have the following proposition.

Comparative dynamics proposition 10

An increase in $T_2^d(C_B(t))$ at each $t \in S \in [0, T]$ with $C_B(t)$ unchanged induces the household to revise its market activities and consumption activities such that $C_B(t)$ is higher on a nonempty set $M \subset S$ and $C_B(t)$ is lower at each $t \notin M$, whereas $C_M(t)$ is lower and $b_M(t)\Pi(t)$ is higher at each $t \in [0, T]$.[59] Hence, as the marginal cost of acquiring consumption goods in the consumption-good-cum-bonds market decreases, the household increases $C_B(t)$ and decreases $C_M(t)$, its rate of acquiring consumption goods in the consumption-good-cum-money market, after having decreased its rate of acquiring money in the money-cum-bonds market. If $\overline{m}$ is the least element in M, then $C(t)$ is lower and $b(t)$ is higher at $t \leq \overline{m}$, whereas $C(t)$ is higher and $b(t)$ is lower at some $t > \overline{m}$ such that $C(T)$ increases and $b(T)$ decreases. The effect of the change in $T_2^d(C_B(t))$ on the money stock is ambiguous.

In the context of the instantaneous maximization problem, a decrease in the marginal cost of acquiring bonds in the bonds-cum-money market (i.e., a decrease in $T_3^d(b_M(t)\Pi(t))$ at each $t \in S \subset [0, T]$ with $b_M(t)\Pi(t)$ unchanged at $t \in S$) results in an increase in $b_M(t)\Pi(t)$ at each $T \in S$. The first-order condition that determines $b_M(t)\Pi(t)$ at each $T \in [0, T)$ is

$$T_3^d(b_M(t)\Pi(t)) = \frac{\lambda_B(t)}{\lambda_C(t)} \Pi(t) - \frac{\lambda_M(t)}{\lambda_C(t)} \qquad \forall\, t \in [0, T] \quad \text{(IV.12.5)}$$

(see equation III.2.14). Because the shadow and market prices are given in the instantaneous maximization problem, a decrease in $T_3^d(b_M(t)\Pi(t))$ at each $t \in S$ must result in an increase in $b_M(t)\Pi(t)$ at each $t \in S$.

The increase in $b_M(t)\Pi(t)$ at each $t \in S$ causes an increase in $b(t)$ and a decrease in $m(t)$ at each $t \in S$. Hence, $b(t)$ increases and $m(T)$ decreases. The increase in $b(T)$ brings about a decrease in $\lambda_B(t)$, which induces the household to increase $C_B(t)$ and decrease $b_M(t)\Pi(t)$ at each $t \in [0,T]$. The decrease in $m(T)$ causes an increase in $\lambda_M(t)$ at each $t \in [0, T]$; hence, the household decreases $C_M(t)$ and $b_M(t)\Pi(t)$ at each $T \in [0, T]$. The increase in $b(T)$ implies that

$$\int_S \Delta\,(b_M(t)\Pi(t))\,dt$$
$$+ \int_0^T \left(\frac{d(b_M(t)\Pi(t))}{d\lambda_B(t)}\Delta\lambda_B(t) + \frac{d(b_M(t)\Pi(t))}{d\lambda_M(t)}\Delta\lambda_M(t) \right) dt > 0 \quad \text{(IV.12.6)}$$

We have thus proved the following proposition.

Comparative dynamics proposition 11

After a reduction in $T_3^d(b_M(t)\Pi(t))$ at each $t \in S \subseteq [0, T]$ with $b_M(t)\Pi(t)$ unchanged, the household increases $b_M(t)\Pi(t)$ at each $t \notin M \subseteq S$ and decreases $b_M(t)\Pi(t)$ at each $t \notin M$. Also, the household increases $C_B(t)$ and decreases $C_M(t)$ at each $t \in [0, T]$. Hence, as the marginal cost of acquiring bonds in the bonds-cum-money market decreases, the household increases $b_M(t)\Pi(t)$ and decreases its acquisition of bonds in the consumption-good-cum-bonds market, and it increases its acquisition of money in the money-cum-consumption-goods market. The real bond stock declines and the real money stock increases at each $t \le \overline{m}$, whereas $m(t)$ decreases and $b(t)$ increases at some $t > \overline{m}$, where $\overline{m}$ is the least element in M. The effect of a decrease in $T_3^d(b_M(t)\Pi(t))$ on the consumption-good stock is ambiguous.

CHAPTER V

General-equilibrium theory

V.1   Introduction

In this chapter we shall investigate the properties of an intertemporal economy composed of agents who live an interval of time $[0, T]$ and behave as described in previous chapters. We shall first establish the consistency properties of the price system of the economy and analyze the arbitrage mechanism that generates those properties. In Section V.3 we shall discuss the existence, stability, and uniqueness of equilibrium price vectors. In Section V.4 the partial-equilibrium comparative dynamics results derived in the preceding chapter are extended to account for general-equilibrium interactions. Lastly, endogenous price movements in this intertemporal economy are investigated under varying assumptions about the sequencing of generations of agents.

V.2   Arbitrage, price systems, and monetary economies

When executing an exchange among consumption goods, bonds, and money the household can trade directly any of those commodities for another in the appropriate market, or it can use one commodity as a medium of exchange to effect a trade between the other two and thus enter two markets. The marginal arbitrage conditions that determine trading routes are implicit in the first-order conditions for a maximum of the household's intertemporal optimization problem. In addition, these conditions form a basis for a characterization of price systems and monetary economies; therefore they will be derived explicitly.

The household can acquire a unit of the consumption good in exchange for money directly in the consumption-good-cum-money market at time $t \in [0, T]$ at a marginal money cost of

$$P_{CM}(t) + T_1^d(C_M(t))P_{CM}(t) \tag{V.2.1}$$

Alternatively, at time t the household can buy a unit of the consumption good in exchange for money by purchasing $P_{CB}(t)$ units of bonds with $P_{CB}(t)P_{BM}(t)$ units of money and then exchanging bonds for consumption

85

goods at a marginal money cost of

$$P_{CB}(t)P_{BM}(t) + T_2^d(C_B(t))P_{CM}(t)$$
$$+ T_3^d(b_M(t)\Pi(t))P_{CB}(t)P_{BM}(t) \quad \text{(V.2.2)}$$

If

$$\Pi(t) < \frac{1 + T_3^d(\cdot)}{1 + T_1^d(\cdot) - T_2^d(\cdot)} \quad \text{where} \quad \Pi(t) = \frac{P_{CM}(t)}{P_{CB}(t)P_{BM}(t)} \quad \text{(V.2.3)}$$

then equations V.2.1 and V.2.2 imply that the household uses the direct trading route (i.e., exchanges money for consumption goods at time t in the consumption-good-cum-money market). However, if the inequality V.2.3 is reversed, then the household uses bonds as a medium of exchange when trading consumption goods for money.

The household can obtain a unit of money at time t in exchange for consumption goods directly in the money-cum-consumption-good market at a marginal consumption-good cost of[1]

$$P_{MC}(t) - T_1^d(C_M(t))P_{MC}(t) \quad \text{(V.2.4)}$$

Alternatively, the household can obtain a unit of money at time t in exchange for consumption goods by purchasing $P_{MB}(t)$ units of bonds with $P_{MB}(t)P_{BC}(t)$ units of consumption goods and then buying a unit of money with $P_{MB}(t)$ units of bonds. The marginal cost of acquiring a unit of money via this indirect route equals

$$P_{MB}(t)P_{BC}(t) - T_3^d(b_M(t)\Pi(t))\frac{1}{P_{CM}(t)} - T_2^d(C_B(t))P_{MB}(t)P_{BC}(t) \quad \text{(V.2.5)}$$

If

$$\Pi(t) > \frac{1 - T_1^d(\cdot) + T_3^d(\cdot)}{1 - T_2^d(\cdot)} \quad \text{(V.2.6)}$$

then equations V.2.4 and V.2.5 imply that the household chooses to exchange consumption goods directly for money. A reversal of the inequality V.2.6 induces the household to use bonds as a medium of exchange when purchasing money in exchange for consumption goods.

The marginal cost in terms of money of obtaining one unit of bonds in exchange for money directly in the money-cum-bonds market at time t is given by

$$P_{BM}(t) + T_3^d(b_M(t)\Pi(t))P_{BM}(t) \quad \text{(V.2.7)}$$

The marginal cost of obtaining bonds in exchange for money by using the consumption good as a medium of exchange equals

$$P_{BC}(t)P_{CM}(t) - T_2^d(C_B(t))P_{BC}(t)P_{CM}(t)$$
$$+ T_1^d(C_M(t))P_{BC}(t)P_{CM}(t) \quad \text{(V.2.8)}$$

Hence, the household purchases bonds in exchange for money directly in the bonds-cum-money market at time t if

$$\Pi(t) > \frac{1 + T_3^d(\cdot)}{1 + T_1^d(\cdot) - T_2^d(\cdot)} \quad \text{(V.2.9)}$$

However, it uses the consumption good as a medium of exchange if the inequality is reversed.

The marginal cost in terms of bonds of obtaining an additional unit of money in exchange for bonds directly in the bonds-cum-money market at time t is given by

$$P_{MB}(t) - T_3^d(b_M(t)\Pi(t)) \frac{P_{CB}(t)}{P_{CM}(t)} \quad \text{(V.2.10)}$$

However, if the household uses the consumption good as a medium of exchange when trading bonds for money, then the marginal cost of obtaining one more unit of money in terms of bonds is given by

$$P_{MC}(t)P_{CB}(t) - T_1^d(C_M(t))P_{MC}(t)P_{CB}(t)$$
$$+ T_2^d(C_B(t))P_{MC}(t)P_{CB}(t) \quad \text{(V.2.11)}$$

Hence, the household buys money directly in the money-cum-bonds market at time t if

$$\Pi(t) < 1 + T_2^d(\cdot) + T_3^d(\cdot) - T_1^d(\cdot) \quad \text{(V.2.12)}$$

However, if the inequality is reversed, the household uses the consumption good as a medium of exchange when trading bonds for money.

The marginal cost of acquiring an additional unit of the consumption good in the consumption-good-cum-bonds market is given by

$$P_{CB}(t) + T_2^d(C_B(t))P_{CB}(t) \quad \text{(V.2.13)}$$

If the household uses money as a medium of exchange when trading bonds for consumption goods, then the marginal cost of acquiring an additional unit of consumption goods equals

$$P_{CM}(t)P_{MB}(t) + T_1^d(C_M(t))P_{CB}(t) - T_3^d(b_M(t)\Pi(t))P_{CB}(t) \quad \text{(V.2.14)}$$

Hence, the household obtains consumption goods in exchange for bonds directly in the consumption-good-cum-bonds market if

$$\Pi(t) > 1 + T_3^d(\cdot) + T_2^d(\cdot) - T_1^d(\cdot) \tag{V.2.15}$$

and uses money as a medium of exchange when trading bonds for consumption goods if the inequality V.2.15 is reversed.

The marginal cost in terms of consumption goods of obtaining an additional unit of bonds in the bonds-cum-consumption-good market at time t is given by

$$P_{BC}(t) - T_2^d(C_B(t))P_{BC}(t) \tag{V.2.16}$$

However, if the household uses money as the medium of exchange when trading consumption goods for bonds, then the marginal cost in terms of consumption goods of obtaining an additional unit of bonds is given by

$$P_{BM}(t)P_{MC}(t) + T_3^d(b_M(t)\Pi(t))P_{BM}(t)P_{MC}(t)$$
$$- T_1^d(C_M(t))P_{BM}(t)P_{MC}(t) \tag{V.2.17}$$

Hence, the household trades consumption goods directly for bonds in the bonds-cum-consumption-good market if

$$\Pi(t) < \frac{1 + T_3^d(\cdot) - T_1^d(\cdot)}{1 - T_2^d(\cdot)} \tag{V.2.18}$$

and it uses money as a medium of exchange when trading bonds for consumption goods if the inequality V.2.18 is reversed.

Equality of the two terms in equation V.2.3, V.2.6, V.2.9, V.2.12, V.2.15, or V.2.18 indicates that the marginal cost of acquiring an additional unit of one of the three commodities in exchange for a second commodity is independent of whether the exchange is made directly or by using the third commodity as a medium of exchange. However, because the household is confronted with an arbitrary set of prices at each point in time, the possibility of a corner solution cannot be excluded; that is, strict inequalities may hold in some of equations V.2.3, V.2.6, V.2.9, V.2.12, V.2.15, and V.2.18.

The first-order conditions for an interior maximum of the Hamiltonian imply that equations V.2.6 and V.2.18 hold with equality; that is,[2]

$$\Pi(t) = \frac{1 - T_1^d(\cdot) + T_3^d(\cdot)}{1 - T_2^d(\cdot)} \qquad \forall \, t \in [0, \, T] \tag{V.2.19}$$

Hence, the household organizes its demands at each $t \in [0, \, T]$ so that the marginal cost of buying an additional unit of money in exchange for consumption goods remains the same whether the household exchanges consumption goods and money directly or uses bonds as a medium of exchange. Similarly, because equations V.2.18 and V.2.6 hold with equality, the household will arrange its demands $C_M(t)$, $C_B(t)$, and $b_M(t)\Pi(t)$ at each $t \in [0,\ T]$ so that the marginal cost of acquiring an additional unit of bonds in exchange for consumption goods remains the same regardless of whether the household exchanges bonds and consumption goods directly or uses money as a medium of exchange.

Because the right-hand and left-hand sides of equations V.2.3 and V.2.9 are identical, as are those of equations V.2.12 and V.2.15, the inequalities in V.2.3 and V.2.9 or V.2.12 and V.2.15 cannot hold simultaneously. For instance, if $C_M(t)$, $C_B(t)$, $b_M(t)\Pi(t)$, and $\Pi(t)$ are such that the household acquires additional units of money in exchange for bonds directly in the money-cum-bonds market at time t (i.e., inequality V.2.12 holds at time t), then any desire to acquire further units of the consumption good in exchange for bonds must be satisfied by using money as a medium of exchange. Similarly, at the margin the household cannot acquire both more consumption goods and more bonds in exchange for money directly in the consumption-good-cum-money and bonds-cum-money markets, respectively; rather, it must use a medium of exchange in one of the two types of exchanges. This result is due to the fact that the household is confronted with arbitrary prices rather than consistent prices. We shall see later that whenever prices are not consistent, then incentives will be generated to move prices toward consistency. We shall see further that when prices are consistent, then it is possible for the household to acquire both consumption goods and bonds in exchange for money directly in the consumption-good-cum-money and bonds-cum-money markets.

The household is said to face internally consistent prices at time $t \in [0,\ T]$ if the marginal cost of acquiring an additional unit of one of the three commodities in direct exchange for a second commodity equals the marginal cost of executing the same trade with the third commodity as medium of exchange. Hence, at time t, internally consistent prices will prevail if

$$\Pi(t) = \frac{1 + T_3^d(\cdot)}{1 + T_1^d(\cdot) - T_2^d(\cdot)} \tag{V.2.20}$$

$$\Pi(t) = \frac{1 - T_1^d(\cdot) + T_3^d(\cdot)}{1 - T_2^d(\cdot)} \tag{V.2.21}$$

$$\Pi(t) = 1 + T_2^d(\cdot) + T_3^d(\cdot) - T_1^d(\cdot) \tag{V.2.22}$$

Therefore, if the household determines its choice variables $C_B(t)$, $C_M(t)$, and $b_M(t)\Pi(t)$ at time $t \in [0,\ T]$ such that

$$T_1^d(C_M(t)) = T_2^d(C_B(t)) + T_3^d(b_M(t)\Pi(t)) \tag{V.2.23}$$

then equations V.2.20, V.2.21, and V.2.22 are solved simultaneously. However, substituting V.2.23 into V.2.20, V.2.21, and V.2.22 reveals that the household achieves internally consistent prices only if $\text{III}(t) = 1$. Alternatively, if $\text{III}(t) \neq 1$, then internal prices cannot be consistent. Hence, we have proved the following proposition.

Consistency-of-price-systems proposition

The household's internal prices are consistent if and only if market prices are consistent.[3]

Equations V.2.3, V.2.6, V.2.9, V.2.12, V.2.15, and V.2.18 permit derivation of the necessary conditions under which the household chooses one commodity as the medium of exchange for all its marginal transactions. Specifically, the household uses money as a medium of exchange in all of its marginal transactions at time t if V.2.3, V.2.9, and V.2.12 hold and the inequality in V.2.15 is reversed. Equation V.2.19 implies that V.2.6 and V.2.18 hold with equality. Inequalities V.2.3 and V.2.9 cannot hold simultaneously at time t; hence, V.2.20 must be satisfied. If inequality V.2.12 holds, then V.2.15 implies that the household uses money as a medium of exchange when acquiring additional units of consumption goods in exchange for bonds. Hence, the following represents a necessary condition for money to be used as a medium of exchange in the household's marginal transactions at time t:

$$\text{III}(t) = \frac{1 + T_3^d(\cdot)}{1 + T_1^d(\cdot) - T_2^d(\cdot)} = \frac{1 - T_1^d(\cdot) + T_3^d(\cdot)}{1 - T_2^d(\cdot)}$$

$$\leq 1 + T_2^d(\cdot) + T_3^d(\cdot) - T_1^d(\cdot) \quad (V.2.24)$$

The two middle terms in equation V.2.24 are equal if and only if $T_1^d(\cdot)$ $(T_2^d(\cdot) + T_3^d(\cdot) - T_1^d(\cdot)) = 0$. By equation III.4.2 we know that $dC_M(t)/dt \gtreqqless 0$ as $\delta - \dot{P}_{CM}(t) \gtreqqless 0$, and hence $T_1^d(\cdot) \neq 0$, which implies that equation V.2.23 must be satisfied. Therefore, the necessary condition for the household to use money as a medium of exchange in its marginal transactions at time t is that internal prices be consistent at time t or, equivalently, that market prices be consistent at time t. We need to assume further that if the marginal cost of a direct exchange equals the marginal cost of the same exchange with money as a medium of exchange, then the household will choose the latter type of exchange. This monetary-preference assumption, together with consistent internal prices, is sufficient to ensure that the household uses money as a medium of exchange for its marginal transactions at time t. We can summarize these results in the following proposition.

Medium-of-exchange proposition

The household will use money as a medium of exchange in all its marginal transactions if and only if internal prices and hence market prices are consistent.

In the special case in which $T_1^d(\cdot)$, $T_2^d(\cdot)$, and $T_3^d(\cdot)$ are constant, we can conclude that if the internal or market prices are consistent from time $t^* \geq 0$ onward and the household has monetary preference, then it will use money as a medium of exchange in all transactions for all $t \geq t^*$.

If one or more of the inequalities in V.2.3, V.2.6, V.2.9, V.2.12, V.2.15, or V.2.18 are satisfied, then there exists an incentive for the household to adjust its market behavior to favor direct exchanges over exchanges that involve a medium of exchange. The adjustments in $C_M(t)$, $C_B(t)$, and $b_M(t)\Pi(t)$ resulting from the shift in trading routes will tend to restore equality between the marginal costs of direct and indirect exchanges, as given by V.2.20, V.2.21, and V.2.22, as long as the market prices are consistent.

For example, if equation V.2.3 is satisfied (i.e., if the marginal cost of acquiring consumption goods directly in exchange for money is less than the marginal cost of executing the same exchange using bonds as a medium of exchange), then the household increases $C_M(t)$ and decreases $C_B(t)$ and $b_M(t)\Pi(t)$. These marginal changes in $C_M(t)$, $C_B(t)$, and $b_M(t)\Pi(t)$ induce an increase in $T_1^d(\cdot)$ and decreases in $T_2^d(\cdot)$ and $T_3^d(\cdot)$ that will tend to lower the value of the right-hand side of equation V.2.3.

The incentive to arbitrage persists until internal prices are consistent. However, a necessary and sufficient condition for the existence of consistent internal prices at time t is that market prices be consistent at time t. If $\Pi(t) \neq 1$, then there exists, nevertheless, a tendency toward equality in equations V.2.3, V.2.6, V.2.9, V.2.12, V.2.15, and V.2.18 through adjustments in $C_M(t)$, $C_B(t)$, and $b_M(t)\Pi(t)$ and the resulting changes in $T_1^d(\cdot)$, $T_2^d(\cdot)$, and $T_3^d(\cdot)$; but as long as external market prices are inconsistent, consistent internal prices cannot be realized. However, if we allow the changes in $C_M(t)$, $C_B(t)$, and $b_M(t)\Pi(t)$ (which occur as long as market prices are inconsistent) to affect market prices, then the equilibrating process that established consistent internal prices also leads market prices toward consistency.

For instance, if equation V.2.3 holds, then $C_M(t)$ increases and $C_B(t)$ and $b_M(t)\Pi(t)$ decrease. The comparative dynamics results in Section IV.4 demonstrate that such changes induce an increase in $P_{CM}(t)$ and decreases in $P_{CB}(t)$ and $P_{BM}(t)$. Hence, $\Pi(t)$ increases. A similar chain of events takes place when any of the inequalities in V.2.6, V.2.9, V.2.12, V.2.15, or V.2.18 hold. Hence, as long as any of these inequalities hold, there will exist a tendency toward internally consistent prices and thus a tendency toward consistent market prices.

The existence of internally consistent prices, together with the assumption of monetary preference, establishes the necessary and sufficient condition for the household to use money as a medium of exchange for all of its marginal transactions at time t. However, if the marginal costs of transacting are variable, then the household must adjust $C_B(t)$ as well as $C_M(t)$ and $b_M(t)\Pi(t)$ at time t. For instance, if equations V.2.20, V.2.21, and V.2.22 hold (i.e., internal prices are consistent), then a desire on the part of the household to acquire additional units of consumption goods in exchange for money will, by the assumption of monetary preference, lead to an increase in $C_M(t)$. The resulting increase in $T_1^d(\cdot)$ leads to inconsistent internal prices, because the left-hand side of equation V.2.20 now exceeds the right-hand side of that equation. Hence, if the adjustment in demand for consumption goods in exchange for money exceeds a marginal increment, then the household must also increase $C_B(t)$ and $b_M(t)\Pi(t)$ in order to restore consistency of internal prices. Hence, we have the following proposition.

Monetary-economy proposition

Variable marginal costs of transacting exclude the existence of a purely monetary economy, that is, an economy in which $C_B(t) = 0 \ \forall \ t > t^* \in [0, T)$.

However, the comparative dynamic analysis of Section IV.5 that establishes the effects of structural changes in $T^d(\cdot)$ on $C_M(t)$, $C_B(t)$, and $b_M(t)\Pi(t)$ demonstrates that an increase in $T_2^d(\cdot)$ or a decrease in $T_1^d(\cdot)$ or $T_3^d(\cdot)$ induces the household to increase $C_M(t)$ and $b_M(t)\Pi(t)$ and decrease $C_B(t)$ at each $t \in [0, T]$. Hence, although variable costs of transacting exclude the existence of purely monetary economies, such an economy can be approximated as closely as desired by raising the marginal cost of nonmonetary transactions $T_2^d(\cdot)$ relative to the marginal costs of monetary transactions (i.e., $T_1^d(\cdot)$ and $T_3^d(\cdot)$), because these structural cost changes result in a decrease in $C_B(t)$ relative to $C_M(t)$ and $b_M(t)\Pi(t)$. It is possible to think of these changes in $T_1^d(\cdot)$, $T_2^d(\cdot)$, and $T_3^d(\cdot)$ as occurring over time due to technological progress in the exchange technology.[4]

V.3   Existence, stability, and uniqueness of intertemporal competitive equilibria

Each household in the economy is endowed with initial stocks of money, bonds, and consumption goods, as well as an instantaneous utility function, a utility-of-bequest function, a transactions technology, and income in the form of a continuous stream of consumption goods. At time $t = 0$ the ith household $(i = 1, 2, \ldots, n)$ solves its intertemporal maximization problem with a price vector $P(t)_i = (P_{CM}(t)_i, P_{CB}(t)_i, P_{BM}(t)_i, P_{MC}(t)_i, P_{BC}(t)_i, P_{MB}(t)_i)$ defined on $[0, T]$ to obtain the vector of flow demands $d(t)_i = (C_M(t)_i, C_B(t)_i, B_M(t)_i, M_C(t)_i, B_C(t)_i, M_B(t)_i)$ also defined on $[0, T]$. Hence the demand of the ith household at a given $t^* \in [0, T]$ depends on the value of $P(t)_i$ at each $t \in [0, T]$. The transactions flow constraints given in equations II.5.1., II.5.2., and II.5.3 allow the elimination of $M_C(t)_i$, $B_C(t)_i$, and $M_B(t)_i$ from the analysis. Also, the inverse relationship among prices given by $P_{CM}(t)_i = 1/P_{MC}(t)_i$, $P_{CB}(t)_i = 1/P_{BC}(t)_i$, and $P_{BM}(t)_i = 1/P_{MB}(t)_i$ permits disregard of $P_{MC}(t)_i$, $P_{DC}(t)_i$, and $P_{MD}(t)_i$.

A competitive Walrasian rational-expectations equilibrium is defined by a market price vector $\tilde{P}(t) = (\tilde{P}_{CM}(t), \tilde{P}_{CB}(t), \tilde{P}_{BM}(t))$ on $[0, T]$ such that

$$\tilde{P}(t) = P(t)_i \qquad \forall\, i = 1, 2, \ldots, n \quad \text{and} \quad \forall\, t \in [0, T] \tag{V.3.1}$$

$$\sum_{i=1}^{n} C_M(\tilde{P}(t))_i = 0 \qquad \forall\, t \in [0, T] \tag{V.3.2}$$

$$\sum_{i=1}^{n} C_B(\tilde{P}(t))_i = 0 \qquad \forall\, t \in [0, T] \tag{V.3.3}$$

$$\sum_{i=1}^{n} B_M(\tilde{P}(t))_i = 0 \qquad \forall\, t \in [0, T] \tag{V.3.4}$$

It can easily be seen that equations V.3.2, V.3.3, and V.3.4 imply

$$\sum_{i=1}^{n} M_C(\tilde{P}(t))_i = \sum_{i=1}^{n} B_C(\tilde{P}(t))_i = \sum_{i=1}^{n} M_B(\tilde{P}(t))_i = 0 \qquad \forall\, t \in [0, T] \tag{V.3.5}$$

Hence, in a rational-expectations equilibrium, all n households have identical price expectations, and these expectations are realized in the market at each $t \in [0, T]$.

In Section II.5 it was demonstrated that the intertemporal demand functions of the ith household ($i = 1, 2, \ldots, n$) satisfy a Walrasian budget constraint of the form

$$C_M(t)_i + m_C(t)_i + C_B(t)_i + b_C(t)_i + m_B(t)_i + b_M(t)_i \Pi(t) = 0$$
$$\forall\, i = 1, \ldots, n \quad \text{and} \quad \forall\, t \in [0, T] \tag{V.3.6}$$

Summing over all households and employing equation V.3.1 leads to

$$C_M(t) + m_C(t) + C_B(t) + b_C(t) + m_B(t) + b_M(t) \Pi(t) = 0$$
$$\forall\, t \in [0, T] \tag{V.3.7}$$

where flow demands and prices without superscripts denote market flow demands and market prices. Equation V.3.7 can be written as

$$P_{MC}(t)(M_C(t) + M_B(t)) + (C_M(t)$$
$$+ C_B(t)) + P_{BC}(t)(B_C(t) + \Pi(t)b_M(t)) = 0 \qquad \forall\, t \in [0, T] \tag{V.3.8}$$

which represents the form of Walras's law appropriate for the economy under consideration.

The equilibrium price vector $\tilde{P}(t)$ for all $t \in [0, T]$ can be established at $t = 0$ in a simultaneous or sequential tâtonnement process. In the simultaneous process the auctioneer proposes a price vector $\tilde{P}(t) \ \forall \ t \in [0, T]$. If there exists excess demand or supply at some $t \in [0, T]$, then the auctioneer adjusts the price vector simultaneously for all such t. This process is assumed to be timeless and is repeated at $t = 0$ until the price vector has converged onto the equilibrium price vector $\tilde{P}(t)$ at all $t \in [0, T]$. Alternatively, we can assume that at $t = 0$ the households form expectations about equilibrium prices at all $t \in [0, T]$ and use these price expectations to form their demands at each $t \in [0, T]$. If there exists positive excess demand at some $t \in [0, T]$, then the households' expectations are incorrect, and all plans are void. The households adjust their expectations, and the process starts again until the expected price vector converges onto the equilibrium price vector $\tilde{P}(t) \ \forall \ t \in [0, T]$. This learning process is also assumed to be timeless. If all households have identical expectations, and the mechanism by which households adjust their expected $P(t)$ is the same as the mechanism by which the auctioneer adjusts the price vector $P(t)$, then the expectations adjustment process and the tâtonnement process are isomorphic. It was shown in Chapter II that the tâtonnement or learning process uses real resources. Such costs and the costs of effecting transactions are captured in the transactions technology. In Chapter VII we shall develop the theory of expectations adjustment when trading takes place sequentially in chronological time (i.e., there is no recontracting).

The sequential tâtonnement is also assumed to be timeless and takes place at $t = 0$. Here we perceive instantaneous markets that are indexed by $t \in [0, T]$, and the adjustment process is carried out sequentially in the individual instantaneous markets as the index t progresses from 0 to T. The instantaneous Walrasian equilibrium at $t = t^* \in [0, T]$ is defined as the price vector $\overline{P}(t^*)$. This instantaneous equilibrium need not be an expectations equilibrium in which the equilibrium price vector equals the expected price vector. If the instantaneous equilibrium price vector at $t = t^*$ is not equal to the expected price vector at $t = t^*$, then all the preceding markets are in disequilibrium again. The entire sequential process is thus repeated until the price vector so established on $[0, T]$ converges to the expectations equilibrium price vector defined in equations V.3.2, V.3.3, and V.3.4. The instantaneous demand functions at $t^* \in [0, T]$ are obtained by the household from the maximization of its Hamiltonian in equation III.2.1 at t^*; that is, it maximizes the discounted value of the total flow of utility experienced at time t^*, subject to the implicit budget constraint in equation II.5.14.[5] It was shown in equation V.3.8 that Walras's law is satisfied at $t = t^*$, and the instantaneous demand functions are homogeneous of degree zero in prices. Hence, we can conclude that an instantaneous Walrasian equilibrium exists at each $t = t^* \in$

$[0, T]$ (Arrow and Hahn, 1971). Such an instantaneous equilibrium price vector $\overline{P}(t) = (\overline{P}_{CM}(t), \overline{P}_{CB}(t), \overline{P}_{BM}(t))$ is said to be locally stable at a given t^* $\in [0, T]$ if the price vector $P(t) = (P_{CM}(t), P_{CB}(t), P_{BM}(t))$ approaches $\overline{P}(t^*)$ after any small perturbation and reaches $\overline{P}(t^*)$ as tâtonnement or recontracting time tends to infinity. The process of tâtonnement or recontracting that establishes the instantaneous equilibrium price in the market indexed by t^* is assumed to use no chronological time. The analysis of the stability of instantaneous competitive equilibria employs the fundamental competitive or tâtonnement assumption that a market price increases if there exists excess demand in that market, and a market price decreases if there exists excess supply in the market.

An adjustment mechanism describing the behavior of the competitive auctioneer in the instantaneous market indexed by t^* can be characterized as follows:

$$\frac{d(P_{CM}(\tau; t^*))}{d\tau} = G^1(C_M(P_{CM}(\tau; t^*)P_{CB}(\tau; t^*)P_{BM}(\tau; t^*))) \quad \text{(V.3.9)}$$

$$\frac{d(P_{CB}(\tau; t^*))}{d\tau} = G^2(C_B(P_{CM}(\tau; t^*)P_{CB}(\tau; t^*)P_{BM}(\tau; t^*))) \quad \text{(V.3.10)}$$

$$\frac{d(P_{BM}(\tau; t^*))}{d\tau} = G^3 b_M(\tau; t^*)\Pi(\tau; t^*)(P_{CM}(\tau; t^*)P_{CB}(\tau; t^*)P_{BM}(\tau; t^*)) \quad \text{(V.3.11)}$$

with $P_{CM}(\tau; t^*)$, $P_{CB}(\tau; t^*)$, and $P_{BM}(\tau; t^*)$ as equilibrium values and initial conditions. The adjustment functions $G^1(\cdot)$, $G^2(\cdot)$, and $G^3(\cdot)$ are strictly increasing functions of excess demands; however, the units of the three commodities can be chosen in such a way that (Samuelson, 1947)

$$G^1(C_M(\cdot)) = C_M(\cdot) \quad \text{(V.3.12)}$$

$$G^2(C_B(\cdot)) = C_B(\cdot) \quad \text{(V.3.13)}$$

$$G^3(b_M(\cdot)\Pi(\cdot)) = b_M(\cdot)\Pi(\cdot) \quad \text{(V.3.14)}$$

Therefore, an equilibrium state $\overline{P}(t^*)$ is locally stable at $t^* \in [0, T]$ if there exists a closed sphere $B(\overline{P}(t^*))$ about $\overline{P}(t^*)$ with radius $\delta > 0$ such that for any initial value $P(t^*) \in B(\overline{P}(t^*))$ we have $P(\tau; t^*) \to \overline{P}(t^*)$ as $\tau \to \infty$. In order to prove that equilibria of the economy under consideration are locally stable, one employs the linear approximation theorem, which states that if the linear approximation system associated with the nonlinear differential equation system V.3.9, V.3.10, and V.3.11 is stable, then the nonlinear system is also stable.[6] The linear approximation system associated with equations V.3.9, V.3.10, and V.3.11 is given by

$$
\begin{bmatrix}
\dfrac{dP_{CM}(\tau;\,t^*)}{d\tau} \\[2ex]
\dfrac{dP_{CB}(\tau;\,t^*)}{d\tau} \\[2ex]
\dfrac{dP_{BM}(\tau;\,t^*)}{d\tau}
\end{bmatrix}
$$

$$
=
\begin{bmatrix}
\dfrac{\partial C_M}{\partial P_{CM}} & \dfrac{\partial C_M}{\partial P_{CB}} & \dfrac{\partial C_M}{\partial P_{BM}} \\[2ex]
\dfrac{\partial C_B}{\partial P_{CM}} & \dfrac{\partial C_B}{\partial P_{CB}} & \dfrac{\partial C_B}{\partial P_{BM}} \\[2ex]
\dfrac{\partial (b_M\Pi)}{\partial P_{CM}} & \dfrac{\partial (b_M\Pi)}{\partial P_{CB}} & \dfrac{\partial (b_M\Pi)}{\partial P_{BM}}
\end{bmatrix}
\begin{bmatrix}
P_{CM}(\tau;\,t^*) - \overline{P}_{CM}(t^*) \\[2ex]
P_{CB}(\tau;\,t^*) - \overline{P}_{CB}(t^*) \\[2ex]
P_{BM}(\tau;\,t^*) - \overline{P}_{BM}(t^*)
\end{bmatrix}
\quad \text{(V.3.15)}
$$

where the Jacobian matrix of the excess-demand functions is evaluated at $\overline{P}(t^*)$, the equilibrium point of the nonlinear system.

In turn, the linear approximation system is stable if and only if the real parts of the eigenvalues of the Jacobian are negative. A theorem due to McKenzie (1960) determines that the real parts of the eigenvalues of the Jacobian matrix are negative if this matrix has a negative dominant diagonal.[7] By employing the comparative dynamics results of the previous chapters, one can show that the foregoing Jacobian matrix indeed has a negative dominant diagonal.

In the previous chapter it was demonstrated that an increase in $P_{CM}(t)$ at each $t \in [0, T]$, with $P_{CB}(t)$ and $P_{BM}(t)$ unchanged, results in a lower $C_M(t)$ and a higher $C_B(t)$ at each $t \in [0, T]$, whereas $b_M(t)\Pi(t)$ will be higher on some nonempty subset of $[0, T]$. An increase in $P_{CB}(t)$ at each $t \in [0, T]$, with $P_{CM}(t)$ and $P_{BM}(t)$ unchanged, induces a lower $C_B(t)$ and higher $C_M(t)$ at each $t \in [0, T]$, whereas $b_M(t)\Pi(t)$ will be lower on some nonempty subset of $[0, T]$. An increase in $P_{BM}(t)$ at each $t \in [0, T]$ results in a lower $b_M(t)\Pi(t)$ on some nonempty subset of $[0, T]$, and $C_B(t)$ will be lower, whereas $C_M(t)$ will be higher at each $t \in [0, T]$. The total acquisition of bonds in exchange for money increases when $P_{CM}(t)$ increases and decreases when $P_{CB}(t)$ or $P_{BM}(t)$ increases on $[0, T]$. These results are summarized in the following sign matrix associated with the Jacobian matrix V.3.15:

$$
\begin{bmatrix}
- & + & + \\
+ & - & - \\
+ & - & -
\end{bmatrix}
\quad \text{(V.3.16)}
$$

From this information alone it is not possible to determine that the Jacobian matrix has a negative dominant diagonal. However, in Section 2 of this chapter it was established that prices and therefore price changes tend to be consistent. Thus, instead of the household being confronted with individual price changes, the household can be confronted with increases in $P_{CM}(t)$, $P_{CB}(t)$, and $P_{BM}(t)$ such that after the changes $P_{CM}(t) = P_{CB}(t)P_{BM}(t)$ $\forall\, t \in [0, T]$.

The comparative statics results in Section IV.2 demonstrate that such price changes do not result in any substitution effects but only in wealth effects. The increase in $P_{CM}(t)$ at each $t \in [0, T]$ reduces $m(T)$ and thus, through an increase in $\lambda_M(t)$ at each $t \in [0, T]$, leads to a decrease in $C_M(t)$ at each $t \in [0, T]$ and a decrease in $b_M(t)\Pi(t)$ at each $t \in [0, T]$. The increase in $P_{CB}(t)$ on $[0, T]$ reduces $b(T)$ and thus results in a decrease in $C_B(t)$ and an increase in $b_M(t)\Pi(t)$ at each $t \in [0, T]$. The net effect of the increases in $P_{CM}(t)$ and $P_{CB}(t)$ at each $t \in [0, T]$ on $b_M(t)\Pi(t)$ is to decrease this flow demand, because the percentage change in $P_{CM}(t)$ exceeds the percentage change in $P_{CB}(t)$ at each $t \in [0, T]$. Hence, after all effects have manifested themselves, increases in $P_{CM}(t)$, $P_{CB}(t)$, and $P_{BM}(t)$ that maintain $P_{CM}(t) = P_{CB}(t)P_{BM}(t)$ induce reductions in $C_M(t)$, $C_B(t)$, and $b_M(t)\Pi(t)$ at each $t \in [0, T]$. This proves that the Jacobian matrix of the instantaneous excess-demand functions has a negative dominant diagonal at each $t \in [0, T]$.[8] Thus, if the price system tends toward consistency, then the instantaneous Walrasian equilibria are locally stable at each $t^* \in [0, T]$.

In order to prove the uniqueness of an instantaneous equilibrium, an index theorem from differential topology is employed (Guillemin and Pollack, 1974). The theorem, when applied to the present problem, states that there exists a unique equilibrium if (a) $C_M(t) > 0$, $C_B(t) > 0$, and $B_M(t) > 0$ when $\tilde{P}(t) = 0$ and (b)

$$\text{sgn} \begin{vmatrix} \dfrac{\partial C_M}{\partial P_{CM}} & \dfrac{\partial C_M}{\partial P_{CB}} \\[2ex] \dfrac{\partial C_B}{\partial P_{CM}} & \dfrac{\partial C_B}{\partial P_{CB}} \end{vmatrix}$$

is positive when this determinant is evaluated at the equilibrium price vector. Condition (a) is guaranteed by the concavity of the instantaneous utility functions, and condition (b) is satisfied because the Jacobian matrix of the excess-demand functions has a negative dominant diagonal and the determinant in (b) is the second-order principal minor of this Jacobian. Hence, the instantaneous competitive equilibria are unique and stable.

We have thus demonstrated the existence, stability, and uniqueness of equilibria in individual markets indexed by $t^* \in [0, T]$. However, it remains to be shown that such instantaneous equilibria converge onto the rational-expectations equilibrium defined in equations V.3.2, V.3.3, and V.3.4. A formal proof of this convergence conjecture proposition involves arguments in infinite-dimensional function spaces and is beyond the scope of this book.

When the transactions technology $T^d(\cdot)$ is nonconvex, then there may not exist an equilibrium in the usual sense; that is, there may not exist a price vector that clears the three markets at each transactions date $\tau_s \in [0, T] \ \forall$ $s \in \cup_{i-1}^n [I_i^1 \cup I_i^2 \cup I_i^3]$, where I_i^1, I_i^2, and I_i^3 are the index sets of the ith household for transactions dates in the consumption-good-cum-money market, the consumption-good-cum-bonds market, and the money-cum-bonds market, respectively. The discontinuity of the excess-demand functions with respect to time on the interval $[0, T]$ makes impossible the application of a fixed-point theorem for the purpose of proving the existence of an equilibrium price vector. It may nevertheless be possible to prove the existence of an approximate equilibrium price vector $P(t)^* = (P_{CM}(t)^*, P_{CB}(t)^*, P_{BM}(t)^*)$ defined at each $t \in [0, T]$ such that (a) at $P(t)^*$ the excess demands in all three markets are bounded at any $t \in [0, T]$, with the bounds being determined by the degree of the nonconvexity,[9] and (b) the discrepancy between demand and supply at any $t \in [0, T]$ will approach zero as the number of households approaches infinity.[10]

The economy with the nonconvex transactions technologies can be convexified by replacing the nonconvex transactions technologies with their convex hulls (i.e., with the smallest convex sets containing the nonconvex transactions technologies). The approximate equilibrium price vector $P(t)^*$ of the nonconvex economy is then defined as the equilibrium price vector of the · convexified economy.[11] Because the convexified economy has the same properties as the economy discussed so far, a unique approximate equilibrium price vector will exist. The approximation theorem then states that the market excess demands in the nonconvex economy at the price vector $P(t)^*$, that is,

$$C_M(t)^* = \sum_{i-1}^n C_M(P(t)^*)_i \qquad \forall \, t \in [0, T] \tag{V.3.17}$$

$$C_B(t)^* = \sum_{i-1}^n C_B(P(t)^*)_i \qquad \forall \, t \in [0, T] \tag{V.3.18}$$

$$b_M(t)^* \Pi(t)^* = \sum_{i-1}^n b_M(t)_i^* \Pi(t)_i^* P(t)^* \qquad \forall \, t \in [0, T] \tag{V.3.19}$$

are bounded by the degree of the nonconvexity. Furthermore, the approximation theorem states that

$$\lim_{n \to \infty} \frac{1}{n} C_M(t)^* = 0 \qquad \forall \, t \in [0, T] \tag{V.3.20}$$

$$\lim_{n \to \infty} \frac{1}{n} C_B(t)^* = 0 \qquad \forall\, t \in [0, T] \tag{V.3.21}$$

$$\lim_{n \to \infty} \frac{1}{n} b_M(t)^* \Pi(t)^* = 0 \qquad \forall\, t \in [0, T] \tag{V.3.22}$$

where n is the number of households in the economy.

It is this approximation theorem that can provide the justification for analyzing the behavior of intertemporal households in convexified economies rather than in nonconvex economies and thus permit the type of comparative dynamic and welfare theoretical analysis conducted in the previous chapters.[12]

In addition to determining the household's modes of transacting in the various markets, the curvature properties of the transactions technology can also be employed to explain the existence of intermediary traders in the three markets. Nonconvexities in the household's transactions technology induce intermittent arrivals at the marketplace, but at the moment of arrival there may not exist a feasible trading opportunity. Hence, we cannot assume the existence of an equilibrating process that clears such markets by matching demanders and suppliers instantaneously at each moment. Thus the voluntary-exchange assumption implies that some households will not be able to exchange the desired amounts at the time they enter the market. Because the marginal cost of transacting decreases with the volume per transaction, undesired reductions in the sizes of transactions due to mismatching will increase the aggregate transactions costs incurred in this economy. In such circumstances the existence of competitive intermediary traders who hold buffer stocks will result in a reduction in aggregate transactions cost. The costs incurred by these intermediaries because of the holding of buffer stocks do not exceed the costs incurred by individual households that in the absence of intermediaries are forced to hold larger stocks because they cannot make trades of the desired size. On the other hand, because the intermediaries permit the households to execute trades of the desired sizes, the costs of transacting in this economy will be lower. Hence, we have the following proposition.

Proposition on the optimality of intermediary traders

The presence of nonconvex transactions technologies is the necessary and sufficient condition for a Pareto-efficient institutional innovation in the form of intermediary traders.

V.4   Comparative dynamics in general equilibrium

The existence of a unique and stable equilibrium makes it possible to combine the partial-equilibrium comparative dynamics effects of changes in the initial endowments, the transactions technology, and other behavioral parameters with the partial-equilibrium comparative dynamics effects of changes in market prices. This enables us to extend the partial-equilibrium comparative dynamics results to the general-equilibrium model.

The effects of an increase in $P_{CM}(t)$, $P_{BM}(t)$, or $P_{CB}(t)$ on $C_M(t)_i$, $C_B(t)_i$, and $b_M(t)_i\Pi(t)$ are summarized as follows:

	$dC_M(t)_i$	$dC_B(t)_i$	$d(b_M(t)_i\Pi(t))$
$dP_{CM}(t) > 0$	$-$	$+$	$+$
$dP_{CB}(t) > 0$	$+$	$-$	$-$
$dP_{BM}(t) > 0$	$+$	$-$	$-$

$$(V.4.1)$$

where $t \in [0, T]$ and $i = 1, 2, \ldots, n$.[13] Hence, changes in the exogenously given market prices induce adjustments in demands compatible with the household's desire to maintain internally consistent prices, as analyzed in Section 2 of this chapter. Furthermore, each household's demand curve $C_M(t)_i$ at a given $t \in [0, T]$ has a negative slope with respect to $P_{CM}(t)$ at any $t \in [0, T]$, as does its demand curve $C_B(t)_i$ with respect to $P_{CB}(t)$. If $P_{BM}(t)$ is raised at each $t \in [0, T]$, then $b_M(t)_i\Pi(t)$ will be lower on a nonempty connected subset of $[0, T]$; hence, the demand curve $b_M(t)_i\Pi(t)$ at a given t in this subset has a negative slope with respect to $P_{BM}(t)$ at any $t \in [0, T]$. Therefore, because each individual household has negatively sloped demand curves, the market demand curves $C_M(t)$, $C_B(t)$, and $b_M(t)\Pi(t)$ also have negative slopes with respect to $P_{CM}(t)$, $P_{CB}(t)$, and $P_{BM}(t)$, respectively.

An increase in each household's initial endowment of money induces increases in $C_M(t)_i$, $C_B(t)_i$, and $b_M(t)_i\Pi(t)$ at each $t \in [0, T]$ and for all $i = 1, \ldots, n$. Consequently, the aggregate excess-demand functions will shift upward, and excess demand appears in all three markets, stimulating increases in $P_{CM}(t)$, $\dot{P}_{CB}(t)$, and $P_{BM}(t)$ at each $t \in [0, T]$. An increase in $P_{CM}(t)$ at all $t \in [0, T]$ will lead households to reduce $C_M(t)$ at each $t \in [0, T]$. Similarly, increases in $P_{CB}(t)$ and $P_{BM}(t)$ impel all households to reduce $C_B(t)$ and $b_M(t)\Pi(t)$ at each $t \in [0, T]$. These adjustments represent movements along the higher new aggregate excess-demand curves. They cease as soon as aggregate excess demand in each market is zero again. However, the increase in $P_{CM}(t)$ causes upward shifts in the aggregate demand curves $C_B(t)$ and $b_M(t)\Pi(t)$ at each $t \in [0, T]$, and the increase in $P_{CB}(t)$ will produce an upward shift in $C_M(t)$ and a downward shift in $b_M(t)\Pi(t)$ at each $t \in [0, T]$, whereas the increase in $P_{BM}(t)$ will result in an upward shift in $C_M(t)$ and a downward shift in $C_B(t)$ at each $t \in [0, T]$. These changes are summarized as follows:

$dM_0 > 0$ implies:		$dC_M(t)$	$dC_B(t)$	$d(b_M(t)\Pi(t))$
$dC_M(t) > 0$	$dP_{CM}(t) > 0$	$-$	$+$	$+$
$dC_B(t) > 0$	$dP_{CB}(t) > 0$	$+$	$-$	$-$
$d(b_M(t)\Pi(t)) > 0$	$dP_{BM}(t) > 0$	$+$	$-$	$-$

(V.4.2)

It was established in the previous section that the consistency of the price system implies that the Jacobian matrix of the market excess-demand functions has a negative dominant diagonal at each $t \in [0, T]$. The fact that the changes in $P_{CB}(t)$, $P_{CM}(t)$, and $P_{BM}(t)$ in equation V.4.2 resulting from the upward shifts in $C_B(t)$, $C_M(t)$, and $b_M(t)\Pi(t)$ at each $t \in [0, T]$ leave the price system consistent implies that the matrix of changes in excess demands in equation V.4.2 has a negative dominant diagonal. Thus, in the final equilibrium the aggregate excess-demand curves $C_M(t)$, $C_B(t)$, and $b_M(t)\Pi(t)$, as well as $P_{CM}(t)$, $P_{CB}(t)$, and $P_{BM}(t)$, are higher at each $t \in [0, T]$.

Because the sum of the stocks of all outstanding private perpetuities is zero, we can consider only the effects of an experiment in which the stock of claims held by the private sector against the government is increased (i.e., the government increases the issue of perpetuities). In order for the issue of such perpetuities to be considered an increase in net wealth, it is necessary that there exist a new production opportunity that can be exploited optimally by the government (Barro, 1974). An increase in the initial stock of such government bonds results in excess demand in both the consumption-good-cum-money market and the consumption-good-cum-bonds market and causes excess supply in the bonds-cum-money market at each $t \in [0, T]$. The following summarizes the resulting changes in market prices and their effects on excess demand:

$dB_0 > 0$ implies:		$dC_M(t)$	$dC_B(t)$	$d(b_M(t)\Pi(t))$
$dC_M(t) > 0$	$dP_{CM}(t) > 0$	$-$	$+$	$+$
$dC_B(t) > 0$	$dP_{CB}(t) > 0$	$+$	$-$	$-$
$d(b_M(t)\Pi(t)) < 0$	$dP_{BM}(t) < 0$	$-$	$+$	$+$

(V.4.3)

As before, the consistency of the price system and the negative dominant diagonal of the Jacobian matrix of the aggregate excess-demand functions imply that in the final equilibrium the excess-demand curves $C_M(t)$ and $C_B(t)$ shift up, whereas $b_M(t)\Pi(t)$ shifts down at each $t \in [0, T]$. Furthermore, the levels of $P_{CM}(t)$ and $P_{CB}(t)$ are higher at each $t \in [0, T]$, whereas $P_{BM}(t)$ is lower at each $t \in [0, T]$.

An increase in the initial holdings of consumption goods induces excess supply in both the consumption-good-cum-money and the consumption-good-cum-bonds markets, whereas its effect on the bonds-cum-money market is indeterminate. The resulting changes in $P_{CM}(t)$ and $P_{CB}(t)$ and their effects on demands are summarized as follows:

$dC_0 > 0$ implies:	$dC_M(t)$	$dC_B(t)$	$d(b_M(t)\Pi(t))$
$dC_M(t) < 0 \quad dP_{CM}(t) < 0$	$+$	$-$	$-$
$dC_B(t) < 0 \quad dP_{CB}(t) < 0$	$-$	$+$	$+$
$d(b_M(t)\Pi(t)) \gtreqless 0 \quad dP_{BM}(t) \gtreqless 0$	?	?	?

$$(V.4.4)$$

Hence, in the final equilibrium, $C_M(t)$, $C_B(t)$, and $P_{CM}(t)$ and $P_{CB}(t)$ are lower at each $t \in [0, T]$, whereas the effects on $b_M(t)\Pi(t)$ and $P_{MB}(t)$ are indeterminate.

From the homogeneity properties of the flow and stock demand functions (see Section III.4) we know that a simultaneous doubling of each household's initial endowments of money and nominal bonds leads to a doubling of $P_{CM}(t)$, $P_{CB}(t)$, and $B_M(t)$ $\forall\ t \in [0, T]$, whereas $C_M(t)$, $C_B(t)$, and $P_{BM}(t)$ remain unchanged everywhere on $[0, T]$.

An increase in $X(t)$ at each $t \in [0, T]$, a decrease in δ, and an increase in ρ all augment each household's consumption-good stock; hence, these changes generate the same result as an increase in the initial holdings of the consumption good. The effects of a change in the transactions technology on aggregate excess demand and market prices are identical in both the general-equilibrium framework and the partial-equilibrium analysis. The general conclusion is that the partial-equilibrium comparative dynamics results are sustained when all the general-equilibrium repercussions are considered.

V.5   Intrinsic inflation in an intertemporal economy

In this section we shall analyze the rates of change of $P_{CM}(t)$, $P_{CB}(t)$, and $P_{BM}(t)$ on the interval $[0, T]$ in an economy made up of the type of agents whose behavior has been described in the preceding chapters.

The partial-equilibrium analysis of the household determined that (see Section III.4)

$$\frac{dC_M(t)_i}{dt} = \frac{1}{T_{11}^d(t)_i} [\delta - \hat{P}_{CM}(t)] \frac{\lambda_M(t)_i}{\lambda_C(t)_i}$$
$$\forall\ t \in [0,T] \quad \text{and} \quad i = 1, 2, \ldots, n \quad (V.5.1)$$

Because equation V.5.1 is satisfied for each household in the economy, one can conclude that the rate of change of aggregate excess demand, $C_M(t)$, is such that

$$\frac{dC_M(t)}{dt} \gtreqless 0 \quad \text{as} \quad \delta - \hat{P}_{CM}(t) \gtreqless 0 \qquad \forall \, t \in [0,T] \tag{V.5.2}$$

If $\hat{P}_{CM}(t) = 0$, then $dC_M(t)/dt > 0$, by equation V.5.2; however, this implies that there exists positive excess demand in the consumption-good-cum-money market and therefore that $\hat{P}_{CM}(t) > 0$, contradicting the hypothesis. Thus, $\hat{P}_{CM}(t) > 0 \ \forall \, t \in [0, T]$.

The fact that a larger $\hat{P}_{CM}(t)$ implies a smaller $\delta - \hat{P}_{CM}(t)$ and a smaller $dC_M(t)/dt$ reveals that the rate of inflation is bounded from above by δ and from below by 0. Also, partial-equilibrium analysis of the household demonstrated that

$$\frac{dC_B(t)_i}{dt} = \frac{1}{T^d_{22}(t)_i} [\delta + P_{MB}(t) - \hat{P}_{CB}(t)] \frac{\lambda_B(t)_i}{\lambda_C(t)_i}$$

$$\forall \, t \in [0,T] \quad \text{and} \quad i = 1, 2, \ldots, n \tag{V.5.3}$$

Because equation V.5.3 is satisfied for all households in the economy, one can conclude that

$$\frac{dC_B(t)}{dt} \gtreqless 0 \quad \text{as} \quad \delta + P_{MB}(t) - \hat{P}_{CB}(t) \gtreqless 0 \qquad \forall \, t \in [0,T] \tag{V.5.4}$$

If $\hat{P}_{CB}(t) = 0$, then by equation V.5.4 $dC_B(t)/dt > 0$; however, this implies that there exists positive excess demand in the consumption-good-cum-bonds market and therefore that $\hat{P}_{CB}(t) > 0$, contradicting the hypothesis. Thus $\hat{P}_{CB}(t) > 0 \ \forall \, t \in [0, T]$. As $\hat{P}_{CB}(t)$ increases, $\delta + P_{MB}(t) - \hat{P}_{CB}(t)$ decreases, and hence $dC_B(t)/dt$ decreases. Therefore, $\hat{P}_{CB}(t)$ is bounded from above by $\delta + P_{MB}(t)$ and from below by 0.

Finally, partial-equilibrium analysis of the intertemporal household's behavior revealed that

$$\frac{d(b_M(t)\Pi(t))}{dt} = \frac{1}{T^d_{33}(t)_i} \left[(\hat{P}_{CB}(t) - P_{MB}(t) - \delta) \left(\frac{\lambda_B(t)_i}{\lambda_C(t)_i} \right) \Pi(t) \right.$$

$$\left. + (\delta - \hat{P}_{CM}(t)) \left(\frac{\lambda_M(t)_i}{\lambda_C(t)_i} \right) + \frac{\lambda_B(t)_i}{\lambda_C(t)_i} \left(\frac{d\Pi(t)}{dt} \right) \right]$$

$$\forall \, t \in [0,T] \quad \text{and} \quad i = 1, 2, \ldots, n \tag{V.5.5}$$

The sign of $d(b_M(t)\Pi(t))/dt$ cannot be determined from equation V.5.5. However, the price system tends toward consistency, and hence

$$\hat{P}_{BM}(t) = \hat{P}_{CM}(t) - \hat{P}_{CB}(t) \qquad \forall \, t \in [0, T] \tag{V.5.6}$$

That is, the rate of change of the money price of bonds is equal to the difference between the rate of change of the money price of consumption goods and the rate of change of the price of consumption goods in terms of bonds.

The time derivative of equation V.5.1 is given by

$$T_{11}^d \frac{d^2 C_M(t)_i}{dt^2} = \left[(\delta - \hat{P}_{CM}(t))(\hat{P}_{CM}(t) - \delta) - \frac{d\hat{P}_{CM}(t)}{dt} \right] \frac{\lambda_M(t)_i}{\lambda_C(t)_i}$$

$$\forall\, t \in [0, T] \quad \text{and} \quad i = 1, 2, \ldots, n \quad (V.5.7)$$

Where T_{11}^d is a constant. If we assume that $d^2 C_M(t)/dt^2 > 0$ if $d\hat{P}_{CM}(t)/dt > 0$, then $d\hat{P}_{CM}(t)/dt = 0$ implies that $d^2 C_M(t)/dt^2 < 0$, which contradicts the hypothesis. Hence, $d\hat{P}_{CM}(t)/dt < 0$, and

$$\left| \frac{dP_{CM}(t)}{dt} \right| < |(\delta - \hat{P}_{CM})(\hat{P}_{CM} - \delta)| \quad \forall\, t \in [0, T] \quad (V.5.8)$$

Therefore, on the interval $[0, T]$, the rate of inflation of the money price of the consumption good is positive but declining.

The time derivative of equation V.5.3 is given by

$$T_{22}^d \frac{d^2 C_B(t)_i}{dt^2} = \left[(\delta + P_{MB}(t) - \hat{P}_{CB}(t))(\hat{P}_{CB}(t) - P_{MB}(t) - \delta) \right.$$

$$\left. + (\hat{P}_{MB}(t) - \frac{d\hat{P}_{CB}(t))}{dt} \right] \frac{\lambda_B(t)_i}{\lambda_C(t)_i}$$

$$\forall\, t \in [0, T] \quad \text{and} \quad i = 1, 2, \ldots, n \quad (V.5.9)$$

Hence, as long as $dP_{MB}(t)/dt$, the interest rate, is large enough, it is possible for $d\hat{P}_{CB}(t)/dt$ to be positive. However, if $dP_{MB}(t)/dt$ is small, then $d^2 C_B(t)/dt^2 < 0$, and $d\hat{P}_{CB}(t)/dt < 0$. The hypothesis of consistent prices implies again that

$$\frac{d\hat{P}_{BM}(t)}{dt} = \frac{d\hat{P}_{CM}(t)}{dt} - \frac{d\hat{P}_{CB}(t)}{dt} \quad \forall\, t \in [0, T] \quad (V.5.10)$$

We can summarize these results in the following proposition.

Intrinsic inflation proposition 1

An economy that consists of the type of agents described earlier will have rates of inflation of $P_{CM}(t)$, $P_{CB}(t)$, and $P_{MB}(t)$ such that

$$0 < \hat{P}_{CM}(t) < \delta \quad \forall\, t \in [0, T]$$

$$0 < \hat{P}_{CB}(t) < \delta + P_{MB}(t) \quad \forall\, t \in [0, T]$$

$$-(\delta + P_{MB}(t)) < \hat{P}_{MB}(t) < \delta \quad \forall\, t \in [0, T]$$

Furthermore, the rate of inflation of $P_{CM}(t)$ is declining on $[0,T]$, and the rate of inflation of $P_{CB}(t)$ is also declining, unless $dP_{MB}(t)/dt$ is large.

It is also possible to establish the effects of increases in initial endowments of money, bonds, and consumption goods on the rates of change of the three prices. An increase in the initial endowment of money results in increases in $C_M(t)$, $C_B(t)$, and $b_M(t)\Pi(t)$ at all $t \in [0,T]$ and hence in higher levels of $P_{CM}(t)$, $P_{CB}(t)$, and $P_{BM}(t)$ at each $t \in [0,T]$. The increase in $C_M(t)_i$ is given by (see Section IV.4)

$$\Delta C_M(t)_i = \frac{dC_M(t)_i}{d\lambda_M(t)_i} \Delta\lambda_M(t)_i + \frac{dC_M(t)_i}{d\lambda_C(t)_i} \Delta\lambda_C(t)_i > 0$$

$$\forall\, t \in [0,T] \quad \text{and} \quad i = 1, 2, \ldots, n \quad \text{(V.5.11)}$$

Note 12 for Chapter IV demonstrates that both terms on the right-hand side grow at a percentage rate equal to $(\hat{P}_{CM}(t) - \delta)$, and hence

$$\Delta\hat{C}_M(t) = \hat{P}_{CM}(t) - \delta < 0 \quad \forall\, t \in [0,T] \quad \text{(V.5.12)}$$

The increase in $C_B(t)_i$ is given by

$$\Delta C_B(t)_i = \frac{dC_B(t)_i}{d\lambda_C(t)_i} \Delta\lambda_C(t)_i + \frac{dC_B(t)_i}{d\lambda_B(t)_i} \Delta\lambda_B(t)_i > 0$$

$$\forall\, t \in [0,T] \quad \text{and} \quad i = 1, 2, \ldots, n \quad \text{(V.5.13)}$$

Note 13 for Chapter IV demonstrates that both terms on the right-hand side of equation V.5.13 grow at a percentage rate equal to $(\hat{P}_{CB}(t) - P_{MB}(t) - \delta)$ < 0 for all $t \in [0,T]$, and hence

$$\Delta\hat{C}_B(t) = \hat{P}_{CB}(t) - P_{MB}(t) - \delta < 0 \quad \forall\, t \in [0,T] \quad \text{(V.5.14)}$$

The percentage rate of change of $\Delta(b_M(t)\Pi(t))_i$ cannot be determined unambiguously. However, because the changes in $C_M(t)$ and $C_B(t)$ decline over the interval $[0,T]$, one can conclude that even though the levels of $P_{CM}(t)$ and $P_{CB}(t)$ are higher everywhere following the increase in initial endowment of money, the rate of inflation is lower everywhere on $[0,T]$. Hence we have established the following proposition.

Intrinsic inflation proposition 2

An increase in the initial endowment of money results in higher levels of $P_{CM}(t)$ and $P_{CB}(t)$ but lower rates of inflation of $P_{CM}(t)$ and $P_{CB}(t)$ on $[0,T]$.

An increase in initial holdings of bonds induces increases in $C_M(t)$ and $C_B(t)$ and a decrease in $b_M(t)\Pi(t)$ at each $t \in [0,T]$. The increases in $C_M(t)_i$ and $C_B(t)_i$ are given by

$$\Delta C_M(t)_i = \frac{dC_M(t)_i}{d\lambda_C(t)_i} \Delta\lambda_C(t)_i + \frac{dC_M(t)_i}{d\lambda_M(t)_i} \Delta\lambda_M(t)_i > 0$$

$$\forall\, t \in [0, T] \quad \text{and} \quad i = 1, 2, \ldots, n \quad \text{(V.5.15)}$$

$$\Delta C_B(t)_i = \frac{dC_B(t)_i}{d\lambda_B(t)_i} \Delta\lambda_B(t)_i + \frac{dC_B(t)_i}{d\lambda_C(t)_i} \Delta\lambda_C(t)_i > 0$$

$$\forall\, t \in [0, T] \quad \text{and} \quad i = 1, 2, \ldots, n \quad \text{(V.5.16)}$$

Note 26 for Chapter IV demonstrates that the rate of growth of each term on the right-hand side of equation V.5.15 equals $\hat{P}_{CM}(t) - \delta$ and that the rate of growth of each term of the right-hand side of equation V.5.16 equals $\hat{P}_{CB}(t) - P_{MB}(t) - \delta$. Hence, the rates of growth of $\Delta C_M(t)$ and $\Delta C_B(t)$ are

$$\Delta\hat{C}_M(t) = \hat{P}_{CM}(t) - \delta < 0 \qquad \forall\, t \in [0, T] \qquad \text{(V.5.17)}$$

$$\Delta\hat{C}_B(t) = \hat{P}_{CB}(t) - P_{MB}(t) - \delta < 0 \qquad \forall\, t \in [0, T] \qquad \text{(V.5.18)}$$

Hence, we have established the following proposition.

Intrinsic inflation proposition 3

As a result of the increase in initial holdings of bonds, the levels of $P_{CM}(t)$ and $P_{CB}(t)$ will be higher everywhere, but their rates of inflation will be lower everywhere.

Lastly, an increase in the initial stock of consumption goods results in decreases in $C_M(t)$ and $C_B(t)$ everywhere on $[0, T]$. The changes in $C_M(t)$ and $C_B(t)$ are given by

$$\Delta C_M(t) = \frac{dC_M(t)_i}{d\lambda_C(t)_i} \Delta\lambda_C(t)_i + \frac{dC_M(t)_i}{d\lambda_M(t)_i} \Delta\lambda_M(t)_i < 0$$

$$\forall\, t \in [0, T] \quad \text{and} \quad i = 1, 2, \ldots, n \quad \text{(V.5.19)}$$

$$\Delta C_B(t) = \frac{dC_B(t)_i}{d\lambda_C(t)_i} \Delta\lambda_C(t)_i + \frac{dC_B(t)_i}{d\lambda_B(t)_i} \Delta\lambda_B(t)_i < 0$$

$$\forall\, t \in [0, T] \quad \text{and} \quad i = 1, 2, \ldots, n \quad \text{(V.5.20)}$$

The percentage rates of change of the terms on the right-hand sides of equations V.5.19 and V.5.20 are given by $\hat{P}_{CM}(t) - \delta$ and $\hat{P}_{CB}(t) - P_{MB}(t) - \delta$, respectively. Hence,

$$\Delta\hat{C}_M(t) = \hat{P}_{CM}(t) - \delta < 0 \qquad\qquad \forall\, t \in [0, T] \qquad \text{(V.5.21)}$$

and

$$\Delta\hat{C}_B(t) = \hat{P}_{CB}(t) - P_{MB}(t) - \delta < 0 \qquad \forall\, t \in [0, T] \qquad \text{(V.5.22)}$$

Hence, we have proved the following proposition.

Intrinsic inflation proposition 4

An increase in the initial stock of consumption goods causes the levels of $P_{CM}(t)$ and $P_{CB}(t)$ to decrease everywhere, as well as the rates of change of $P_{CM}(t)$ and $P_{CB}(t)$.

Until now, our analysis has dealt with an intertemporal economy made up of agents whose economic lives extend over the interval $[0,T]$. If the economy extends over the partitioned interval $[0,T_1, T_2, \ldots, T_n,\ldots]$, with adjoining sequential generations whose economic lives extend over $[0, T_1], [T_1, T_2], [T_2, T_3], \ldots, [T_{n-1}, T_n]$, then all the results derived in this section remain valid in the interior of these intervals, whereas there will be discontinuous breaks in the price levels at $T_1, T_2, \ldots, T_n$. If initial endowments at $t = 0$ and the bequest utility functions are such as to induce increasing stocks of money, bonds, and consumption goods, then it is possible to apply the analysis of this section and conclude that the price level will be higher in consecutive intervals, but the rates of change of the price levels will be lower in consecutive intervals. On the other hand, if generations overlap continuously in such a way as to leave the total population and its age structure constant, then price levels will be continuous on $[0, \infty)$, and rates of inflation will be zero (Cass and Yaari, 1966). If the total population remains constant, but its average age is increasing, then rates of inflation will be positive, whereas they will be negative if the population is growing younger on the average.

CHAPTER VI

Optimality of intertemporal equilibria and the role of government

VI.1 Introduction

In this chapter we shall examine the optimality of the intertemporal competitive rational-expectations equilibrium. We shall derive the conditions for intertemporal optimality and show that the competitive intertemporal equilibrium is not Pareto-optimal. The explanation for this nonoptimality is found in the finite-life assumption. The third section of this chapter formally introduces a government and defines its policy options. Investigation of the effects of various government policies reveals that some of those policies can be used to move the economy toward Pareto optimality.

VI.2 Intertemporal optimality of competitive equilibria

At a given point in time $t \in [0, T]$ the household cannot alter the levels of its stocks of the three commodities. Instead, it determines the rates of change of its stocks by optimally arranging its flow demands in the three markets according to the instantaneous marginal trading conditions given in equations III.2.12, III.2.13, and III.2.14. Because the instantaneous utility functions are quasi-concave, the transactions technology is strictly convex, and the flow version of Walras's law holds. Therefore, the instantaneously clearing flow markets possess a unique instantaneous competitive general equilibrium. Furthermore, this instantaneous competitive general equilibrium is Pareto-optimal (see Section V.3).

The household attains intertemporal optimality by finding that time path of consumption and final bequest that maximizes its total present stock of utility. The household must arrange its holdings of consumption goods, bonds, and money so as to sustain this rate of consumption and final bequest stock. The marginal conditions for optimal intertemporal behavior of the state variables, given in equations III.2.5 and III.2.6, instruct the household to equate the marginal benefit with the marginal cost of holding a unit of a commodity in stock. In order to identify clearly the marginal cost of holding assets, the maximization problem must be translated from present-value form to current-value form. In particular, define

$$\mu_M(t) = \lambda_M(t) \exp(\rho t) \qquad \forall\, t \in [0, T] \qquad (VI.2.1)$$

$$\mu_B(t) = \lambda_B(t) \exp{(\rho t)} \qquad \forall\, t \in [0, T] \qquad\qquad \text{(VI.2.2)}$$

$$\mu_C(t) = \lambda_C(t) \exp{(\rho t)} \qquad \forall\, t \in [0, T] \qquad\qquad \text{(VI.2.3)}$$

This transformation has no effect on the time path of $C_M(t)$, $C_B(t)$, or $B_M(t)$, because

$$\mu_M(t)_i = \mu_C(t)_i\,(1 - T^{d_i}_1(C_M(t)_i)) \qquad \forall\, t \in [0, T] \qquad\qquad \text{(VI.2.4)}$$

$$\mu_B(t)_i = \mu_C(t)_i\,(1 - T^{d_i}_2(C_B(t)_i)) \qquad \forall\, t \in [0, T] \qquad\qquad \text{(VI.2.5)}$$

$$\mu_B(t)_i = \mu_M(t)_i\,\Pi(t) + \mu_C(t)_i\,\Pi(t)\,T^{d_i}_3(b_M(t)_i\,\Pi(t))$$
$$\forall\, t \in [0, T] \quad \text{and} \quad i = 1, 2, \ldots, n \qquad \text{(VI.2.6)}$$

Equations VI.2.4, VI.2.5, and VI.2.6 are identical with III.2.12, III.2.13, and III.2.14, respectively.

The marginal conditions for asset holding change to[1]

$$\frac{d\mu_M(t)_i}{dt} = (\rho + \hat{P}_{CM}(t))\,\mu_M(t)_i \qquad \forall\, t \in [0, T] \qquad\qquad \text{(VI.2.7)}$$

$$\frac{d\mu_C(t)_i}{dt} = (\rho + \delta)\,\mu_C(t)_i \qquad \forall\, t \in [0, T] \qquad\qquad \text{(VI.2.8)}$$

$$\frac{d\mu_B(t)_i}{dt} = (\rho + \hat{P}_{CB}(t) - P_{MB}(t))\,\mu_B(t)_i \qquad \forall\, t \in [0, T] \qquad \text{(VI.2.9)}$$

and $i = 1, 2, \ldots, n$. The shadow prices $\mu_M(t)_i$, $\mu_C(t)_i$, and $\mu_B(t)_i$ ($\lambda_M(t)_i$, $\lambda_C(t)_i$, $\lambda_B(t)_i$) represent the gains in current (present) utility from the free gift at time t of an additional unit of money, consumption goods, and bonds, respectively. Because the marginal utility of consumption is always positive (i.e., the household is never sated), these shadow prices are strictly positive.

The term $\hat{\mu}_M(t)_i$ represents the percentage gain in current utility derived by individual i from holding a unit of real money in its money inventory, whereas $\rho + \hat{P}_{CM}(t)$ represents the opportunity cost the individual household incurs by holding a unit of money in its inventory. Similarly, $\hat{\mu}_C(t)_i$ and $\hat{\mu}_B(t)_i$ represent the percentage gains in current utility according to the ith household due to holding in its inventories a unit of the consumption good and a unit of bonds, respectively, whereas $\rho + \delta$ and $\rho + \hat{P}_{CB}(t) - P_{MB}(t)$ represent the opportunity costs at time t of holding a unit of the consumption good and a unit of bonds, respectively. Hence, the individual household attains its intertemporal equilibrium when conditions VI.2.7, VI.2.8, and VI.2.9 are fulfilled.

However, because the total money stock outstanding in the economy can be changed costlessly by the government, the optimal aggregate quantity of money is reached only when the gain from holding additional units of money is zero. As long as $\hat{\mu}_M(t)_i$ is nonzero, the intertemporal equilibrium price vector $\tilde{P}(t) = (\tilde{P}_{CM}(t), \tilde{P}_{CB}(t), \tilde{P}_{BM}(t))$ defined on $[0, t]$ is not Pareto-optimal. Alternatively, this proposition can be viewed in the following way: If the government can costlessly intervene in the markets and make the opportunity cost of holding money zero, then it can induce an optimal equilibrium. In the economy defined in the previous chapter, the rate of change of $P_{CM}(t)$ (i.e., $\hat{P}_{CM}(t)$) is strictly positive at every $t \in [0, T]$,[2] and

$$\hat{\mu}_M(t)_i = \rho + \hat{P}_{CM}(t) > 0 \qquad \forall\, t \in [0, T] \qquad i = 1, \ldots, n \qquad \text{(VI.2.10)}$$

which implies that equilibria in such economies are not Pareto-optimal.

In order to bring about an optimal intertemporal equilibrium (i.e., an optimal supply of money), the government must decrease the money stock at a rate that produces a deflation in $P_{CM}(t)$ such that[3]

$$\hat{P}_{CM}(t) = -\rho \qquad \forall\, t \in [0, T] \qquad \text{(VI.2.11)}$$

Alternatively, the government can pay interest on households' money holdings at a rate[4] $r_M(t)$ such that

$$r_M(t) = \rho + \hat{P}_{CM}(t) \qquad \forall\, t \in [0, T] \qquad \text{(VI.2.12)}$$

However, because the interest payment is in money, the money stock outstanding rises at the rate of r_M, which results in an increase in the rate of inflation of $P_{CM}(t)$. In the steady-state overlapping-generations economy this policy thus introduces an instability.[5]

The aggregate real bond stock in the economy is endogenous; however, because households have finite lives, it may not be optimal. Households with income streams skewed towards $t = 0$ tend to buy bonds initially and sell bonds as t approaches T, whereas households with income streams skewed toward $t = T$ sell bonds initially and buy bonds as t approaches T. Hence, unequal time profiles of income, as well as differences in the marginal utility of consumption, prevent all households from being on the same side of the market (i.e., prevent all households from having either excess demand or excess supply of bonds for any positive interest rate). Assume, then, that

$$\mu_B(t)_i = \rho - P_{MB}(t) + \hat{P}_{CB}(t) < 0 \qquad \forall\, t \in [0, T] \qquad \text{(VI.2.13)}$$

and $i = 1, \ldots, n$. Hence,

$$\rho < P_{MB}(t) - \hat{P}_{CB}(t) \qquad \forall\, t \in [0, T] \qquad \text{(VI.2.14)}$$

That is, the intertemporal discount rate ρ is less than the real rate of return on bonds. The inequality VI.2.14 represents an incentive for households to postpone consumption and invest their income in bonds. Such an intertemporal allocation raises the money and consumption-good prices of bonds; that is, $P_{MB}(t)$ and $P_{CB}(t)$ fall, and unless the effect on $dP_{CB}(t)/dt$ is large and negative, the right-hand side of equation VI.2.13 decreases. But even in the favorable case in which the right-hand side of VI.2.14 declines and the economy moves toward establishing VI.2.14 as an equality, the amount of bonds the household can buy is limited both by decreasing marginal utility and the necessity to allocate its consumption over the finite interval $[0, T]$. On the other hand, if households live on the infinite interval $[0, \infty)$, then it is optimal for them to try to postpone consumption forever and acquire bonds until

$$\rho = P_{MB}(t) - \hat{P}_{CB}(t) \qquad \qquad \text{(VI.2.15)}$$

is established. However, as long as households live on finite intervals, there exist time paths of income streams that produce equilibria in which VI.2.15 does not hold. In order for this type of nonoptimality of competitive intertemporal equilibria to occur, it is not necessary that overlapping generations improperly value future consumption. Finite lives and diminishing marginal utility of consumption are sufficient to obtain non-Pareto-optimal equilibria.[6]

It is possible to enrich the structure of the exchange economy and assume that the government has access to a production opportunity that is not available to the private sector. The proceeds from such production accrue in the form of a public good, which is equally available to all households and has been incorporated into the functional form of the instantaneous utility function. The financing of this productive activity can occur through nondistortionary lump-sum taxes or through the issue of government perpetuities. The mode of financing is a matter of indifference to the government. It is now possible for the government, through the choice of an appropriate combination of bond issue or retirement and lump-sum taxes, to bring about condition VI.2.15.

In a production economy, optimality also requires that the marginal productivity of additions to the stock of consumption goods[7] in the production of consumption goods be such that[8]

$$g(C(t)) = \rho + \delta \qquad \forall \, t \in [0, T] \qquad \qquad \text{(VI.2.16)}$$

where $g(C(t))$ is the marginal product of consumption goods in the production of consumption goods.

Intertemporal optimality proposition 1

An economy consisting of the finite-life households described in previous chapters achieves a Pareto-optimal competitive equilibrium at each instant in time, with stocks and their shadow prices held constant at that instant. However, the intertemporal equilibrium, given by the path of the market-clearing price vector $\tilde{P}(t) = (\hat{P}_{CM}(t), \tilde{P}_{CB}(t), \tilde{P}_{MB}(t)) \, \forall \, t \in [0, T]$, is not Pareto-optimal; that is, the household's asset-accumulation behavior is suboptimal.

A government can bring about a Pareto-optimal intertemporal equilibrium by changing the money stock so as to produce a rate of deflation in $P_{CM}(t)$ such that

$$\hat{P}_{CM}(t) = -\rho \qquad \forall t \in [0, T]$$

and through the appropriate financing of the production of a public good it can ensure that

$$\rho = P_{MB}(t) - \hat{P}_{CB}(t) \qquad \forall t \in [0, T]$$

VI.3   Introduction of a government into the intertemporal economy

The previous section established the government's ability to produce the level of the aggregate money stock that will induce a Pareto-optimal intertemporal competitive general equilibrium. If this economy does not possess any productive opportunities that can optimally be exploited by the government, then the optimal stock of government bonds is zero. In this intertemporal exchange economy the activity of the government is thus confined to the execution of an optimal monetary policy. Open market operations in the form of swaps of government perpetuities for money, or fiscal policy in the form of a purchase of consumption goods in the money and government perpetuities, are all suboptimal (Barro, 1974). However, if it is optimal for the government to undertake the production of a public good, then the financing of this activity can be accomplished through nondistortionary lump-sum taxation and bond issue. In this case it is optimal for the government to tax and enter the bonds-cum-money or bonds-cum-consumption-good market until conditon VI.2.15 is established. The choice variables available to the government are $C_M(t)_G$, $B_M(t)_G$, $C_B(t)_G$, $\tau_C(t)$, $\tau_M(t)$, and $\tau_B(t)$, which are its demand for consumption goods in exchange for money, its demand for bonds in exchange for money, its demand for consumption goods in exchange for bonds, and its tax rates, respectively, at $t \in [0, T]$. Hence, the government's intervention in the private economy is restricted to interventions in the three markets and to alterations of the household's stocks of assets and its income stream through taxation.

The government is fully described by the three state variables $m(t)_G$, $b(t)_G$, and $C(t)_G$, which denote its real money, bond, and consumption-good stocks, respectively, at time $t \in [0, T]$. There are no restrictions on the sign of $M(t)_G$ and $B(t)_G$; however, $C(t)_G$ is required to be nonnegative. The equations of motion for the three state variables of the government are

$$\frac{dm(t)_G}{dt} = -C_M(t)_G - b_M(t)_G \Pi(t)$$

$$- \hat{P}_{CM}(t)\, m(t)_G + n\tau_M(t) \qquad (VI.3.1)$$

$$m(0)_G = - \sum_{i=1}^{n} m_0(0)_i \qquad (VI.3.2)$$

$$\frac{dC(t)_G}{dt} = C_M(t)_G + C_B(t)_G - \delta C(t)_G + n\tau_C(t) \qquad (VI.3.3)$$

$$C(0)_G = C_{0G} \qquad (VI.3.4)$$

$$\frac{db(t)_G}{dt} = -C_B(t)_G + b_M(t)_G \Pi(t)$$
$$- (\hat{P}_{CB}(t) - P_{MB}(t)) b(t)_G + n\tau_B(t) \qquad (VI.3.5)$$

$$b(0)_G = - \sum_{i=1}^{n} b_0(0)_i \qquad (VI.3.6)$$

Following the introduction of a government, the market-clearing equations V.3.2, V.3.3, and V.3.4 change to

$$\sum_{i=1}^{n} C_M(\tilde{P}(t))_i + C_M(t)_G = 0 \qquad \forall\, t \in [0, T] \qquad (VI.3.7)$$

$$\sum_{i=1}^{n} C_B(\tilde{P}(t))_i + C_B(t)_G = 0 \qquad \forall\, t \in [0, T] \qquad (VI.3.8)$$

$$\sum_{i=1}^{n} b_M(t)_i \tilde{\Pi}(t) + b_M(t)_G \tilde{\Pi}(t) = 0 \qquad \forall\, t \in [0, T] \qquad (VI.3.9)$$

where $\tilde{P}(t) = (\tilde{P}_{CM}(t), \tilde{P}_{CB}(t), \tilde{P}_{BM}(t))$ is the equilibrium price vector. The aggregate stocks of money and bonds held by the households and the government are zero, because

$$\frac{dm(t)}{dt} = \sum_{i=1}^{n} \frac{dm(t)_i}{dt} + \frac{dm(t)_G}{dt}$$

$$= \sum_{i=1}^{n} C_M(t)_i - C_M(t)_G - \sum_{i=1}^{n} b_M(t)_i \Pi(t) + b_M(t)_G \Pi(t)$$

$$- \hat{P}_{CM}(t) \left(\sum_{i=1}^{n} m(t)_i - m(t)_G \right)$$

$$m(0) = \sum_{i=1}^{n} m_0(0)_i + m_0(0)_G \qquad (VI.3.10)$$

$$\frac{db(t)}{dt} = \sum_{i=1}^{n} \frac{db(t)_i}{dt} + \frac{db(t)_G}{dt}$$

$$= - \sum_{i=1}^{n} C_B(t)_i - C_B(t)_G + \sum_{i=1}^{n} b_M(t)_i \Pi(t) + b_M(t)_G \Pi(t)$$

$$- (\hat{P}_{CB}(t) - P_{MB}(t)) \left(\sum_{i=1}^{n} b(t)_i + b(t)_G \right)$$

$$b(0) = \sum_{i=1}^{n} b_0(0)_i + b_0(0)_G \qquad (VI.3.11)$$

and $dm(t)/dt = db(t)/dt = 0 \; \forall \; t \in [0, T]$, by equations VI.3.7, VI.3.8, VI.3.9, VI.3.2, and VI.3.6. The aggregate stock of consumption goods is given by

$$\frac{dC(t)}{dt} = \sum_{i=1}^{n} \frac{dC(t)_i}{dt} + \frac{dC(t)_G}{dt}$$

$$= \sum_{i=1}^{n} C_M(t)_i + C_M(t)_G + \sum_{i=1}^{n} C_B(t)_i + C_B(t)_G - \sum_{i=1}^{n} \phi(t)_i$$

$$- \sum_{i=1}^{n} T^{di}(\cdot) - \delta \left(\sum_{i=1}^{n} C(t)_i + C(t)_G \right) + \sum_{i=1}^{n} X(t)_i$$

$$C(0) = \sum_{i=1}^{n} C(0)_i + C(0)_G \qquad (VI.3.12)$$

which can be simplified with the aid of the market-clearing equations VI.3.7 and VI.3.8 to yield

$$\frac{dC(t)}{dt} = \sum_{i=1}^{n} (X(t)_i - \phi(t)_i - T^{di}(\cdot)) - \delta C(t) \qquad (VI.3.13)$$

The aggregate stocks of money, bonds, and consumption goods held by the private sector only are given by[9]

$$\frac{dm(t)_H}{dt} = \sum_{i=1}^{n} \frac{dm(t)_i}{dt} - \sum_{i=1}^{n} C_M(t)_i$$

$$- \sum_{i=1}^{n} b_M(t)_i - \sum_{i=1}^{n} \hat{P}_{CM}(t)m(t)_i - n\tau_M(t) \quad (VI.3.14)$$

$$m_0(0)_H = \sum_{i=1}^{n} m_0(0)_i \qquad (VI.3.15)$$

$$\frac{db(t)_H}{dt} = \sum_{i=1}^{n} \frac{db(t)_i}{dt} - \sum_{i=1}^{n} C_B(t)_i + \sum_{i=1}^{n} b_M(t)_i \Pi(t)$$

$$- (\hat{P}_{CB}(t) - P_{MB}(t)) \sum_{i=1}^{n} b(t)_i - n\tau_B(t) \quad (VI.3.16)$$

$$b_0(0)_H = \sum_{i=1}^{n} b_0(0)_i \qquad (VI.3.17)$$

$$\frac{dC(t)_H}{dt} = \sum_{i=1}^{n} \frac{dC(t)_i}{dt} = \sum_{i=1}^{n} C_M(t)_i + \sum_{i=1}^{n} C_B(t)_i - \sum_{i=1}^{n} T^i(\cdot)$$

$$- \delta \sum_{i=1}^{n} C(t)_i + \sum_{i=1}^{n} X(t)_i - n\tau_C(t) \quad (VI.3.18)$$

$$C_{0H} = \sum_{i=1}^{n} C_{0i} \qquad (VI.3.19)$$

Equations VI.3.14, VI.3.16, and VI.3.18 can be simplified with the aid of the market-clearing equations VI.3.7, VI.3.8, and VI.3.9 and equations VI.3.2. and VI.3.6 and can be written as

$$\frac{dm(t)_H}{dt} = C_M(t)_G + b_M(t)_G \Pi(t) + \hat{P}_{CM}(t) m(t)_G + n\tau_M(t) \qquad (VI.3.20)$$

$$\frac{db(t)_H}{dt} = C_B(t)_G - b_M(t)_G \Pi(t)$$
$$+ (\hat{P}_{CB}(t) - P_{MB}(t)) b(t)_G + n\tau_B(t) \qquad (VI.3.21)$$

$$\frac{dC(t)_H}{dt} = -C_M(t)_G - C_B(t)_G$$
$$- \sum_{i=1}^{n} T^i(\cdot) - \delta \sum_{i=1}^{n} C(t)_i + \sum_{i=1}^{n} X(t)_i - n\tau_C(t) \qquad (VI.3.22)$$

Hence,

$$\frac{dm(t)_G}{dt} = -\frac{dm(t)_H}{dt} \quad \text{and} \quad \frac{db(t)_G}{dt} = -\frac{db(t)_H}{dt} \qquad \forall\, t \in [0, T]$$

which, together with equations VI.3.2 and VI.3.6, imply that

$$m(t)_H = -m(t)_G \quad \forall\, t \in [0, T] \qquad (VI.3.23)$$

$$b(t)_H = -b(t)_G \quad \forall\, t \in [0, T] \qquad (VI.3.24)$$

The variable $B_M(t)_G$ gives the rate at which the government conducts open market operations, and $C_M(t)_G$ and $C_B(t)_G$ represent the rates at which the government conducts fiscal policy financed with money and bonds, respectively. An increase in $B_M(t)_G$ at each $t \in [0, T]$ results in an increase in $P_{BM}(t)$ at each $t \in [0, T]$, which, in turn, induces decreases in $b_M(t)_H \Pi(t)$ and $C_B(t)_H$ and an increase in $C_M(t)_H$ at each $t \in [0, T]$. The decrease in $C_B(t)_H$ causes a decrease in $P_{CB}(t)$ at each $t \in [0, T]$, whereas the increase in $C_M(t)_H$ brings about an increase in $P_{CM}(t)$ at each $t \in [0, T]$. The increase in $P_{CM}(t)$ and the decrease in $P_{CB}(t)$, in turn, lead the households to increase $C_B(t)_H$ and $b_M(t)_H \Pi(t)$ and to decrease $C_M(t)_H$ at each $t \in [0, T]$. The analysis of comparative dynamics in general equilibrium (see Section V.4) implies that $b_M(t)_H \Pi(t)$ and $C_B(t)_H$ are lower and that $C_M(t)_H$ is higher everywhere on $[0, T]$. Thus, $P_{CM}(t)$ is higher and $P_{CB}(t)$ and $P_{MB}(t)$ are lower everywhere on $[0, T]$. Hence, if the government increases the rate at which it conducts open market operations on $[0, T]$, it crowds the households out of the money-cum-bonds market and also brings about an increase in the level of the money price of consumption goods and a decrease in the interest rate at each $t \in [0, T]$. We thus have the following proposition.

Government policy proposition 1

An increase in the government's open market operations (i.e., a purchase of bonds with money in the bonds-cum-money market by the government) results in an increase in $P_{CM}(t)$ on $[0, T]$ and decreases in $P_{CB}(t)$ and $P_{MB}(t)$ on the same interval. The private demand for bonds in exchange for money is lower, whereas the private demands for consumption goods in exchange for money and bonds increase everywhere on $[0, T]$. If such a policy is anticipated at time $t = 0$, then its effects are spread over all of $[0, T]$. An unanticipated policy at $t^* \in (0, T]$ results in a discontinuous readjustment of plans at t^*, and its effects will be spread over the shorter interval $[t^*, T]$, with the largest effect occurring at $t = t^*$.

An increase in $C_M(t)_G$ at each $t \in [0, T]$ causes an increase in $P_{CM}(t)$ at each $t \in [0, T]$, which then results in a decrease in $C_M(t)_H$ and increases in $C_B(t)_H$ and $b_M(t)_H \Pi(t)$ at each $t \in [0, T]$. The increases in $C_B(t)_H$ and $b_M(t)_H$ lead to higher $P_{CB}(t)$ and $P_{BM}(t)$ on $[0, T]$, which, in turn, induce the households to decrease $C_B(t)_H$ and $b_M(t)_H \Pi(t)$ and to increase $C_M(t)_H$ at each $t \in [0, T]$. However, from Chapter V we know that the decrease in $C_M(t)_H$ and the increases in $C_B(t)_H$ and $b_M(t)_H \Pi(t)$ at each $t \in [0, T]$ dominate. Hence, an increase in the $C_M(t)_G$ demand results in a higher $P_{CM}(t)$ as well as a lower interest rate at each $t \in [0, T]$. Hence we have proved the following proposition.

Government policy proposition 2

An increase in fiscal policy (i.e., an increase in the government's demand for goods in exchange for money) will result in increases in $P_{CM}(t)$, $P_{CB}(t)$, and $P_{BM}(t)$, a decrease in $C_M(t)_H$, and increases in $C_B(t)_H$ and $b_M(t)_H \Pi(t)$ everywhere on $[0, T]$.

Lastly, we have the following proposition.

Government policy proposition 3

An increase in $C_B(t)_G$ at each $t \in [0, T]$ results in a higher $P_{CB}(t)$ on $[0, T]$ and hence a lower $C_B(t)_H$ and $b_M(t)_H \Pi(t)$ and a higher $C_M(t)$ at each $t \in [0, T]$. Therefore, the price level $P_{CM}(t)$ is higher everywhere on $[0, T]$, as is the interest rate. An increase in the tax rates has effects that are identical with those of a decrease in M_0, B_0, or $X(t)_i \forall i = 1, \ldots, n$. This is analyzed in Section V.4.

Hence, it has been possible to ascertain the price and crowding-out effects of the various government policies, taking into consideration all budget and financing constraints of the private and public sectors (Blinder and Solow, 1974; Sargent, 1979).

It is also possible to ascertain the effects on excess demands and market prices at each $t \in [0, T]$ of changes in the government's policy variables that occur on some subset $S \subset [0, T]$ only. For example, if $C_M(t)_G$ shifts upward at each $t > t^* \in (0, T]$, then $P_{CM}(t)$ must be higher at each $t > t^*$, and all results derived previously must hold for $t > t^*$; that is, $C_M(t)_H$ is lower and $C_B(t)_H$, $b_M(t)_H \Pi(t)$, $P_{CM}(t)$, $P_{CB}(t)$, and $P_{BM}(t)$ are higher at each $t > t^*$. However, changes in aggregate private demands, $C_M(t)_H$, $C_B(t)_H$, and $b_M(t)_H \Pi(t)$, extend over each household's entire life span, $[0, T]$, because consistency of the price system prevents the substitution effects from dominating. Hence, $C_M(t)_H$ is lower at each $t \in [0, T]$, whereas $C_B(t)_H$ and $b_M(t)_H \Pi(t)$ are higher at each $t \in [0, T]$. Therefore, $P_{CM}(t)$ is lower at each $t < t^*$ and higher at each $t > t^*$, and $P_{CB}(t)$, and $P_{BM}(t)$ are higher on the entire interval $[0, T]$. Similar results can be derived by considering changes in the remaining government policy variables on some subset of $[0, T]$. In each case, the households distribute the adjustments in their choice variables over their entire life spans, and the price change in the market in which the government intervenes exhibits a sign reversal in a neighborhood of t^*.

The results of the analysis of the effects of government policies can be applied to determine which policy choices the government might use to induce a Pareto-optimal quantity of money. The government induces Pareto optimality by ensuring that the following conditions are satisfied:

$$\rho + \hat{P}_{CM}(t) = 0 \qquad \forall\, t \in [0, T] \tag{VI.3.25}$$

Section V.5 demonstrates that $\hat{P}_{CM}(t)$ varies with changes in the average age of the population and is zero for stationary populations. The government must change the private money stock at a rate that establishes condition VI.3.25. This can be done optimally only through lump-sum taxation. Any other method, such as open market operations, will result in a suboptimal stock of government debt.

CHAPTER VII

A theory of disequilibrium adjustments

VII.1 Introduction

The previous two chapters established some of the dynamic and structural properties of a perfectly competitive economy composed of finite-life households whose behavior was defined and analyzed in Chapters II through IV. In this chapter we shall apply the results obtained previously in an analysis of an economy composed of the same households, but without the assumption that the equilibrium price vector is established in a timeless tâtonnement or learning process. So as to abstract from the intertemporal allocation dynamics, we shall assume throughout this chapter that the economy consists of overlapping generations whose average age remains constant with the passage of time.

The following three assumptions define a perfectly competitive economy: (a) Households are price-takers. (b) At $t = 0$, households solve costlessly and instantaneously the convex intertemporal maximization problem defined in Chapter II, with a given price vector $P(t) = (P_{CM}(t), P_{CB}(t), P_{BM}(t))$ defined on $[0, T]$. (c) The price vector $P(t)$, which is taken as given by the households when solving their maximization problem, is identically equal to the market-clearing price vector $\tilde{P}(t)$ on $[0, T]$ (see equations V.3.1 through V.3.4).

The literature on general-equilibrium models of monopolistic competition relaxes assumption (a) (Johansen, 1977; Roberts and Sonnenschein, 1977). The implications of assumption (b) are discussed in Section VII.3. Assumption (c) can be interpreted in two ways. The equilibrium price vector $\tilde{P}(t)$ may be generated in a timeless converging Walrasian tâtonnement. Alternatively, the households may arrive at $\tilde{P}(t)$ through a timeless converging learning process (i.e., the households have rational expectations). It was shown in Chapter II that assumption (c), together with the assumption that financial markets are complete, leads to universal forward contracting at $t = 0$. The household forms plans at $t = 0$ with the known equilibrium price vector $\tilde{P}(t)$, and all trades are executed as planned.

In this chapter we shall develop a theoretical framework for the analysis of economies in which assumption (c) and the assumption of complete financial markets have been relaxed. Specifically, there does not exist an instantaneous tâtonnement or learning process that at $t = 0$ establishes $\tilde{P}(t)$ $\forall$ $t \in [0, T]$ and a universal set of forward contracts. Instead, the household is endowed at $t = 0$ with a mechanism through which it formulates expectations about future prices and quantities and updates these expectations as new information is revealed with the passage of time. The households have available a set of information that is costlessly updated as time goes on. With the aid of this information, the household then makes optimal forecasts of the future values of its exogenous variables (i.e., it forms expectations). As time goes by, the household will discover how accurate the expected values of its variables are. If the expected values do not coincide with the actual values, then the household will adjust the rules by which it forms forecasts from the information set. This is the household's learning process.

If the household discovers that it had mistaken expectations about prices or quantities, it updates its expectations and employs the adjusted expectations when remaximizing its intertemporal problem to obtain new demand flows. This process reveals the significance of assumption (b). If planning (i.e., updating expectations and solving the intertemporal maximization problem) uses real resources, it may be optimal for the household to adjust its expectations and demands intermittently rather than continuously.

Because we have abandoned the assumption that there exist comprehensive forward markets, it is no longer true a priori that the households' plans for their future market behavior are consistent. Thus, even if spot markets are always in equilibrium, such equilibria are temporary. Inconsistent plans will require changes in market prices and quantities as incorrect expectations lead to changes in amounts demanded. The explicit specification of the households' intertemporal behavior and their expectations-adjustment behavior permit us to describe the path of the temporary equilibrium of the economy.

In addition to the introduction of imperfect information, we shall also allow markets to be in disequilibrium. The convergence of market prices toward the equilibrium market-clearing prices is retarded when price changes are costly or when household expectations adjustments and remaximizations consume real resources. Price change may be costly because the collecting and extracting of information from signals may be costly. Furthermore, the presence of nonconvexities in the households' transactions technologies is a necessary and sufficient condition for the existence of intermediaries. Such intermediaries may enjoy monopolistic market power and thereby influence the speed of adjustment of prices and quantities.[1] In either of these cases, the sign and size of market excess demand at any $t \in [0, T]$ determine, respectively, the direction and speed of concurrent changes in market prices. That is, prices rise faster when positive aggregate excess demand is larger and fall faster when negative aggregate excess demand is smaller. Thus, whether price changes are costly or planning consumes real resources, the adjustment of market prices mimics the adjustment of prices in the competitive tâtonnement process; however, whenever the rate of price change is finite, market prices do not adjust to their equilibrium values instantaneously. The disequilibrium dynamics of prices and quantities are dealt with in Section VII.3.

These introductory remarks reveal that households can never be in disequilibrium, because at any time $t \in [0, T]$ their behavior is determined by a choice-theoretical mechanism and thus is optimal given the state of the economy at time t. However, markets can be in disequilibrium in the sense that ex ante demand is not equal to ex ante supply at the prevailing market price. It will be seen that the comparative dynamics results obtained in the previous chapters permit us to analyze the adjustment in plans that occurs because of mistaken expectations. We shall also explore the effects of changes in expectations on current prices and quantities and the spillover effects of a disequilibrium situation in one market on the other two markets. We shall assume throughout this chapter that expectations are held with certainty.

VII.2   Expectations formation and the household's intertemporal maximization problem

This section imposes rudimentary analytical structure on the process by which a household forms and updates its expectations about future prices and quantities at each $t \in [0, T]$. It then modifies the intertemporal maximization problem that the household solves at each $t \in [0, T]$ to accommodate these price and quantity expectations.

The household has access to a set of information Ω that, together with an optimal set of inference rules, is used to generate forecasts of future prices and quantities. Changes in expectations come about because of (a) learning, which occurs as a result of mistaken expectations, and (b) changes in Ω, the set of information. We shall first discuss how the learning process changes expectations and then analyze the effects of changes in expectations, which may occur either as a result of learning or through the accumulation of new information, on the household's market behavior.

At each $t \in [0, T]$ the household forms expectations about the market price vector at time $\tau \in [0, T]$ by applying a set of optimal forecast rules to the information set Ω. The price expectations vector thus formed is denoted by $P(\tau, t)^e$. Similarly, at each $t \in [0, T]$ the household forms expectations about the quantities it can purchase at time $\tau \in [t, T]$ at the expected price of $P(\tau, t)^e$. The quantity expectations are obtained by the same method and are denoted by[2]

$$d(\tau, t)^e = (C_M(\tau, t)^e, C_B(\tau, t)^e, b_M(\tau, t)^e \, \Pi \, (\tau, t)^e)$$

Quantity expectations are expected constraints on the amounts of the three commodities the household can buy or sell at future dates when the market is not expected to clear instantaneously. If at time $t \in [0, T]$ the quantity constraint $d(\tau, t)^e$ is unexpectedly relaxed by enough to become nonbinding at all $\tau \in [t, T]$, then the demands at $\tau = t$ obtained by solving the household's maximization problem with the new quantity constraints are the household's notional demands at time τ. Notional demands are thus found at each $t \in [0, T]$ and are written as $d(\tau, t)^N$. The quantities that the household expects to demand over the interval $[0, T]$ when the quantity constraints are never binding are the household's Walrasian demands.[3] The amounts of three commodities the household plans to demand once it has fully taken into consideration the expected quantity constraints are its effective demands. Effective demands formed at time t for execution at time τ are denoted by $d(\tau, t)^e$ $\forall$ $\tau \in [t, T]$. The market prices that prevail at any time $t \in [0, T]$ and the quantities that are transacted at that time are the ex post prices and quantities and are denoted by $P(t)^a$ and $d(t)^a$, respectively.

The process by which the household at time $t \in [0, T]$ updates the prices and quantities expected at time $\tau \in [t, T]$ is assumed to depend on the difference between expected and notional values, as well as on the difference between expected and actual values of prices and quantity variables. Thus, this process can be written as

$$E[P(s)^a, d(s)^a, P(l, s)^e, d(l, s)^e, d(l, s)N, t] = (P(\tau, t)^e, d(\tau, t)^e)$$
$$\forall \, s \in [0, T], \quad \forall \, l \in [s, t], \quad \text{and} \quad \forall \, \tau \in [t, T] \quad (\text{VII.2.1})$$

The household is assumed to have an initial endowment of information about the structure of the economy.[4] Furthermore, it is assumed that this information allows the household to deduce that unsatisfied notional demands imply market disequilibria and that a positive (negative) market excess demand at time $t \in [0, T]$ implies positive (negative) time rates of change of prices and of quantities supplied. This latter assumption justifies including the differences between expected and notional quantities among the variables determining expected prices and quantities, because a positive difference between the notional demand and expected demand (supply) at time $t \in [t, T]$ implies positive (negative) market excess demand at time t. Hence,

$$d(\tau, t)^N > d(\tau, t)^e \quad \text{implies} \quad \frac{dP(\tau, t)^e}{d\tau} > 0 \quad \text{when} \quad d(\tau, t)^N > 0$$

$$d(\tau, t)^N < d(\tau, t)^e \quad \text{implies} \quad \frac{dP(\tau, t)^e}{d\tau} < 0 \quad \text{when} \quad d(\tau, t)^N < 0$$

$$(\text{VII.2.2})$$

Postulating that in addition to the initial information the household is endowed with a learning process provides a rationale for including differences between expected and actual prices and quantities among the variables determining expected prices and quantities. The household's learning process can be characterized by the effects on its behavior of deviations of expected values from actual values of price and quantity variables.

The first assumption about the household's learning process is a continuity or consistency requirement (Burmeister and Turnovsky, 1976); that is,

$$\lim_{\substack{\tau \to t \\ \tau \ge t}} |P(\tau, t)^e - P(t)^a| = 0 \qquad \forall\, t \in [0, T] \qquad\qquad \text{(VII.2.3)}$$

$$\lim_{\substack{\tau \to t \\ \tau \ge t}} |d(\tau, t)^e - d(t)^a| = 0 \qquad \forall\, t \in [0, T] \qquad\qquad \text{(VII.2.4)}$$

The foregoing equations ensure that expectations formed at time t about prices and quantities at time t are equal to the actual prices and quantities at time t. The second assumption regarding household learning requires expectations to be adjusted monotonically; that is, if

$$P(t, t - \tau)^e - P(t)^a > 0 \quad \text{for} \quad \tau \in S \subseteq [0, t) \qquad\qquad \text{(VII.2.5)}$$

then $P(t + \tau, t)^e$ will be adjusted downward at each $\tau \in [0, T - t]$.[5] Similarly, if

$$d(t, t - \tau)^e - d(t)^a > 0 \quad \text{for} \quad \tau \in S \subseteq [0, t) \qquad\qquad \text{(VII.2.6)}$$

then $d(t + \tau, t)^e$ will be adjusted downward at each $\tau \in [0, T - t]$. This monotonic adjustment assumption is the least restrictive structural assumption that permits the application of the comparative dynamics results obtained in Chapter IV. The third assumption requires that the learning process converge in the sense that at each $t \in [0, T]$ the absolute value of the difference between expected and actual values, that is,

$$|P(t, t - \tau)^e - P(t)^a| \qquad\qquad \text{(VII.2.7)}$$

and

$$|d(t, t - \tau)^e - d(t)^a| \qquad\qquad \text{(VII.2.8)}$$

must decrease as τ decreases from t to 0. A more restrictive convergence assumption is given by the requirement that the differences

$$P(t, t - \tau)^e - P(t)^a \qquad\qquad \text{(VII.2.9)}$$

and

$$d(t, t - \tau)^e - d(t)^a \qquad\qquad \text{(VII.2.10)}$$

must decrease if these differences are positive and increase if these differences are negative. This latter postulate rules out the phenomenon of overshooting in the learning mechanism. The last two convergence assumptions are employed in the analysis of market dynamics in Section VII.3.

At every point $t \in [0, T]$ the household's expectations about prices and quantities at time $\tau \in [t, T]$ are given by $P(\tau, t)^e$ and $d(\tau, t)^e$, respectively. Thus the household's intertemporal maximization problem as developed in Chapter II must be modified to include the expected future quantity constraints in such a way that the household solves at each $t \in [0, T]$

$$\max J[P(\tau, t)^e, t] \quad \text{subject to} \quad d(\tau, t)^e \le d(\tau, t)^e \quad \forall \tau \in [t, T]$$
$$(\text{VII.2.11})$$

where $J[P(\tau, t)^e, t]$ denotes the intertemporal optimization problem as specified in equation II.5.23, except that the initial point can be at any $t \in [0, T]$ rather than $t = 0$. Hence, current as well as future ex ante demand in each market depends on expected quantity constraints in each market at every $\tau \in [t, T]$.[6] Thus the vector of choice variables in equation VII.2.11 is the household's effective demand vector. Therefore, if the quantity constraint is expected to be binding at $\tau \in [t, T]$, then effective demand equals expected demand at τ, whereas a nonbinding quantity constraint implies that effective demand is equal to notional demand at τ. The household's notional demands at time $\tau \in [t, T]$, $d(\tau, t)^N$, are obtained by solving its modified optimization problems at time t with nonbinding quantity constraints. For example, at time $t \in [0, T]$ the household's notional demands at time $\tau \in [t, T]$ are obtained by solving its modified maximization problem with a value for $d(\tau, t)^e$ that does not constrain $d(\tau, t)^e$. Hence, the household solves at time t

$$\max J[P(\tau, t)^e, t] \qquad\qquad (\text{VII.2.12})$$

Assumption (c) from Section VII.1 makes it optimal for the household to revise its expectations continuously in accordance with the process defined in equation VII.2.1 and to remaximize continuously its intertemporal problem given by equation VII.2.11. If the expected prices and quantities are realized, then a remaximization of the intertemporal problem, by Bellman's principle of optimality (see Section IV.7), does not yield new demand flows. However, if the expected values of prices and quantities are not realized, then the remaximization yields different planned demand flows, because the expected values of the price and quantity variables must have been adjusted.[7]

The adjustments in expected prices and quantities resulting from the divergence of expected values from actual values of these variables were not anticipated before the divergence occurred. Thus it is possible to apply the results of the analysis of the comparative dynamic effects of price changes in Chapter IV to investigate the effects of mistaken expectations on current and planned demands. If, for example, the expectations formed at time $t - \tau$, where $\tau \in S \subset [0, T)$, about prices at time t are higher than actual prices at time t, that is, if

$$P(t, t - \tau)^e > P(t)^a \quad \text{for} \quad \tau \in S \subset [0, t) \qquad \text{(VII.2.13)}$$

then by assumptions VII.2.3 and VII.2.5 the household revises its expectations downward on $(t, T]$. This change in $P(t + \tau, t)^e \; \forall \; \tau \in [0, T - t]$ is equivalent to an unanticipated downward shift on $(t, T]$ of the price vector used at time t to compute planned demands on $(t, T]$, and the effects of such unanticipated changes in prices on the household's market and consumption behavior are given in Chapter IV. We summarize the results in the following proposition.

Price expectations adjustment proposition

If $P_{CM}(t, t - \tau)^e < P_{CM}(t)^a$ for $\tau \in S \subset [0, t)$, then $P_{CM}(\tau, t)^e$ will be raised $\forall \; \tau \in (t, T]$, and $C_M(\tau, t)^e$ will be reduced, whereas $b_M(\tau, t)^e \, \Pi \, (\tau, t)^e$ and $C_B(\tau, t)^e$ will be raised $\forall \; \tau \in (t, T]$.

If $P_{CB}(t, t - \tau)^e < P_{CB}(t)^a$ for $\tau \in S \subset [0, t)$, then $P_{CB}(\tau, t)^e$ will be raised $\forall \; \tau \in (t, T]$, and $C_B(\tau, t)^e$ and $b_M(\tau, t)^e \, \Pi \, (\tau, t)^e$ will be lowered, whereas $C_M(\tau, t)^e$ will be higher $\forall \; \tau \in (t, T]$.

If $P_{MB}(t, t - \tau)^e < P_{MB}(t)^a$ for $\tau \in S \subset [0, t)$, then $P_{MB}(\tau, t)^e$ will be raised $\forall \; \tau \in (t, T]$, and $b_M(\tau, t)^e \, \Pi \, (\tau, t)^e$ and $C_M(\tau, t)^e$ will be higher, whereas $C_B \, (\tau, t)^e$ will be lower $\forall \; \tau \in (t, T]$.

The effects of changes in the expected quantity constraints on the household's planned demands can also be ascertained. In particular, if

$$C_M(t, t - \tau)^e < C_M(t)^a \quad \text{for} \quad \tau \in S \subset [0, t) \qquad \text{(VII.2.14)}$$

then by assumptions VII.2.4 and VII.2.6, the household adjusts $C_M(\tau, t)^e$ upward $\forall \; \tau \in (t, T]$. If the quantity constraint is binding, then the upward shift of $C_M(\tau, t)^e$ will lead to upward shifts of $C_M(\tau, t)^e$ and $\phi(\tau, t)^e$ and downward shifts of $C_B(\tau, t)^e$ and $B_M(\tau, t)^e$ for all $\tau \in (\tau, t]$.[8] The relaxation of the quantity constraint in the consumption-good-cum-money market given by the upward shift of $C_M(\tau, t)^e$ induces a reduction in the household's notional demand in that market; that is, $C_M(\tau, t)^N$ will shift down $\forall \; \tau \in (t, T]$. Furthermore, the decreases in $C_B(\tau, t)^e$ and $B_M(\tau, t)^e$ on the interval $[t, T]$ result in downward shifts of $C_B(\tau, t)^N$ and $B_M(\tau, t)^N \; \forall \; \tau \in (t, T]$. Similarly, if

$$C_B(t, t - \tau)^e < C_B(t)^a \quad \text{for} \quad \tau \in S \subset [0, t) \qquad \text{(VII.2.15)}$$

then the household increases $C_B(\tau, t)^e$, $B_M(\tau, t)^e$ and $\phi(\tau, t)^e$ and decreases $C_M(\tau, t)^e \; \forall \; \tau \in (t, T]$. In this case, notional demand in the consumption-good-cum-bonds market diminishes on the interval $(t, T]$, whereas $C_M(\tau, t)^N$ shifts down and $B_M(\tau, t)^N$ shifts up $\forall \; \tau \in (t, T]$.

Lastly, if

$$B_M(t, t - \tau)^e < B_M(t)^a \quad \text{for} \quad \tau \in S \subset [0, t) \tag{VII.2.16}$$

then the household raises $B_M(\tau, t)^e$ and $C_B(\tau, t)^e$ and lowers $C_M(\tau, t)^e \; \forall \; \tau \in (t, T]$. The notional demands $B_M(\tau, t)^N$ and $C_M(\tau, t)^N$ shift down, whereas $C_B(\tau, t)^N$ shifts up $\forall \; \tau \in (t, T]$. We summarize these results in the following proposition.

Quantity expectations adjustment proposition

If $C_M(t, t - \tau)^e < C_M(t)^a$ for $\tau \in S \subseteq [0, t)$, then $C_M(\tau, t)^e$ will be raised for $\forall \; \tau \in (t, T]$, and $C_M(\tau, t)^e$ and $\phi\,(\tau, t)^e$ will be higher, whereas $C_B(\tau, t)^e$ and $b_M(\tau, t)^e$ $\Pi\,(\tau, t)^e$ will be lower $\forall \; \tau \in (t, T]$. $C_M(\tau, t)^N$, $C_B(\tau, t)^N$, and $b_M(\tau, t)^N \Pi\,(\tau, t)^e$ decline $\forall \; \tau \in (t, T]$.

If $C_B(t, t - \tau)^e < C_B(t)^a$ for $\tau, \in S \subseteq [0, t)$, then $C_B(\tau, t)^e$ will be raised $\forall \; \tau \in (t, T]$, and $C_B(\tau, t)^e$, $b_M(\tau, t)^e \Pi\,(\tau, t)^e$, and $\phi(\tau, t)^e$ will be higher, whereas $C_M(\tau, t)^e$ will be lower $\forall \; \tau \in (t, T]$. $C_B(\tau, t)^N$ and $C_M(\tau, t)^N$ are lower and $b_M(\tau, t)^N \Pi\,(\tau, t)^e$ is higher $\forall \; \tau \in (t, T]$.

If $B_M(t, t - \tau)^e < B_M(t)^a$ for $\tau \in S \subseteq [0, t)$, then $B_M(\tau, t)^e$ will be raised $\forall \; \tau \in (t, T]$, $B_M(\tau, t)^e$ will be higher and $C_M(\tau, t)^e$ and $C_B(\tau, t)^e$ will be lower $\forall \; \tau \in (t, T]$. $B_M(\tau, t)^N$ and $C_M(\tau, t)^N$ will be reduced, and $C_B(\tau, t)^N$ will be increased $\forall \; \tau \in (t, T]$.

VII.3   Market disequilibrium dynamics

This section employs the results of the analysis of quantity constraints and mistaken price and quantity expectations on the household's market behavior to investigate the dynamics of excess demands and prices in the three markets when all or some of these markets are in disequilibrium. First, disequilibrium adjustments in one isolated market are considered, and then the simultaneous adjustments in the three interrelated markets are examined.

For expository purposes, demanders are distinguished from suppliers in each market. Let

$$C(\tau, t)^x = \sum_{i \in L} d_i(\tau, t)^x \qquad \forall \; \tau \in [t, T] \tag{VII.3.1}$$

be the aggregate demand function in a market when $d_i(\tau, t)^x$ is the demand function of the ith $(i \in L)$ household in that market and L is the index set of demanders. Similarly, let

$$S(\tau, t)^x = \sum_{i \in K} d_i(\tau, t)^x \qquad \forall \; \tau \in [t, T] \tag{VII.3.2}$$

be the aggregate supply function in the same market when $d_i(\tau, t)^x$ is the supply function of the ith $(i \in K)$ household in the market and K is the index set of suppliers. The superscript x equals a, e, ϵ, or N, according to whether the variable takes on its actual, expected, effective, or notional value.

The dynamics of market demand, supply, and prices in disequilibrium situations are illustrated by assuming that at the present time $t \in [0, T]$ there exists excess demand at the arbitrarily chosen price $P(t)^a$; that is,

$$D(t, t)^N > S(t, t)^N \qquad (VII.3.3)$$

At this time t the expected value of the demand and supply variables must equal the actual value by the continuity assumption of equation VII.2.4; that is,

$$D(t, t)^e = D(t)^a = S(t)^a = S(t, t)^e \qquad (VII.3.4)$$

According to equation VII.2.11, effective demand cannot exceed expected demand, and the voluntary-exchange assumption ensures that effective demand cannot be less than the actual amount transacted. Hence,

$$D(t, t)^\epsilon = D(t)^a \qquad (VII.3.5)$$

By the voluntary-exchange assumption, actual supply cannot exceed effective supply, and effective supply cannot exceed expected supply. Hence, by equation VII.3.4,

$$S(t, t)^\epsilon = S(t)^a \qquad (VII.3.6)$$

Combining equations VII.3.4, VII.3.5, and VII.3.6 yields[9]

$$D(t, t)^\epsilon = S(t, t)^\epsilon \qquad (VII.3.7)$$

Furthermore, because the actual amount transacted at time t cannot exceed $S(t, t)^N$, the notional value of demand must exceed the actual value of demand at time t; that is,

$$D(t, t)^N > D(t)^a \qquad (VII.3.8)$$

The actual aggregate amount transacted has been rationed among the households in the index set L, according to some rationing rule, in such a way that

$$D(t)^a = \sum_{i \in L} d_i(t)^a \qquad (VII.3.9)$$

Hence, the members of a nonempty subset of the demanders are not on their notional demand curves.

In order for some members of the set of suppliers not to be on their notional supply curves, it is necessary that[10]

$$S(t)^a < S(t, t)^N \qquad (VII.3.10)$$

which implies by equations VII.3.4, VII.3.5, and VII.3.7 that

$$D(t, t)^x = S(t, t)^x < S(t, t)^N \qquad (x = \epsilon, e, a) \qquad \text{(VII.3.11)}$$

However, in a market with positive excess demand, this situation is unstable, because a slight upward perturbation in $S(t)^a$ reveals to suppliers that demanders are willing immediately to absorb larger quantities at the prevailing price of $P(t)^a$. Thus, suppliers increase $S(t, t)^\epsilon$, and demanders willingly absorb larger quantities until

$$S(t)^a = S(t, t)^N \qquad \text{(VII.3.12)}$$

Therefore, in situations of excess demand, all suppliers are on their notional supply curves. Similarly, in situations of excess supply, all demanders are on their notional demand curves.

If in a situation of excess demand the quantity and price expectations of demanders and suppliers are such that neither group expects its notional plans to be realized, but

$$D(\tau, t)^e = S(\tau, t)^e < S(\tau, t)^N < D(\tau, t)^N \qquad \forall \, \tau \in [t, T] \quad \text{(VII.3.13)}$$

then this situation is not an expectations equilibrium, which requires that actual quantities transacted equal expected quantities. Hence, it is not possible for both suppliers and demanders to have correct expectations and still have their notional plans unrealized. The market variables satisfy

$$D(t, t)^N > D(t, t)^x = S(t, t)^x = S(T, t)^N \qquad (x = a, e, \epsilon) \quad \text{(VII.3.14)}$$

If the household's price and quantity expectations are accurate, then by assumption VII.2.2 households expect the price to increase when there exists excess demand; that is,

$$\frac{d}{d\tau}[P(\tau, t)^e] > 0 \qquad \forall \, \tau \in [t, T] \qquad \text{(VII.3.15)}$$

Thus, the individual's notional demand $d_i(\tau, t)^N$ ($\forall \, i \in L \cup K$) decreases on the interval $[t, T]$ (see Sections III.4 and IV.4). Hence, when the household's expectations are accurate, instantaneous quantity equilibrium moves along the notional supply curve toward the market-clearing price. The speed of this equilibration depends on the properties of the process by which prices are changed.

However, when the household's price and quantity expectations are not realized, the resulting adjustments in these expectations induce shifts in notional demands and supplies. If price and quantity expectations fall short of the actual prices and quantities, that is, if

$$P(t, t - \tau)^e < P(t)^a \qquad \forall \, \tau \in S \subset (0, t] \qquad \text{(VII.3.16)}$$

$$d(t, t - \tau)^e < d(t)^a \qquad \forall \, \tau \in S \subset (0, t] \qquad \text{(VII.3.17)}$$

then, by equations VII.2.5 and VII.2.6, $P(\tau, t)^e$ and $d(\tau, t)^e$ are revised upward at all $\tau \in (t, T]$. The upward shift of $P(\tau, t)^e$ on $(t, T]$ induces the household to adjust $d(\tau, t)^c$ downward on $(t, T]$. The resulting downward shift of $d(\tau, t)^N$ reduces excess demand at each $\tau \in (t, T]$.[11] The upward shift of $d(\tau, t)^e$ on $(\tau, t]$ constitutes a relaxation of the quantity constraints and thus induces the household to revise $d(\tau, t)^c$ upward and $d(\tau, t)^N$ downward at each $\tau \in (t, T]$. Hence, the excess demand diminishes at each $\tau \in (t, T]$. Similarly, it is easily established that excessive price and quantity expectations result in an increase in excess demand at each $\tau \in (t, T]$. Hence, in the first example of inaccurate expectations, the resulting shifts in demand and supply accelerate the movements of prices and quantities toward their market-clearing values, whereas in the second instance of inaccurate expectations, the adjustments in demand and supply retard the movement toward the equilibrium.

It was shown earlier that the adjustments of prices and quantities in a market with positive excess demand are stable (i.e., prices and quantities converge onto their equilibrium values) when all expectations are fully realized. On the other hand, if price and quantity expectations are not realized, then a convergence assumption such as equations VII.2.7 and VII.2.8 is needed to ensure the stability of price and quantity adjustments.[12]

If the expectations-adjustment mechanism in equation VII.2.1 does not satisfy VII.2.7 and VII.2.8, then explosive or cyclical behavior of prices and quantities cannot be ruled out.[13]

In contrast to the tâtonnement process described in Chapter V, the equilibrating process in an individual market investigated here is of nonzero duration and thus allows trading at disequilibrium prices. Furthermore, the intertemporal nature of the household permits explicit modeling of the expectations, and therefore the implications of unrealized expectations on the market dynamics can be analyzed.

The disequilibrium dynamics of market demand, supply, and prices in a multimarket economy are determined by the movements of prices and quantities that arise with nonzero excess demand. Changes in prices and quantities thus caused are movements along the given notional demand or supply curves. In addition, however, the noninstantaneous movements of prices and quantities are responsible for two further effects that are causes of shifts in demand and supply functions: (a) There exist spillover effects; that is, present and expected quantity constraints in one market will be taken into consideration by the household when forming its demands in the remaining two markets. (b) Inaccurate expectations induce expectations adjustments in accordance with equation VII.2.1 and thus affect excess demands in all markets.

If a household faces a present or expected quantity constraint on one of its choice variables (e.g., $C_M(\tau, t)^N_i > C_M(\tau, t)^c_i = C_M(\tau, t)^e_i$ for some $\tau \in [t, T]$), then its remaining effective and notional demands are also affected. The effects of quantity constraints on the household's effective and notional demands have been established in Section VII.2. In turn, the shifts in notional demands cause changes in excess demands and thus alter the movements of prices and quantities toward the equilibrium. Hence, the effects of quantity constraints in one market spread over all markets.

In particular, define

$$C_M^D(\tau, t)^x = \sum_{i \in L} C_M(\tau, t)_i^x \qquad \forall \, \tau \in [t, T] \tag{VII.3.18}$$

$$C_M^S(\tau, t)^x = \sum_{i \in K} C_M(\tau, t)_i^x \qquad \forall \, \tau \in [t, T] \tag{VII.3.19}$$

to represent aggregate demand and aggregate supply, respectively, in the consumption-good-cum-money market. The variable x equals N, ϵ, e, or a according to whether the demand or supply variable assumes its notional, effective, expected, or actual value. The sets L and K are the index sets of demanders and suppliers, respectively. Aggregate demand and supply in the consumption-good-cum-bonds and the bonds-cum-money markets can be defined similarly.

A downward shift of $C_M^D(\tau, t)^e$ at some $\tau \in [t, T]$ due to present or expected excess demand in the consumption-good-cum-money market results in an increase in notional demands in the consumption-good-cum-bonds and bonds-cum-money markets. Hence, we have the following proposition.

Multiple-markets disequilibrium proposition

If $C_M^D(\tau, t)^N - C(\tau, t)^N > 0$ at some $\tau \in [t, T]$, then $[C_M^D(\tau, t)^N - C_B^S(\tau, t)^N]$ and $[B_M^D(\tau, t)^N - B_M^S(\tau, t)^N]$ are higher everywhere on $[t, T]$ than in the situation in which $C_M^D(\tau, t)^N = C_M^S(\tau, t)^N$.

If $C_B^D(\tau, t)^N - C_B^S(\tau, t)^N > 0$ at some $\tau \in [t, T]$, then $[C_M^D(\tau, t)^N - C_M^S(\tau, t)^N]$ is higher and $[B_M^D(\tau, t)^N - B_M^S(\tau, t)^N]$ is lower everywhere on the interval $[t, T]$ than in the $C_B^D(\tau, t) = C_B^S(\tau, t)$ situation.

If $B_M^D(\tau, t)^N - B_M^S(\tau, t)^N > 0$ at some $\tau \in [t, T]$, then $[C_B^D(\tau, t)^N - C_B^S(\tau, t)^N]$ is lower and $[C_M^D(\tau, t)^N - C_M^S(\tau, t)^N]$ is higher everywhere on the interval $[t, T]$ than in the $B_M^D(\tau, t)^N = B_M^S(\tau, t)^N$ situation.

If all price and quantity expectations are fully realized by all households, then the disequilibrium dynamics of excess demand and prices in the three markets can be represented by

$$\frac{dP_{CM}(t)^a}{dt} = G^1(C_M(P(t)^a)^N) \qquad G^1(0) = 0 \tag{VII.3.20}$$

$$\frac{dP_{CB}(t)^a}{dt} = G^2(C_B(P(t)^a)^N) \qquad G^2(0) = 0 \tag{VII.3.21}$$

$$\frac{dP_{BM}(t)^a}{dt} = G^3(B_M(P(t)^a)^N) \qquad G^3(0) = 0 \qquad \text{(VII.3.22)}$$

such that $F(C_M(\tau, t)^N, C_B(\tau, t)^N, B_M(\tau, t)^N) = 0$ $\forall$ $t \in [0, T]$ and $\forall$ $\tau \in [t, T]$. The implicit function F indicates that there exists a relationship among the notional excess demands in the three markets at any $\tau \in [t, T]$ because of the spillover effects discussed earlier.[14] The notional excess demands in equations VII.3.20 through VII.3.22 also depend on the expected values of prices and quantities, but because expectations are realized, these variables have been absorbed into the functional form of G^1, G^2, and G^3. The functions $G^1(\cdot)$, $G^2(\cdot)$, and $G^3(\cdot)$ are increasing and sign preserving, and they represent the mechanism by which prices are moved. From the analysis of tâtonnement processes it is known that the system VII.3.20 through VII.3.22 by itself is stable, and it is conjectured that for those functions F that are determined by the household's maximization problem the system with spillover effects is also stable.[15]

In addition to the spillover effects that occur in a multimarket economy due to quantity constraints in one of the markets, it is necessary to investigate the spillover effects on excess demand in all markets due to inaccurate quantity or price expectations in one of the three markets. The latter spillover effects will be analyzed in the situation in which positive excess demand exists in the consumption-good-cum-money market. If the quantity expectations in the consumption-good-cum-money market are low, that is, if

$$C_M(t, t - \tau)^e < C_M(t)^a \qquad \text{(VII.3.23)}$$

for $\tau \in S \subset (0, t]$, then by equation VII.2.6 the expected quantities will be revised upward at each $\tau \in [t, T]$. The increase in $C_M(\tau, t)^e$ will cause the household to increase $C_M(\tau, t)^e$ and decrease $C_M(\tau, t)^N$, $C_B(\tau, t)^N$, and $B_M(\tau, t)^N$ at each $\tau \in [t, T]$. Hence, the effect of low quantity expectations in the consumption-good-cum-money market not only reduces excess demand in that market but also reduces excess demand in the remaining two markets.

If the price expectations in the consumption-good-cum-money market are low, that is, if

$$P_{CM}(t, t - \tau)^e < P_{CM}(t)^a \qquad \text{(VII.3.24)}$$

for $\tau \in S \subset (0, t]$, then by equation VII.2.5 the expected prices are revised upward and the notional demands $C_M(\tau, t)^N$ and $C_B(\tau, t)^N$ shift downward on the interval $[t, T]$. The effect of the upward revision of $P_{CM}(\tau, t)^e$ on the notional demand $B_M(\tau, t)^N$ is indeterminate (see Section IV.4). Hence, the spillover effects on excess demands in the consumption-good-cum-bonds and the bonds-cum-money markets due to low quantity and price expectations in the consumption-good-cum-money market reduce the spillover effects due to the positive excess demand in the consumption-good-cum-money market. A similar result can be derived for initial positions with excess demand in the consumption-good-cum-bonds or bonds-cum-money market. If there exists excess supply initially in one of the three markets, then the resulting spillover effects will be counteracted by the spillover effects of high rather than low quantity and price expectations in the market with excess supply. In those situations in which the spillover effects from mistaken expectations counteract the spillover effects from excess demand or supply, the movement toward the equilibrium is expedited, whereas in the other cases it is retarded. If the economy with accurate expectations and disequilibrium spillovers is stable,[16] then the system with inaccurate expectations is stable as long as the expectations-adjustment mechanism satisfies equations VII.2.7 and VII.2.8. However, if the adjustment mechanism in equation VII.2.1 does not satisfy VII.2.7 and VII.2.8, then explosive or cyclical movements in quantities and prices may occur.

In order to be able to establish further qualitative and quantitative properties of the paths of quantities and prices in this economy in which some markets are out of equilibrium, it is necessary to develop more specifically the properties of the expectations-adjustment process, as well as those of the mechanism that retards the instantaneous movement of prices toward a Walrasian equilibrium.

The properties of the expectations-adjustment process can be derived from a more comprehensive model of the household's learning behavior, which would include a derivation of optimal rules of inference. The inclusion of resource requirements for the household's accumulation of information and learning activities will also affect its expectations-formation process. The properties of the mechanism that retards equilibrating price movements can be established by investigating the communications process in markets, as well as the cost of price adjustments (Hellwig, 1980).

The analysis of the disequilibrium dynamics of prices and quantities in multiple markets, as described in this chapter, relies only on convergence properties of the expectations- and price-adjustment processes. Thus, whereas the extensions proposed earlier will lead to more refined quantitative knowledge about the dynamics of prices and quantities, they will not alter the framework and the convergence results illustrated in this chapter. Furthermore, because the economic behavior of households is rational, in that all available information is used and there exist no unexploited arbitrage opportunities, the disequilibrium model developed here is fully compatible with the modern equilibrium theory of business cycles (Lucas, 1975). Therefore, this model of disequilibrium adjustment of prices and quantities in an economy in which intertemporal households are subject to a transactions technology can serve as a canonical disequilibrium model.

Stocks, flows, and the budget constraint

We shall reduce Sidrauski's original problem to that of an exchange economy and let $C(t)$ be the rate at which the household consumes, let $M(t)$ be the money balances the household holds, let ρ be its subjective rate of time preference, and let $Y(t)$ be the rate at which it receives endowment. Following Sidrauski, the household maximizes

$$J = \int_0^T U(C(t), M(t)) \exp(-\rho t) \, dt$$

subject to

$$A(t) = M(t) \quad \text{and} \quad Y(t) = C(t) + \frac{dA(t)}{dt} = M(0) = M_0$$

The augmented function

$$\int_0^T U(C(t), M(t)) + \lambda\left[Y(t) - C(t) - \frac{dA(t)}{dt} + \mu[A(t) - M(T)]\right] \exp(-\rho t) \, dt$$

yields the Euler equations

$$\frac{\partial U}{\partial C} = \lambda, \qquad \frac{\partial U}{\partial M} = \mu, \qquad -\frac{d\lambda}{dt} = \mu$$

The Euler equations, together with the two constraints and the initial condition, determine $C(t)$, $M(t)$, $A(t)$, $\lambda(t)$, and $\mu(t)$ as functions of $Y(t)$, ρ, and M_0. We can, however, reformulate Sidrauski's problem by omitting the stock constraint $A(t) = M(t)$ and let the household maximize

$$J = \int_0^T U(C(t), M(t)) \exp(-\rho t) \, dt$$

subject to

$$Y(t) = C(t) + \frac{dM(t)}{dt}, \qquad M(0) = M_0$$

The augmented objective function

$$\int_0^T [U(C(t), M(t)) + \lambda \cdot (Y(t) - C(t) - M(t))] \exp{(-\rho t)} \, dt$$

and the associated Euler conditions

$$\frac{\partial U}{\partial C} = \lambda, \qquad \frac{\partial \lambda}{\partial t} = -\frac{\partial U}{\partial M}$$

together with the one flow constraint and the initial condition for the money stock, determine $C(t)$, $M(t)$, and $\lambda(t)$ as functions of $Y(t)$, ρ, and M_0. These two problems are equivalent in that they determine the same $C(t)$ and $M(t)$ as functions of $Y(t)$, ρ, and M_0, as can be seen by substituting $\partial U/\partial M = \mu$ into the third Euler equation of the first problem.

Because Brainard and Tobin did not specify behavior at the microeconomic level, it is not possible to conduct a similar analysis of their model.

Josef May (1970) also tried to show that in continuous-time stock flow models the use of two constraints (i.e., a stock constraint and a flow constraint) is necessary. May started with a discrete-time-period model, then allowed the time period to approach zero and analyzed the limiting budget constraint.

Let the length of the period be Δt, and let $\overline{L}$, $\overline{B}$, and $\overline{Y}$ be the initial endowments of money, bonds, and income received over period Δt, respectively. Further, let L, B, and C be the household's end-of-period holdings of money and bonds and its consumption during the period, respectively. Then

$$\overline{L} + \overline{B} + \overline{Y} + r \cdot \Delta t \cdot B = L + B + C \qquad (A.1)$$

is the budget constraint in the discrete-time model. The stock variables C and Y can be rewritten as flow variables by defining

$$c = \frac{C}{\Delta t} \quad \text{and} \quad \overline{y} = \frac{\overline{Y}}{\Delta t}$$

then equation A.1 becomes

$$\overline{L} + \overline{B} + \Delta t \cdot \overline{y} + r\Delta t \cdot B = L + B + \Delta t \cdot c \qquad (A.2)$$

or

$$\Delta t[\bar{y} + rB - c] = (L - \bar{L}) + (B - \bar{B}) \tag{A.3}$$

May then argued that in the limiting case, as $\Delta t \to 0$, the individual faces

$$(L - \bar{L}) + (B - \bar{B}) = 0 \tag{A.4}$$

as stock constraint, as well as

$$s = \bar{y} + r \cdot B - c \tag{A.5}$$

as flow constraint. In constraint A.5 the variable s denotes saving or addition to stocks. However, it is easily verified that both A.4 and A.5 can be obtained from A.2 or A.3. In particular, A.4 is obtained from A.3 by letting $\Delta t \to 0$, and A.5 is obtained by dividing A.3 by Δt and then letting $\Delta t \to 0$, which yields $\bar{y} + r \cdot B - c = dL/dt + dB/dt$. Hence only a single constraint is required.

A derivation of the necessary and sufficient conditions for optimal household choice

$$\max \int_0^T f_0(q, v, t)\, dt + \beta\, (q(T), T) \tag{B.1}$$

subject to

$$\frac{dq}{dt} = f(q, v, t)$$

$$q\,(0) = q_0$$

$$q \in R^n, \qquad v \in R^r$$

Let $\lambda(t) = (\lambda_1(t), \ldots, \lambda_n(t))$ be a piecewise-smooth vector-valued function. We then introduce the following Lagrangian function:

$$L(q, v; \lambda) = \int_0^T \left(f_0(q, v, t) + \lambda \left(f(q, v, t) - \frac{dq}{dt} \right) \right) dt + \beta\, (q\,(T), T)$$

Theorem B.1

If (q^*, v^*, λ^*) is a saddle point of L, then q^* and v^* solve problem B.1.

Proof: A saddle point of L is defined as $L(q, v; \lambda^*) \le L(q^*, v^*; \lambda^*) \le L(q^*, v^*; \lambda)$. First, $L(q^*, v^*; \lambda^*) \le L(q^*, v^*; \lambda)$ implies that

$$\int_0^T \lambda(t)^* \left(f(q^*, v^*, t) - \frac{dq^*}{dt} \right) dt \le \int_0^T \lambda(t) \left(f(q^*, v^*, t) - \frac{dq^*}{dt} \right) dt$$

which can be written as

$$\int_0^T (\lambda(t)^* - \lambda(t)) \left(f(q^*, v^*, t) - \frac{dq^*}{dt} \right) dt \le 0$$

and because $\lambda(t)$ is continuous, the last inequality holds for all admissible

135

$\lambda(t)$ only if

$$\frac{dq}{dt} = f(q^*, v^*, t)$$

Hence, if (q^*, v^*, λ^*) is a saddle point of L, then q^* and v^* satisfy the differential equation constraint.

Second, $L(q, v; \lambda^*) \le L(q^*, v^*; \lambda^*)$ implies that

$$\int_0^T f_0(q, v, t) \, dt + \beta(q(T), T) + \int_0^T \lambda^* \left(f(q, v, t) - \frac{dq}{dt} \right) dt$$

$$\le \int_0^T f_0(q^*, v^*, t) \, dt + \beta(q(T)^*, T)$$

Hence, for all q and v satisfying $dq/dt = f(q, v, t)$, this inequality reduces to

$$\int_0^T f_0(q, v, t) \, dt + \beta(q(T), T) \le \int_0^T f_0(q^*, v^*, t) \, dt + \beta(q(T)^*, T)$$

That is, if the vectors q^*, v^*, and λ^* form a saddle point of L, then q^* and v^* maximize the objective function in B.1 subject to $dq^*/dt = f(q^*, v^*, t)$.

Theorem B.2

Three conditions

$$H(q^*, v^*, \lambda) \ge H(q, v; \lambda) \qquad \forall\, v, q$$

subject to

$$\frac{dq}{dt} = f(q, v, t)$$

$$q(0) = q_0$$

and $\forall\, t \in [0, T]$

$$\frac{dq^*}{dt} = f(q^*, v^*, t) \qquad q^*(0) = q_0$$

$$\frac{d\lambda^*}{dt} = -\frac{\partial H}{\partial q^*} \qquad \lambda(T)^* = \frac{\partial \beta(q(T), T)}{\partial q(T)^*}$$

are necessary for (q^*, v^*, λ^*) to be a saddle point of L.

Proof: For L to be maximized with respect to v and q at (q^*, v^*, λ^*), it is necessary that

$$\Delta L = L(q^*, v^*; \lambda^*) - L(q, v; \lambda^*) \ge 0$$

$$= \int_0^T \left(H(q^*, v^*; \lambda^*) - H(q, v; \lambda^*) - \lambda^* \left(\frac{dq^*}{dt} - \frac{dq}{dt} \right) \right) dt$$
$$+ \beta \left(q(T)^*, T \right) - \beta(q(T), T)$$

Integrating by parts yields

$$\Delta L = \int_0^T \left(H(q^*, v^*; \lambda^*) - H(q, v; \lambda^*) - \frac{d\lambda^*}{dt} (q^* - q) \right) dt - \lambda(T)^*$$
$$\cdot (q(T)^* - q(T)) + \lambda(0)(q(0)^* - q(0)) + \beta(q(T)^*, T) - \beta(q(T), T)$$

and because $q(0)^* = q(0)$, this simplifies to

$$\Delta L = \int_0^T \left(\frac{\partial H}{\partial q^*} \Delta v + \left(\frac{\partial H}{\partial q^*} + \frac{d\lambda^*}{dt} \right) \Delta q \right) dt + \left(\frac{\partial F}{\partial q(T)} - \lambda(T)^* \right) \Delta q (T) \ge 0$$

Because Δq is arbitrary, we need $d\lambda^*/dt = -\partial H/\partial q^*$ and $\partial F/\partial q(T)^* = \lambda(T)^*$, as well as $\partial H/\partial v^* = 0$, in order that $\Delta L \ge 0$. For L to be minimized with respect to λ at (q^*, v^*, λ^*), it is necessary that

$$\Delta L = L(q^*, v^*; \lambda^*) - L(q, v; \lambda) \le 0$$

$$= \int_0^T \Delta \lambda \left(f(q^*, v^*; t) - \frac{dq^*}{dt} \right) dt \le 0$$

and because $\Delta \lambda$ is arbitrary, this requires $dq^*/dt = f(q^*, v^*, t)$. Q.E.D.

The equations of motion

The equations of motion for the state and co-state variables are

$$\frac{dm}{dt} = -C_M - b_M \Pi - \hat{P}_{CM} m \qquad M(0) = M_0 \tag{C.1}$$

$$\frac{dC}{dt} = C_M + C_B - \phi - T^d(C_M, C_B, b_M \Pi) - \delta C + X \qquad C(0) = C_0 \tag{C.2}$$

$$\frac{db}{dt} = -C_B + b_M - (\hat{P}_{CB} - P_{MB})b \qquad B(0) = B_0 \tag{C.3}$$

$$\frac{d\lambda_M}{dt} = \hat{P}_{CM}\lambda_M, \qquad \lambda_M(T) = \frac{\partial \beta(T)}{\partial m(T)} \equiv \beta_1(T) \tag{C.4}$$

$$\frac{d\lambda_C}{dt} = \delta\lambda_C, \qquad \lambda_C(T) = \frac{\partial \beta(T)}{\partial(C,(T))} \equiv \beta_2(T) \tag{C.5}$$

$$\frac{d\lambda_B}{dt} = (\hat{P}_{CB} - P_{CB})\lambda_B, \qquad \lambda_B(T) = \frac{\partial \beta}{\partial b(T)} \equiv \beta_3(T) \tag{C.6}$$

The paths of the state variables are given by

$$m(t) = \exp\left(-\int_0^t \hat{P}_{CM} \, d\tau\right)$$

$$\cdot \left[\int_0^t \exp\left(\int_0^\tau \hat{P}_{CM} \, ds\right)(-C_M - b_M\Pi)d\tau + m(0)\right]$$

$$m(t) = \frac{P_{CM}(0)}{P_{CM}(t)}\left[\int_0^t \frac{P_{CM}(\tau)}{P_{CM}(0)}(-C_M - b_M\Pi) \, d\tau + m(0)\right] \tag{C.7}$$

$$m(t) = \left[\int_0^t (m_C(\tau) + m_B(\tau)) \, d\tau + m(0)\right] \tag{C.8}$$

$$C(t) = \exp\left(-\delta t\right)\left[\int_0^t \exp\left(\delta t\right)(C_M + C_B - \phi - T^d + X)\,d\tau + C(0)\right]$$

$$b(t) = \exp\left(-\int_0^t (\hat{P}_{CB} - P_{MB})\,d\tau\right)$$
$$\cdot\left[\int_0^t \exp\left(\int_0^t (\hat{P}_{CB} - P_{MB})\,ds\right)(-C_B + b_M)d\tau + b(0)\right] \quad \text{(C.9)}$$

$$b(t) = \frac{P_{CB}(0)}{P_{CB}(t)}\exp\left(\int_0^t P_{MB}\,d\tau\right)$$
$$\cdot\left[\int_0^t \frac{P_{CB}(\tau)}{P_{CB}(0)}\exp\left(-\int_0^\tau P_{MB}ds\right)(-C_B + b_M)\,d\tau + b(0)\right] \quad \text{(C.10)}$$

$$b(t) = \frac{1}{P_{CB}}\exp\left(\int_0^t P_{MB}\,d\tau\right)$$
$$\cdot\left[\int_0^t \exp\left(-\int_0^\tau P_{MB}\,ds\right)(B_C + B_M)\,d\tau + B(0)\right] \quad \text{(C.11)}$$

The paths for the co-state variables are

$$\lambda_M(t) = \beta_1(T)\exp\left(-\int_0^T \hat{P}_{CM}\,d\tau\right) \quad\quad\quad\quad\quad\quad \text{(C.12)}$$

$$\lambda_M(t) = \beta_1(T)\frac{P_{CM}(t)}{P_{CM}(T)} \quad\quad\quad\quad\quad\quad\quad\quad \text{(C.13)}$$

$$\lambda_C(t) = \beta_2(T)\exp\left(-(T - t)\right)\delta \quad\quad\quad\quad\quad\quad \text{(C.14)}$$

$$\lambda_B(t) = \beta_3(T)\frac{P_{CB}(t)}{P_{CB}(T)}\exp\left(\int_t^T P_{MB}(\tau)\,dt\right) \quad\quad\quad \text{(C.15)}$$

These solutions are obtained by applying an elementary Fourier transform to equations C.1 through C.6.

Comparative statics

The Hamiltonian for the intertemporal problem of the household is given by

$$
\begin{aligned}
H(q(t), v(t), \lambda(t), t) = \ & U(\theta(t)) \exp(-\rho t) \\
& + \lambda_M(t) \left(-C_M(t) - b_M(t) \Pi(t) - \hat{P}_{CM}(t) m(t)\right) \\
& + \lambda_C(t) \left(C_M(t) + C_B(t) - \theta(t) - T^d(t) - \delta C(t) \right. \\
& \left. + X(t)\right) \\
& + \lambda_B(t) \left(-C_B(t) + b_M(t) - (\hat{P}_{CB}(t) \right. \\
& \left. - P_{MB}(t)\right) b(t)
\end{aligned}
$$

$$\text{(D.1)}$$

with

$$q(t) = (m(t), C(t), b(t))$$

and

$$v(t) = (C_M(t), C_B(t), b_M(t), \phi(t)) \in \Omega$$

In its instantaneous maximization problem, as defined by the Maximum Principle, the household maximizes $H(q(t), v(t), \lambda(t), t)$ with respect to $v(t)$ at all $t \in [0, T]$. The necessary conditions for $H(t)$ to attain an extremum at $v(t)^*$ are

$$-\lambda_M(t) + \lambda_C(t) - \lambda_C(t) T_1^d(v(t)^*) = 0 \tag{D.2}$$

$$\lambda_C(t) - \lambda_B(t) - \lambda_C(t) T_2^d(v(t)^*) = 0 \tag{D.3}$$

$$\frac{\lambda_B(t)}{P_{CB}(t)} - \frac{\lambda_M(t)}{P_{CM}(t) P_{MB}(t)} - \frac{\lambda_C(t)}{P_{CM}(t) P_{MB}(t)} T_3^d(v(t)^*) = 0 \tag{D.4}$$

$$U'(\phi(t)) \exp(-\rho t) \lambda_C(t) = 0 \qquad \forall \, t \in [0, T]$$

The qualitative effects of changes in the shadow prices, market prices, and parameters on the choice variables are established by total differentiation of this system of first-order conditions. The result is summarized in matrix equation D.5. Application of Cramer's rule and the implicit-function theorem, together with the assumption that $T_{ij}^d(t) = 0 \; \forall \, t \in [0, T]$ whenever $i \neq j \; (i, j = 1, 2, 3)$, yields the comparative statics results discussed in Chapter IV, Section 2.

$$
\begin{bmatrix}
\lambda_C T^d_{11} & \lambda_C T^d_{12} & \dfrac{\lambda_C T^d_{13}}{P_{CM}P_{MB}} & 0 \\[2mm]
\lambda_C T^d_{21} & \lambda_C T^d_{22} & \dfrac{\lambda_C T^d_{23}}{P_{CM}P_{MB}} & 0 \\[2mm]
\lambda_C \Pi T^d_{31} & \lambda_C \Pi T^d_{32} & \dfrac{\lambda_C \Pi^2 T^d_{33}}{P_{CB}} & 0 \\[2mm]
0 & 0 & 0 & U'' \exp(-\rho t)
\end{bmatrix}
\begin{bmatrix}
dC_M \\ dC_B \\ dB_M \\ d\phi
\end{bmatrix}
$$

$$
=
\begin{bmatrix}
1 - T^d_1 & -1 & 0 & \lambda_C b_M \Pi T^d_{13} & \lambda_C b_M \Pi T^d_{13} & 0 & 0 \\[2mm]
1 - T^d_2 & 0 & -1 & \lambda_C b_M \Pi T^d_{23} & \lambda_C b_M \Pi T^d_{23} & 0 & 0 \\[2mm]
-\Pi T^d_3 & -\Pi & 1 & \begin{array}{c}\Pi(\lambda_M + \lambda_C T^d_3) \\ + b_M \Pi \lambda_C T^d_{33}\end{array} & \begin{array}{c}\Pi(\lambda_M + \lambda_C T^d_3) \\ + b_M \Pi \lambda_C T^d_{33}\end{array} & -(\lambda_M + \lambda_C T^d_3)\Pi & 0 \\[2mm]
-\mu' \exp(-\rho t) & 0 & 0 & 0 & 0 & 0 & tU' \exp(-\rho t)
\end{bmatrix}
\begin{bmatrix}
d\lambda_C \\ d\lambda_M \\ d\lambda_B \\ \dfrac{dP_{CM}}{P_{CM}} \\[2mm] \dfrac{dP_{MB}}{P_{MB}} \\[2mm] \dfrac{dP_{CB}}{P_{CB}} \\[2mm] dp
\end{bmatrix}
\tag{D.5}
$$

The effects of nonnegativity constraints on state variables

The nonnegativity constraints on the household's holdings of consumption goods and money, given by

$$m(t) \geq 0 \qquad \forall\, t \in [0, T] \tag{E.1}$$

$$C(t) \geq 0 \qquad \forall\, t \in [0, T] \tag{E.2}$$

were disregarded in analyzing the first-order conditions of the household's intertemporal maximization problem, as well as in deriving the comparative statics and dynamics results. This appendix demonstrates how explicit introduction of the nonnegativity constraints affects the first-order conditions and the qualitative properties of the household's optimal behavior.

If $m(t) = 0$ on some interval $[t_0, t_1] \subset [0, T]$, then the nonnegativity constraint E.1 requires the choice variables $C_M(t)$, $C_B(t)$, and $b_M(t)\,\Pi(t)$ to behave such that $dm(t)/dt \geq 0 \ \forall\, t \in [t_0, t_1]$. However, by equation II.5.9, the rate of change of the real money stock is given by

$$\frac{dm(t)}{dt} = -C_M(t) - b_M(t)\Pi(t) - \hat{P}_{CM}(t)m(t) \qquad \forall\, t \in [0, T] \tag{E.3}$$

Hence, the constraint

$$-C_M(t) - b_M(t)\Pi(t) - \hat{P}_{CM}(t)m(t) \geq 0 \tag{E.4}$$

is effective on the interval $[t_0, t_1]$ and thus can be regarded as an additional constraint on the household's choice variables. Similarly, if $C(t) = 0$ on an interval $[t_0, t_1]$, then

$$C_M(t) + C_B(t) - \phi(t) - T^d(t) - \delta C(t) + X(t) \geq 0 \tag{E.5}$$

is also effective on the interval $[t_0, t_1]$.

In the presence of nonnegativity constraints, the household's instantaneous maximization problem consists of maximizing the Hamiltonian given in equation III.2.1 subject to equations E.4 and E.5. Defining the multipliers $\mu_M(t)$ and $\mu_C(t)$ for constraints E.4 and E.5, respectively, such that

$$\mu_M(t) \geq 0 \qquad \forall \, t \in [0, T], \qquad \mu_M(t) = 0 \quad \text{if} \quad m(t) > 0 \qquad \text{(E.6)}$$
$$\mu_C(t) \geq 0 \qquad \forall \, t \in [0, T], \qquad \mu_C(t) = 0 \quad \text{if} \quad C(t) > 0 \qquad \text{(E.7)}$$

the constraints can be written in complementary slackness form as follows:

$$\mu_M(t) m(t) = 0 \qquad \forall \, t \, [0, T] \tag{E.8}$$

or as

$$\mu_M(t)(-C_M(t) - b_M(t)\Pi(t) - \hat{P}_{CM}(t)m(t)) = 0 \qquad \forall \, t \in [0, T] \tag{E.9}$$

and

$$\mu_C(t) C(t) = 0 \qquad \forall \, t \in [0, T] \tag{E.10}$$

or as

$$\mu_C(t)(C_M(t) + C_B(t) - \phi(t)$$
$$- T^d(t) - \delta C(t) + X(t)) = 0 \qquad \forall \, t \in [0, T] \tag{E.11}$$

Thus, instead of the Hamiltonian given in equation III.2.1, the household maximizes the following Lagrangian function:

$$L(t) = U(\phi(t)) \exp\left(-\rho t\right)(\lambda_M(t) + \mu_M(t))$$
$$\cdot \, (-C_M(t) + b_M(t)\Pi(t) - \hat{P}_{CM}(t)m(t)) + (\lambda_C(t) + \mu_C(t))$$
$$\cdot \, (C_M(t) + C_B(t) - \phi(t) - T^d(t) - \delta C(t) + X(t))$$
$$+ \lambda_B(t)(-C_B(t) - b_M(t)\Pi(t) - (\hat{P}_{CB}(t) - P_{MB}(t))b(t)) \tag{E.12}$$

The necessary conditions for this Lagrangian to attain a maximum with respect to the choice variables and a minimum with respect to the multipliers are given by

$$-(\lambda_M(t) + \mu_M(t)) + (\lambda_C(t) + \mu_C(t)) - (\lambda_C(t) + \mu_C(t))T_1^d(t) = 0 \tag{E.13}$$

$$(\lambda_C(t) + \mu_C(t)) - \lambda_B(t) - (\lambda_C(t) + \mu_C(t))T_2^d(t) = 0 \tag{E.14}$$

$$\frac{\lambda_B(t)}{P_{CB}(t)} - \frac{\lambda_M(t) + \mu_M(t)}{P_{CM}(t)P_{MB}(t)} - \frac{\lambda_C(t) + \mu_C(t)}{P_{CM}(t)P_{MB}(t)} T_3^d(t) = 0 \tag{E.15}$$

$$U^1(\phi(t)) \exp\left(-\rho t\right)(\lambda_C(t) + \mu_C(t)) = 0 \tag{E.16}$$

which must hold simultaneously for all $t \in [0, T]$. Furthermore, $\mu_M(t) \geq 0$, $\mu_C(t) \geq 0$, and equations E.8, E.9, E.10, and E.11 must hold. A comparison of equations E.13, E.14, E.15, and E.16 with equations III.2.8, III.2.9, III.2.10, and III.2.11 reveals that $\mu_C(t)$ and $\mu_M(t)$ enter into E.13, E.14, E.15, and E.16 in the same way that $\lambda_C(t)$ and $\lambda_M(t)$ enter into equations III.2.8, III.2.9, III.2.10, and III.2.11. Hence, the comparative statics effects of changes in $\mu_M(t)$ and $\mu_C(t)$ on the household's choice variables are identical with the comparative statics changes caused by changes in $\lambda_M(t)$ and $\lambda_C(t)$. Equations E.8, E.9, E.10, and E.11 do not affect the comparative statics results, because all shadow prices and inventories are regarded as exogenous variables in the instantaneous maximization problem.

The equations of motion of the consumption-good, bonds, and money stocks remain unchanged on introduction of the nonnegativity constraints E.1 and E.2. However, the equations of motion of the shadow prices of these stocks become

$$\frac{d\lambda_M(t)}{dt} = (\lambda_M(t) + \mu_M(t))\hat{P}_{CM}(t), \qquad \lambda_M(T) = \beta_1(T) \qquad \text{(E.17)}$$

$$\frac{d\lambda_C(t)}{dt} = (\lambda_C(t) + \mu_C(t))\delta, \qquad \lambda_C(T) = \beta_2(T) \qquad \text{(E.18)}$$

$$\frac{d\lambda_B(t)}{dt} = (\hat{P}_{CB}(t) - P_{MB}(t))\lambda_B(t), \qquad \lambda_B(T) = \beta_3(T) \qquad \text{(E.19)}$$

Thus the nonnegativity constraints affect the trajectories of the household's assets through changes in the paths of the shadow prices.

If the household's unconstrained plans involved a negative money stock on the interval $[t_0, t_1]$, then in the constrained maximization problem the inequality E.1 is binding, and $\mu_M(t) > 0$ on this interval. Following the comparative statics results, one can conclude that $C_M(t)$ and $b_M(t)\Pi(t)$ are lower on $[t_0, t_1]$ in the constrained problem than they are in the unconstrained problem. In particular, $C_M(t)$ and $b_M(t)\Pi(t)$ will be low enough to keep $M(t) > 0$ on $[t_0, t_1]$. For $t > t_1$, the multiplier $\mu_M(t)$ equals zero, and in both the constrained and unconstrained maximization problems the choice variables, ceteris paribus, assume identical values. However, this implies that on the interval $[t_0, t_1]$ the real money stock $m(t)$ is larger in the constrained problem than in the unconstrained problem. The transversality condition determining the final value of $\lambda_M(t)$ then forces a reduction in $\lambda_M(t)$ at each $t \in [0, T]$, which in turn results in increases in $C_M(t)$ and $b_M(t)\Pi(t)$ at each $t \in [0, T]$. However, these increases in $C_M(t)$ and $b_M(t)\Pi(t)$ cannot dominate the decreases in $C_M(t)$ and $b_M(t)\Pi(t)$ on $[t_0, t_1]$ that are due to the increase in $\mu_M(t)$ on the same interval. That is, on the interval $[t_0, t_1]$ the sum of $\lambda_M(t)$ and $\mu_M(t)$ in the constrained problem exceeds $\lambda_M(t)$ in the unconstrained problem, but on the intervals $[0, t_0]$ and $[t_1, T]$ this sum is smaller than the unconstrained value of $\lambda_M(t)$.

Thus $m(t)$ is smaller on $[0, t_0]$ and larger on $[t_0, T]$ in the constrained case than in the unconstrained case. Similarly, the analysis can be applied to the consumption-good stock, and identical results can be derived. This behavior can be interpreted as follows: When a household desires to hold negative stocks on some interval $[t_0, t_1]$, but is constrained to nonnegative inventory holdings, it reduces its stock holding at all $t < t_1$ to approximate the average of its desired holdings. However, the household holds stocks larger than desired on the interval $[t_0, t_1]$ because of the constraints E.1 and E.2, and at $t > t_1$ its holdings are larger, because the increase in holdings on $[t_0, t_1]$ acts as an increase in endowments.

The qualitative comparative dynamics effects of changes in parameters on the household's behavior on the interval $[0, T]$ remain unchanged. This can be seen by reversing the steps in the analysis; that is, first derive the comparative dynamics results in the unconstrained case, as in Chapter IV, and then analyze the effects of the nonnegativity constraints as done here.

Notes

Chapter I: Introduction

1 The term "partial equilibrium" is used in the sense of considering individual agents as well as individual decisions separately.
2 The assumption that an auctioneer costlessly and timelessly clears the set of complete spot and futures markets rules out the use of a medium technology (Hahn, 1965).
3 Arbitrary restrictions on expectations formation are widely employed in order to achieve identification in empirical macroeconomic models (Sargent and Wallace, 1976).
4 A duality relation establishes that along the optimal asset-and-consumption trajectory, transactions costs are minimized.
5 Such a characterization was first obtained by Niehans (1975) in a similar setting. The stability of the agent's plans is determined by the saddle-point property of its Hamiltonian system.
6 The equilibrium price vector also includes all future prices.
7 If there exist n agents and m goods, then the problem of finding the set of equilibrium exchanges is one of locating and accomplishing the desired trades. This is the problem of double coincidence of wants.
8 The result has been obtained in a variety of models (Friedman, 1969; Niehans, 1975).
9 The mode of financing government projects produces no real effects (Barro, 1974).
10 Monopolistic market power may also be a cause for slowly adjusting prices (Benassy, 1976; Hellwig, 1980).

Chapter II: A model of the intertemporal household

1 R^n denotes the n-dimensional Euclidean space.
2 The Weierstrass theorem guarantees the existence of an extremum, and the quasi concavity of the utility function assures that this extremum is a maximum.
3 See the work of Becker (1965). For the purposes at hand, the interposition of a household production function between the market activities of the household and its final consumption of goods is of no great interest.
4 If we let $R^\infty = \Pi_k^\infty (R^n)^k$, where $(R^n)^k$ is a replica of R^n, and if we endow R^∞ with the product topology, then the consumption set Y may be regarded as a proper subset of R^∞ such that Y is convex and closed in the product topology and

146

the utility function is defined on Y and derived as before from a complete preference ordering on Y.

5 Stationarity of preference ordering is defined in the following way: Let X and Y be two consumption streams of infinite dimensions, and let X' and Y' be two consumption streams obtained from X and Y by deleting the first component. Then X, Y and X', Y' are ordered in the same way.

6 Ryder and Heal (1973) have shown that allowing for complementarity by representing recent history as an exponentially weighted average of past consumption levels and including this variable in the instantaneous utility function does not fundamentally change the results obtained in the optimal-growth literature.

7 As a special case, we permit $\beta \equiv 0$.

8 In Chapter V we derive further necessary conditions for an economy to have a consistent price system.

9 For a view of how this framework might develop and change, see the work of Brunner and Meltzer (1971). The implications of a changing transactions technology are discussed in Chapter IV, Section 12.

10 $T^d(t)$ is determined by the institutional framework for making transactions as well as the household's ability to collect information and execute transactions. We shall, however, take $T^d(t)$ as given.

11 This assumption is analogous to a similar assumption about the fixed relative price between investment goods and consumption goods in one-sector macroeconomic models.

12 When some of the X_i are interpreted as addition or subtraction from assets such as money, bonds, etc., and prices are current prices rather than present prices, then this constraint can be written in a more familiar form as $p \cdot X = 0$.

13 Substitute $C_M(t) = -M_C(t)/P_{CM}(t)$, $C_B(t) = -B_C(t)/P_{CB}(t)$, and because $M_B(t) = -B_M(t)/P_{MB}(t)$, we know that $M_B(t) = -B_M(t)/P_{MC}(t)P_{CB}(t)$ if and only if $P_{MC}(t)P_{CB}(t) = P_{MB}(t)$ (i.e., if and only if the price system is consistent).

14 The use of total demand flow variables without transactions costs and forward contracts from one week to the next also forced Patinkin (1965) to rely on the artificial assumption of random disbursements during a contract week, in order to motivate a nonzero demand for money. Hence Patinkin's attempt to reconcile monetary theory and value theory did not result in a theory of a monetary economy.

15 This argument provides a rigorous foundation for the assumption that monetary exchange is cheaper than barter (Niehans, 1971). The origin of centralized markets can also be explained in terms of the reduction it affords in the computational complexity of the algorithm for establishing the set of equilibrium trades, which is a proxy for the actual costs (Berge, 1962; Borodin and Munro, 1975; Niehans, 1969).

16 It will be shown in Chapter III that cost minimization is the dual problem of the utility maximization hypothesis. Some form of the cost-minimization hypothesis to explain the use of money as a medium of exchange has been employed in various partial-equilibrium settings by Baumol (1952a), Tobin (1959), Feige and Parkin (1971), and Grossman and Policano (1975), in a discrete-time-period general-equilibrium model by Niehans (1971), and in sequential transactions models

by Hahn (1973) and Kurz (1974, 1976). All of these models have some costs associated with discrete stock-shift types of transactions.

17 Clower proposed to distinguish between monetary and nonmonetary commodities by defining a monetary commodity as any commodity that can be traded directly for any other commodity, and a monetary economy as an economy in which exactly one commodity has this property. Clower then represented the restricted exchange possibility of a monetary economy by two transactions constraints

$$pX + M = 0 \quad \text{when} \quad X \geq 0$$

$$pX + m = 0 \quad \text{when} \quad X < 0$$

where p is the price vector and X, M, and m represent excess demand for commodities, excess demand for money, and money receipts during the trading period, respectively. Hence an inflow of commodities ($x \geq 0$) must be paid for with money, and an outflow of commodities ($x < 0$) must lead to receipts of money. Clower's method of defining transactions constraints for a monetary economy can easily be derived from the transactions constraints proposed earlier, by letting all entries in $d(t)$ be zero except the first column and first row. Starr (1972) pointed out that in a bilateral exchange economy with the double-coincidence requirement, some exchange equilibria may not be attainable, which might lead to the introduction of money as a commodity not subject to the double-coincidence requirement in order to attain previously unattainable exchange equilibria.

18 Let

$$P_{CM}m = \frac{dP_{CM}}{dt}m + P_{CM}\frac{dm}{dt} = M_C + M_B \qquad \frac{dm}{dt} = m_C + m_B - \hat{P}_{CM}m$$

and similarly for the remaining two accumulation equations.

19 The accumulation equations could also have been expressed in terms of M_C, M_B, and C_B without changing any of the results that follow.

20 Because the amount borrowed must have been lent by some household, and because the amounts of money, consumption goods, and labor are finite, the amount borrowed must be finite. Hence the problem is not to prevent the stock of bonds held by any one household from approaching minus infinity but to assure that the household will always be able to redeem its issued bonds (i.e., to avoid bankruptcy or the passing on of a negative stock of wealth to the next generation).

21 The interest on bonds $P_{MB}(t)$ is used as a discount factor.

22 Even though transactions occur at discrete points in time, it is not necessary to assume that time is divided into periods.

23 We have adopted as resource constraint the requirement that final wealth be nonnegative. This is the least restrictive of the three versions of the resource constraint.

24 A similar assumption in the form of $\lim_{\phi \to 0^+} U(0) = \infty$ has been employed by Koopmans (1965).

25 For discussions of a method of solving problems of this kind, see the work of Arrow and Kurz (1969), Bryson and Ho (1969), Hestenes (1966), Pontryagin and associates (1962), and Shell (1969).

Chapter III: Structure of the intertemporal problem of the household

1 $q(t)^*$ is the vector of state variables that corresponds to $v(t)^*$, the vector of choice variables.

2 For the reader unfamiliar with Pontryagin's theorem, a derivation of these conditions and the saddle-point theorem is given in Appendix B.

3 These first-order conditions do not take account of the nonnegativity conditions on the real money stock and the consumption-good stock. For a discussion of the effects of nonnegativity constraints on the preceding formulation of the household's intertemporal maximization problem, see Appendix E.

4 The transactions flow constraints of equations II.5.1, II.5.2, and II.5.3 allow us to write $T^d(t)$ as a function of $C_M(t)$, $C_B(t)$, and $b_M(t)\,\Pi\,(t)$ only. It is also possible to take $M_C(t)$, $B_C(t)$, and $M_B(t)$ as choice variables. By the transactions flow constraint, all results remain unchanged.

5 $T_i^d(t)$ denotes the ith partial derivative of $T^d(t)$.

6 The factor $\Pi(t)$ in equation III.2.14 represents the number of real bonds that can be purchased with a unit of real money.

7 $\lambda_C(t)$, $\lambda_B(t)$, and $\lambda_M(t)$ are positive on $[0, T]$. See Appendix C.

8 If $C_M(t)^* < 0$, then $\lambda_C(t)^* - \lambda_M(t)^* < 0$, and hence $T^d(C_M(t), \cdot) - T^d(C_M(t)^*, \cdot) > 0$ whenever $C_M(t) - C_M(t)^* < 0$. As before, $T^d(\cdot)$ is minimized along the optimal trajectory.

9 This property of the instantaneous utility function is assumed (see Section II.5).

10 Equations III.3.4, III.3.5, and III.3.6 are obtained by taking time derivatives of III.3.1, III.3.2, and III.3.3, respectively.

11 In Chapter VI we shall make use of the expressions for the gain in utility due to the holding of stocks and derive conclusions about the socially optimal levels of stocks in an economy.

12 $U(\phi(t))$, $\beta(m(T), C(T), b(T))$, and $-T^d(\cdot)$ are all strictly concave, and thus we can apply Mangasarian's theorem on sufficiency (Mangasarian, 1966).

13 From the transactions flow constraints II.5.1, II.5.2, and II.5.3 we can infer that $m_C(t)$, $b_C(t)$, and $m_B(t)$ are also homogeneous of degree zero in $P_{CM}(t)$, $P_{CB}(t)$, $M_C(t)$, $B_C(t)$, $M_B(t)$, M_0, and B_0.

14 However, in the model developed by Patinkin (1965) it is not possible to derive the homogeneity result when an interest rate appears explicitly.

15 $T_{ii}^d(t)$ ($i = 1, 2, 3$) denotes the second-order partial derivative of $T^d(t)$ with respect to its ith variable.

16 This is a plausible assumption if $P_{MB}(t) - \hat{P}_{CB}(t) > \hat{P}_{CM}(t)$ for all $t \in [0, T]$.

17 This assumption implies that $P_{CM}(t) = P_{CB}(t) P_{BM}(t)$ for all $t \in [0, T]$.

18 Continuity of demand functions with respect to market prices is guaranteed by the strict convexity of the two utility functions $U(\phi(t))^i$ and $\beta(m(T), C(T), b(T))_i$ and by the continuity of $T^{di}(C_M(t), C_B(t), b_M(t)\Pi(t))$.

19 Furthermore, the solution to the nonconvex optimization problem will not be an interior solution.

20 Generalized functions (Lighthill, 1958) can be visualized as a sequence of func-

tions that have progressively taller and thinner peaks at τ_s, with the area under the curve remaining constant and equal to $\Delta C(\tau_s | C_M)$ (see equation III.5.3), whereas the value of $C_M(t)$ tends to zero except at $t = \tau_s$, at which point it diverges to infinity:

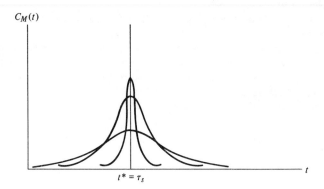

The corresponding shape of the stock-holding function $C(t)$ will approach the rectangular jump of the stock-shift transactions:

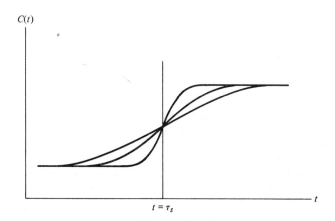

21 Thus $\Delta C(\tau_s | C_M)$ gives the change in $C(t)$ at $t = \tau_s$ that is due to a stock-shift transaction in the consumption-good-cum-money market at the same time.

22 The use of the negatives of the numbers of times the household transacts in the three markets as variables in $\Gamma_i(\cdot)$ permits an easy characterization of the curvature of $\Gamma_i(\cdot)$.

23 The subscript i on the functions $U(\cdot), \beta(\cdot), \phi(t), C_M(t), C_B(t), B_M(t),$ and $\Gamma(\cdot)$, which indicates the ith household, has been omitted. The sets $I_1, I_2,$ and I_3 are the index sets of dates of transactions by the household in the consumption-good-cum-

money market, the consumption-good-cum-bonds market, and the money-cum-bonds market, respectively.

24 Controversies surrounding the appropriate model of adjustment and the implications for the specification of demand functions have surfaced in the neoclassical theory of investment, international capital flows, and portfolio theory (Brainard and Tobin, 1967; Gould, 1968; Grandmont, 1973; Lucas, 1967; Nadiri and Rosen, 1969; Witte, 1963).

Chapter IV: Comparative static and dynamic analyses of household behavior

1 In many instances it suffices to assume that the matrix $[T_{ij}^d(t)]$ has a dominant diagonal.

2 Because of arbitrage between the three markets, an increase in $P_{CB}(t)$ induces an increase in $P_{CM}(t)P_{MB}(t)$. If $\Pi(t) = 1$, then the price system is consistent. If $\Pi(t) \neq 1$, then the price system is inconsistent.

3 When $\Pi(t)$ is constant, the following relations among the elasticities of demand with respect to price changes hold:

$$\frac{dM_C}{dP_{CM}}\frac{P_{CM}}{M_C} - \frac{dC_M}{dP_{CM}}\frac{P_{CM}}{C_M} = 1, \quad \frac{dM_C}{dP_{CM}}\frac{P_{CM}}{M_C} = 1, \quad \frac{dC_M}{dP_{CM}}\frac{P_{CM}}{C_M} = 0$$

$$\frac{dB_M}{dP_{MB}}\frac{P_{MB}}{B_M} - \frac{dM_B}{dP_{MB}}\frac{P_{MB}}{M_B} = 1, \quad \frac{dB_M}{dP_{MB}}\frac{P_{MB}}{B_M} = 1, \quad \frac{dM_B}{dP_{MB}}\frac{P_{MB}}{M_B} = 0$$

$$\frac{dB_C}{dP_{CB}}\frac{P_{CB}}{B_C} - \frac{dC_B}{dP_{CB}}\frac{P_{CB}}{C_B} = 1, \quad \frac{dB_C}{dP_{CB}}\frac{P_{CB}}{B_C} = 1, \quad \frac{dC_B}{dP_{CB}}\frac{P_{CB}}{C_B} = 0$$

All other cross-elasticities are zero.

Without arbitrage, the elasticities in the bonds-cum-money market are such that

$$\frac{dB_M}{dP_{MB}}\frac{P_{MB}}{B_M} = 1 + \frac{P_{CM}P_{CM}\lambda_B}{P_{CM}P_{BM}\lambda_C B_M P_{BM}T_{33}}, \quad \frac{dM_B}{dP_{MB}}\frac{P_{MB}}{M_B} = -\frac{P_{CM}P_{CM}\lambda_B}{P_{CM}P_{BM}\lambda_C M_B T_{33}},$$

$$\frac{dB_M}{dP_{MB}}\frac{P_{MB}}{B_M} - \frac{dM_B}{dP_{MB}}\frac{P_{MB}}{M_B} = 1$$

The cross-elasticities are given by

$$\frac{dB_M}{dP_{CM}}\frac{P_{CM}}{B_M} = 1 + \frac{P_{CM}P_{CM}\lambda_B P_{MB}}{\lambda_C T_{33}P_{CB}B_M P_{BM}}, \quad \frac{dM_B}{dP_{CM}}\frac{P_{CM}}{M_B} = 1 - \frac{P_{CM}P_{CM}\lambda_B P_{MB}}{\lambda_C T_{33}P_{CB}M_B}$$

$$\frac{dB_M}{dP_{CB}}\frac{P_{CB}}{B_M} = -\frac{P_{CM}P_{CM}\lambda_B}{\lambda_C T_{33}P_{CB}P_{BM}B_M P_{BM}}, \quad \frac{dM_B}{dP_{CB}}\frac{P_{CB}}{M_B} = \frac{P_{CM}P_{CM}\lambda_B}{\lambda_C T_{33}P_{CB}P_{BM}M_B}$$

These cross-elasticities are equal in each market.

4 The change in the shadow price is given by

$$\Delta\lambda_M(t) = (\beta_1(\overline{m}(T) + \Delta m_0) - \beta_1(m(T))) \exp\left(-\int_t^T \hat{P}_{CM}d\tau\right)$$

$$= \beta_{11}(\overline{m}(T)) \exp\left(-\int_t^T \hat{P}_{CM}d\tau\right) M_0 < 0 \qquad \forall\, t \in [0, T] \quad \text{if } \Delta M_0 > 0$$

In the comparative dynamic analysis in this chapter, a change in a variable at time t refers to a change in its value at time t due to a change in the endowment or parameter vector at time t. It does not refer to the time derivative of the variable; these are discussed in Section III.4.

5 The changes in the choice variables $C_M(t)$ and $b_M(t)\Pi(t)$ are given by

$$\frac{dC_M(t)}{d\lambda_M(t)}\Delta\lambda_M(t) = -\frac{\beta_{11}\overline{m}(T)}{T_{11}\cdot\beta_2(\overline{C}(T))}\exp\left(-\int_t^T(\hat{P}_{CM}-\delta)\,d\tau\right)\Delta m_0(T) > 0$$
$$\forall\, t \in [0, T]\quad\text{if }\Delta M_0 > 0$$

$$\frac{d(b_M(t)\Pi(t))}{d\lambda_M(t)}\Delta\lambda_M(t) = -\frac{\beta_{11}(\overline{m}(T))}{T_{33}\cdot\beta_2(\overline{C}(T))}\exp\left(-\int_t^T(\hat{P}_{CM}-\delta)\,d\tau\right)\Delta m_0(T) > 0$$
$$\forall\, t \in [0, T]\quad\text{if }\Delta M_0 > 0$$

6 Alternatively, one may think of the household as being compensated for changes that occur in $C(t)$ and $b(t)$.

7 The asterisk indicates that the variable has attained an equilibrium value after all stage I adjustments have been completed, and bars denote the values of variables prior to the change in M_0.

8 The changes in the shadow prices are given by

$$\Delta\lambda_C(t) = \beta_{22}(\overline{C}(T))\exp\left(-(T-t)\delta\right)(C(T)^* - \overline{C}(T)) < 0$$
$$\forall\, t \in [0, T]\quad\text{if }C(T)^* > \overline{C}(T)$$

$$\Delta\lambda_B(t) = \beta_{33}(\overline{b}(T))\exp\left(-\int_t^T(P_{MB}-\hat{P}_{CB})\,d\tau\right)\cdot(b(T)^* - \overline{b}(T)) < 0$$
$$\forall\, t \in [0, T]\quad\text{if }B(T)^* > \overline{B}(T)$$

9 The changes in the choice variables $C_M(t)$, $C_B(t)$, $\phi(t)$, and $B_M(t)$ due to a decrease in $\lambda_C(t)$ and the changes in choice variables $B_M(t)$ and $C_B(t)$ due to a decrease in $\lambda_B(t)$ are given by

$$\frac{dC_M(t)}{d\lambda_C(t)}\Delta\lambda_C(t) = \frac{1 - T_1^d(\overline{C}_M(t))}{T_{11}^d(\overline{C}_M(t))}\frac{\beta_{22}(\overline{C}(T))}{\beta_2(\overline{C}(T))}(C(T)^* - \overline{C}(T)) < 0$$
$$\forall\, t \in [0, T]\quad\text{if }C(T)^* - \overline{C}(T) > 0$$

$$\frac{dC_B(t)}{d\lambda_C(t)}\Delta\lambda_C(t) = \frac{1 - T_2^d(\overline{C}_B(t))}{T_{22}^d(\overline{C}_M(t))}\frac{\beta_{22}(\overline{C}(T))}{\beta_2(\overline{C}(T))}(C(T)^* - \overline{C}(T)) < 0$$
$$\forall\, t \in [0, T]\quad\text{if }C(T)^* - \overline{C}(T) > 0$$

$$\frac{d\phi(t)}{d\lambda_C(t)}\Delta\lambda_C(t) = \frac{\beta_{22}(\overline{C}(T))\exp\left(-\int_t^T\delta\,d\tau + \rho\right)}{U''(\overline{\phi}(t))}(C(T)^* - \overline{C}(T)) > 0$$
$$\forall\, t \in [0, T]\quad\text{if }C(T)^* - \overline{C}(T) > 0$$

$$\frac{d(b_M(t)\Pi(t))}{d\lambda_C(t)} \Delta\lambda_C(t) = \frac{-T_3^d(\bar{b}_M(t)\Pi(t))}{T_{33}^d(\bar{b}_M(t)\Pi(t))} \frac{\beta_{22}(\overline{C}(T))}{\beta_2(\overline{C}(T))} (C(T)^* - \overline{C}(T)) \gtreqless 0$$

$$\forall\ t \in [0, T]\quad \text{as } \overline{B}_M(t) \gtreqless 0\quad \text{and}\quad C(T)^* - \overline{C}(T) > 0$$

$$\frac{d(b_M(t)\Pi(t))}{d\lambda_B(t)} \Delta\lambda_B(t) = \Pi(t) \frac{\beta_{33}(\bar{b}(T)) \exp\left(-\int_t^T (\hat{P}_{CB}(t) - P_{MB} - \delta)\, d\tau\right)}{T_{33}(\bar{b}_M(t)\Pi(t))\beta_2(\overline{C}(T))}$$

$$\cdot (B(T)^* - \overline{B}(T)) > 0\qquad \forall\ t \in [0, T]\quad \text{if } B(T)^* - \overline{B}(T) > 0$$

$$\frac{dC_B(t)}{d\lambda_B(t)} \Delta\lambda_B(t) = \frac{(\beta_{33}(\bar{b}(T)) \exp\left(-\int_t^T (\hat{P}_{CB} - P_{MB} - \delta)\, d\tau\right)}{T_{22}(\overline{C}_B(t))\beta_2(\overline{C}(T))} \cdot (B(T)^* - \overline{B}(T)) > 0$$

10 $\lambda_B(t)$ is a continuous decreasing function of $B(T)$.

11 It was shown earlier that $dC_M(t)$ does not change signs on $[0, T]$. Hence, if $dC_M(t) > 0$ for some $t \in [0, T]$, then $dC_M(t) > 0$ for all $t \in [0, T]$.

12

$$\left[\widehat{\frac{dC_M(t)}{d\lambda_M(t)}} \Delta\lambda_M(t)\right] = \hat{P}_{CM}(t) - \delta$$

(see note 5 for this chapter) and

$$\left[\widehat{\frac{dC_M(t)}{d\lambda_C(t)}} \Delta\lambda_C(t)\right] = \frac{-T_{11}^d(C_M(t))}{1 - T_1(C_M(t))} \frac{dC_M}{dt}$$

(see note 9 for this chapter).

$$\left[\widehat{\frac{dC_M(t)}{d\lambda_C(t)}} \Delta\lambda_C(t)\right] = (\hat{P}_{CM}(t) - \delta) \frac{\lambda_M(t)}{1 - T_1(C_M(t))\lambda_C(t)}$$

because

$$\frac{dC_M(t)}{dt} = \frac{(\delta - \hat{P}_{CM})\lambda_M(t)}{T_{11}^d(C_M(t))\lambda_C(t)} = \hat{P}_{CM}(t) - \delta$$

because

$$\frac{\lambda_M(t)}{\lambda_C(t)} = 1 - T_1^d(C_M(t))$$

13

$$\left[\widehat{\frac{d(b_M(t)\Pi(t))}{d\lambda_M(t)}} \Delta\lambda_M(t)\right] = \hat{P}_{CM}(t) - \delta$$

(see note 5 for this chapter) and

$$\overline{\left[\frac{\widehat{d(b_M(t)\Pi(t))}}{d\lambda_B(t)}\Delta\lambda_B(t)\right]} = -P_{MB}(t) - \delta + \hat{P}_{CM}(t) + \hat{P}_{MB}(t)$$

(see note 9 for this chapter).

14

$$\overline{\left[\frac{\widehat{dC_B(t)}}{d\lambda_C(t)}\Delta\lambda_C(t)\right]} = \frac{-T_{22}^d}{1 - T_2^d(C_B(t))}\frac{dC_B(t)}{dt} = \hat{P}_{CB}(t) - P_{MB}(t) - \delta$$

because

$$\frac{dC_B(t)}{dt} = \frac{1}{T_{22}}(\delta + P_{MB}(t) - \hat{P}_{CB}(t))\frac{\lambda_B(t)}{\lambda_C(t)} \quad \text{and} \quad \frac{\lambda_B(t)}{\lambda_C(t)} = 1 - T_2^d(C_B(t))$$

$$\overline{\left[\frac{\widehat{dC_B(t)}}{d\lambda_B(t)}\Delta\lambda_B(t)\right]} = \hat{P}_{CB}(t) - P_{MB}(t) - \delta$$

(see note 9 for this chapter).

15 $B(t)^* < B(T)$ contradicts the utility maximization hypothesis, because it implies that an increase in real money stock causes reductions in $C(T)$ and $b(T)$ and consumption at each $t \in [0, T]$; that is, the household spends the increase in its real money stock on transacting. However, the household would be better off with no transaction, in which case $B(T)^* = \overline{B}(T)$ and $C(T)^* = \overline{C}(T)$.

16 The stock of consumption goods must increase in stage II; that is, $C(T)^{**} > \overline{C}(T)$. Otherwise $\phi(t)$ would decrease everywhere on $[0, T]$, contradicting the assumption that the household achieved an optimal allocation of resources with its original endowment vector.

17 Two asterisks indicate that all stage I and stage II adjustments have been made. the norm $|\quad|$ is the max norm; that is, $|q(t)| = \max(q_1(t), q_2(t), \dots, q_n(t))$, where $q \in R^n$ and $q_j(t)$ is the jth component of X.

18 See Section III.4 for a discussion of the existence and uniqueness of solutions to the household's intertemporal maximization problem.

19 From the assumptions that $U(\phi(t))$ and $\beta(M(T), C(T), b(T))$ are strictly concave and that $T^d(C_M(t), C_B(t), b_M(t)\Pi(t))$ is strictly convex, one can conclude that a decrease in one of the state variables implies that the initial values of the state variables were not optimal. Hence, as proved earlier, the inequalities must hold for all $t \in [0, T]$, and not only at $t = T$.

20 The change in $\lambda_B(t)$ is given by

$$\Delta\lambda_B(t) = \beta_{33}(\overline{b}(T)) \exp\left(-\int_t^T (\hat{P}_{CB} - P_{MB})\, d\tau\right)\Delta b_0(T) < 0$$

$$\forall\, t \in [0, T] \quad \text{if } \Delta B_0(T) > 0$$

21 The changes in $B_M(t)$ and $C_B(t)$ due to changes in $\lambda_B(t)$ are given by

$$\frac{d(b_M(t)\Pi(t))}{d\lambda_B(t)}\Delta\lambda_B(t) = \beta_{33}(\overline{b}(T))\frac{\Pi(t)\exp\left(-\int_t^T (\hat{P}_{CB} - P_{MB} - \delta)\, d\tau\right)}{T_{33}\cdot\beta_2(\overline{C}(T))}\Delta b_0(T) < 0$$

$$\forall\, t \in [0, T] \quad \text{if } \Delta B_0 > 0$$

$$\frac{dC_B(t)}{d\lambda_B(t)} \Delta\lambda_B(t) = -\beta_{33}(\overline{b}(T)) \frac{\exp\left(-\int_t^T (\hat{P}_{CB} - P_{MB} - \delta)\,d\tau\right)}{T_{22} \cdot \beta_2(\overline{C}(T))} \Delta b_0(T) > 0$$

$$\forall\, t \in [0, T] \quad \text{if } \Delta B_0 > 0$$

22 The function $\beta_3(b(T))$ is continuous and decreasing in the variable $b(T)$; $\lambda_B(t)$ is a continuous and increasing function of $\beta_3(\cdot)$ at each $t \in [0, T]$; $-B_M(t)$ and $C_B(t)$ are continuous and increasing in the variable $\lambda_B(t)$ at each $t \in [0, T]$. Hence $b(T)^*$ cannot fall below $\overline{b}(T)$.

23 As before, one asterisk denotes that the variable has assumed its stage I equilibrium value, and two asterisks denote that the variable has assumed its stage II equilibrium value. A bar denotes that the variable is at its original initial value.

24 The changes in $\lambda_M(t)$ and $\lambda_C(t)$ are given by

$$\Delta\lambda_M(t) = \beta_{11}(\overline{m}(T)) \exp\left(-\int_t^T \hat{P}_{CM}\,d\tau\right)(m(T)^* - \overline{m}(T)) < 0$$

$$\forall\, t \in [0, T] \quad \text{if } m(T)^* - \overline{m}(T) > 0$$

$$\Delta\lambda_C(t) = \beta_{22}(\overline{C}(T)) \exp\left(-T - t)\delta\right)(C(T)^* - \overline{C}(T)) < 0$$

$$\forall\, t \in [0, T] \quad \text{if } C(T)^* - C(T) > 0$$

25 The choice-variable changes induced by the decrease in $\lambda_C(t)$ are given in note 9 for this chapter, and the choice-variable changes induced by the decrease in $\lambda_M(t)$ are

$$\frac{dC_M(t)}{d\lambda_M(t)} \Delta\lambda_M(t) = -\beta_{11}(\overline{m}(T)) \frac{\exp\left(-\int_t^T (\hat{P}_{CM} - \delta)\,d\tau\right)}{T_{11} \cdot \beta_2(\overline{C}(T))}(m(T)^* - m(T)) > 0$$

$$\forall\, t \in [0, T] \quad \text{if } m(T)^* - \overline{m}(T) > 0$$

$$\frac{d(b_M(t)\Pi(t))}{d\lambda_M(t)} \Delta\lambda_M(t) = -\beta_{11}(\overline{m}(T)) \frac{\exp\left(-\int_t^T (\hat{P}_{CM} - \delta)\,d\tau\right)}{T_{33} \cdot \beta_2(\overline{C}(T))}(m(T)^* - \overline{m}(T)) > 0$$

$$\forall\, t \in [0, T] \quad \text{if } m(T)^* - \overline{m}(T) > 0$$

26 The expression for $(dC_B(t)/d\lambda_B(t))\,\Delta\lambda_B(t)$ in note 9 for this chapter implies that its percentage rate of change over time is equal to $\hat{P}_{CB} - P_{MB} - \delta$. Also, note 14 for this chapter shows that the percentage rate of change over time of $(dC_B(t)/d\lambda_C(t))\,\Delta\lambda_C(t)$ equals $\hat{P}_{CB} - P_{MB} - \delta$.

27 The decrease in $\lambda_C(t)$ is given by

$$\Delta\lambda_C(t) = \beta_{22}(C(T)) \exp\left(-(T - t)\right)\Delta C_0 < 0 \qquad \forall\, t \in [0, T] \quad \text{if } \Delta C_0 > 0$$

28 See note 9 for this chapter for a derivation of these changes in the choice variables.

29 The decreases in $\lambda_M(t)$ and $\lambda_B(t)$ are derived in notes 24 and 8 for this chapter.

30 Note 5 for this chapter contains expressions for these changes when $\Delta M_0 = M(T)^* - \overline{M}(T)$.

31 Note 21 for this chapter contains expressions for these changes when $\Delta B_0 = B(T)^* - \overline{B}(T)$.

32 See note 12 for this chapter for a proof.

33 See note 14 for this chapter.

34 This can be established by observing that $(dC_M(t)/d\lambda_M(t)) \, \Delta\lambda_M(t) < 0$ when $m(t)^* < \overline{m}(t)$ and that $(dC_B(t)/d\lambda_B(t)) \, \Delta\lambda_B(t) < 0$ when $b(t)^* < \overline{b}(t)$ and by using equation IV.4.15.

35 If the exogenous changes in $M(t)$ occur continuously, then the household adjusts its choice and state variables as if the initial change in the nominal money stock were equal to $\int_0^T \Delta M(t)\,dt$.

36 $M(t_1)$, $B(t_1)$, and $C(t_1)$ are the optimal values of the stocks at time t_1 in the original problem, which starts at $t = 0$ with M_0, B_0, and C_0 as initial conditions for the state variables.

37 It is possible that $t''' = 0$ if $S = [0, T]$ or if the intertemporal substitution effect is strong enough.

38 If R''' is empty, then $t''' = T$.

39 The changes in $b(t)$ and $m(t)$ that are due to the comparative statics change in $b_M(t)\,\Pi(t)$ are given by

$$\Delta^S(b(t)) = \int_0^t \left[\frac{d(b_M(\tau)\Pi(\tau))}{dP_{CM}(\tau)} \Delta P_{CM}(\tau) - (\hat{P}_{CB}(\tau) - P_{MB}(\tau))\Delta^S(b(\tau)) \right] d\tau > 0$$

$$\forall\, t \in [0, T] \quad \text{if } \frac{d(b_M(\tau)\Pi(\tau))}{dP_{CM}(\tau)} > 0 \qquad \forall\, \tau \in [0, t]$$

$$\Delta^S(m(t)) = \int_0^t \left[-\frac{d(b_M(\tau)\Pi(\tau))}{dP_{CM}(\tau)} \Delta P_{CM}(\tau) - \hat{P}_{CM}(\tau)\Delta^S(m(\tau)) \right] d\tau < 0$$

$$\forall\, t \in [0, T] \quad \text{if } \frac{d(b_M(\tau)\Pi(\tau))}{dP_{CM}(\tau)} > 0 \qquad \forall\, \tau \in [0, t]$$

40 The changes in the shadow prices are given by

$$\Delta\lambda_B(t) = \beta_{33}(b(T)) \exp\left(-\int_t^T (\hat{P}_{CB}(\tau) - P_{MB}(\tau))\,d\tau \right)\Delta^S(b(T)) < 0$$

$$\forall\, t \in [0, T] \quad \text{if } \Delta^S(b(T)) > 0$$

$$\Delta\lambda_M(t) = \beta_{11}(m(T)) \exp\left(-\int_t^T (\hat{P}_{CM}(\tau)\,d\tau \right)\Delta^S(m(T)) > 0$$

$$\forall\, t \in [0, T] \quad \text{if } \Delta^S(m(T)) < 0$$

41 The changes in $C_B(t)$ and $b_M(t)\,\Pi(t)$ at each $t \in [0, T]$ due to the decrease in $\lambda_B(t)$ are given in note 9 for this chapter, if $B(T)^* - \overline{B}(T)$ is replaced with $\Delta^S(b(T))$.

42 The changes in $C_M(t)$ and $b_M(t)\,\Pi(t)$ at each $t \in [0, T]$ due to the increase in $\lambda_M(t)$ are given in note 5 for this chapter, if Δm_0 is replaced with $\Delta^S(m(T))$.

43 If the integral inequality IV.4.2 does not hold, then $b(T)$ will be lower and $m(T)$ will be higher than before the change in $P_{CM}(t)$ took place. This would contradict

the continuity of $C_M(t)$, $C_B(t)$, and $b_M(t) \Pi(t)$ at time $t \in [0, T]$ with respect to changes in $\lambda_M(t)$ and $\lambda_B(t)$ at the same time $t \in [0, T]$, as well as the continuity of $\lambda_M(t)$ and $\lambda_B(t)$ at time $t \in [0, T]$ with respect to changes in $m(T)$ and $b(T)$.

44 The increase in $C_B(t)$ induced by the rise in $\lambda_C(t)$ reinforces the increase in $C_B(t)$ caused by the decrease in $\lambda_B(T)$. The increase in $C_M(t)$ resulting from the increase in $\lambda_C(t)$ cannot dominate the decrease in $C_M(t)$ caused by the increase in $\lambda_M(t)$. Because $\int_0^T (dC_M(t)/d\lambda_C(t)) \, \Delta\lambda_C(t) + (dC_M(t)/d\lambda_M(t)) \, \Delta\lambda_M(t) \, dt < 0$, and because $(dC_M(t)/d\lambda_C(t)) \, \Delta\lambda_C(t)$ and $(dC_M(t)/d\lambda_M(t)) \, \Delta\lambda_M(t)$ have the same rates of growth,they cannot cross on $[0, T]$.

45 The change in $m(t)$ that is due to the change in $P_{CM}(t)$ only is given by

$$\Delta^W(m(t)) = - \int_t^T \hat{P}_{CM}(\tau) m(\tau) \frac{\Delta P_{CM}(\tau)}{P_{CM}(\tau)} \, d\tau < 0 \qquad \forall \, t \in [0, T)$$

where $\Delta P_{CM}(\tau) > 0$ is the exogenously given change in $P_{CM}(t)$ at time $t = \tau$.

46 The changes in $\lambda_M(t)$, $C_M(t)$, and $b_M(t) \Pi(t)$ at each $t \in [0, T]$ are given in notes 40 and 5 for this chapter, if $\Delta^S(m(T))$ and $\Delta \, m_0(T)$ are replaced with $\Delta^W(m(T))$ (see also note 42 for this chapter).

47 The decrease in the stock of consumption goods is given by

$$\Delta^W C(t) = \int_0^t \left[\frac{dC_M(\tau)}{d\lambda_M(\tau)} \Delta\lambda_M(\tau) - \delta\Delta^W C(\tau) \right] d\tau < 0$$
$$\forall \, t \in [0, T] \quad \text{if } \Delta\lambda_M(t) > 0 \qquad \forall \, \tau \in [0, T]$$

The increase in the shadow price of the consumption good is given by $\Delta\lambda_C(t)$

$$= \beta_{22}(C(T)) \exp\left(-(T - t)\right) \Delta^W C(T) > 0 \, \forall \, t \in [0, T], \text{ if } \Delta^W C(T) < 0.$$

48 The increase in $\lambda_C(t)$ also leads to an increase in $C_M(t)$, but this increase is dominated by $(dC_M(t)/d\lambda_M(t)) \, \Delta\lambda_M(t)$ at all $t \in [0, T]$.

49 The decrease in the real stock of bonds is given by

$$\Delta^W(b(t)) = \int_0^t \left[\frac{d(b_M(\tau)\Pi(\tau))}{d\lambda_M(\tau)} \Delta\lambda_M(\tau) - (\hat{P}_{CB}(\tau) - P_{MB}(\tau))\Delta^W(b(\tau)) \right] d\tau < 0$$

and the change in $\lambda_B(t)$ is given by

$$\Delta\lambda_B(t) = \beta_{33}(b(t)) \exp\left(- \int_t^T (\hat{P}_{CB}(\tau) - P_{MB}(\tau)) \, d\tau \right) \Delta^W(b(T)) > 0 \qquad \forall \, t \in [0, T]$$

50 The increase in $\lambda_B(t)$ also results in an increase in $b_M(t)\Pi(t)$ at each $t \in [0, T]$, but this change in the demand for bonds is dominated by the decrease in $b_M(t) \Pi(t)$ at each $t \in [0, T]$ due to the increase in $\lambda_M(t)$.

51 The solution to the equation of motion for $\lambda_M(t)$ is given by $\lambda_M(t) = \beta_1(m(T) + \Delta m(T)) \exp\left(-\int_t^T \hat{P}_{CM}(\tau) \, d\tau\right) \forall \, T \in [0, T]$, where $\Delta m(T)$ is the change in the real stock of money caused by the substitution and wealth effects. Hence, the higher is $\hat{P}_{CM}(\tau)$, the lower is $\lambda_M(t)$, and the decrease in $\lambda_M(t)$ becomes larger as t approaches 0, whereas at $t = T \, \lambda_M(t)$ will not change.

52 The decrease in $m(T)$ and the subsequent increase in $\lambda_M(t)$ at each $t \in [0, T]$ also cause the household to reduce $C_M(t)$ and $b_M(t) \Pi(t)$ at each $t \in [0, T]$. However, these decreases are dominated by the increases in $C_M(t)$ and $b_M(t)\Pi(t)$ at each $t \in [0, T]$ because of the initial decrease in $\lambda_M(t)$ at each $t \in [0, T]$.

53 It is necessary that $0 < t^* < T$, because the increases in $C_M(t)$ and $b_M(t)\Pi(t)$ at each $t \in [0, T]$ due to the downward shift of $\lambda_M(t)$ must cause a decrease in $m(t)$ at each $t \in [0, T]$ and hence an increase in $\lambda_M(t)$, implying that $t^* < T$. However, the subsequent decreases in $C_M(t)$ and $b_M(t)\Pi(t)$ at each $t \in [0, T]$ due to the decreases in $\lambda_C(t)$ and $\lambda_B(t)$ and the increase in $\lambda_M(t)$ at each $t \in [0, T]$ cannot dominate the increases in $C_M(t)$ and $b_M(t)\Pi(t)$ at each $t \in [0, T]$ due to the initial decrease in $\lambda_M(t)$, because then the increases in $C(t)$ and $b(t)$ and the decrease in $m(t)$ at each $t \in [0, T]$ could not have occurred. This argument proves that $0 < t^*$ and that $C(t)$ and $b(t)$ increase at each $t \in [0, T]$.

54 The analysis of the effects of a change in $P_{CB}(t)$ on the household's choice variables and state variables is analogous to the analysis of the effects of a change in $P_{CM}(t)$, and the results are similar. Hence the derivation of the quantitative changes in the choice, state, and co-state variables has not been repeated.

55 The increases in $\lambda_C(t)$ and $\lambda_M(t)$ will also result in an increase in $C_B(t)$ and a decrease in $b_M(t)\Pi(t)$ at each $t \in [0, T)$. However, these changes are dominated by the decrease in $C_B(t)$ and the increase in $b_M(t)\Pi(t)$ at each $t \in [0, T]$ due to the increase in $\lambda_B(t)$ at each $t \in [0, T]$.

56 Increases in ρ on S result in a reduction in $\phi(t)$ on S and hence cause $C(T)$ to increase. This increase in $C(T)$ then leads the household to reduce $\phi(t)$ everywhere. However, by the continuity of $C(t)$, $\lambda_C(t)$, and $\phi(t)$, the net change in $\phi(t)$ must be such as to increase $C(T)$.

57 The set M is nonempty, because

$$\int_S \Delta C_M(t)\, dt + \int_0^T \frac{dC_M(t)}{d\lambda_C(t)} \Delta\lambda_C(t)\, dt > 0$$

where $\Delta C_M(t)$ is the instantaneous increase in $C_M(t)$ induced by the decrease in $T_1^d(C_M(t))$.

58 The changes in $C_B(t)$ and $b_M(t)\Pi(t)$ also cause a change in $b(t)$, the direction of which is ambiguous.

59 If the marginal transactions cost of an increase in $b_M(t)\Pi(t)$ is large, and if $B_M(t) > 0$, then it is possible that the household might lower $b_M(t)\Pi(t)$ on $[0, T]$ (see Table IV.1).

Chapter V: General-equilibrium theory

1 The second term in equation V.2.4 and the transactions-cost term in equation V.2.5 are obtained with the aid of the following identities:

$$T_1^d(C_M(t)) = T_1^d(-M_C(t)P_{MC}(t))$$

$$T_2^d(C_B(t)) = T_2^d(-B_C(t)P_{BC}(t))$$

$$T_3^d(b_M(t)\Pi(t)) = T_3^d(-m_B(t))$$

2 Equation V.2.19 can be derived by substituting equations III.2.12 and III.2.13 into equation III.2.14.

3 Substituting $P_{CM}(t)/(P_{CB}(t)P_{BM}(t)) = \mathbf{III}\,(t) = 1$ into equations III.2.12, III.2.13, and III.3.14 yields the converse (i.e., if market prices are consistent, then internal

prices are consistent). The possibility of obtaining an economy with consistent market prices and $T^d(\cdot) \neq 0 \; \forall \; t \in [0, T]$ has been denied by Niehans (1971).

4 The introduction of an electronic monetary transfer system is an example of such technological progress in the exchange technology. The existence of barter can be observed empirically in modern economies.

5 The expected equilibrium prices for markets indexed with $t > t^* \in [0, T]$ affect current demands through the shadow prices $\lambda_M(t^*)$, $\lambda_C(t^*)$, and $\lambda_B(t^*)$, which are parametric to the maximization problem at t^*.

6 See the work of Hirsch and Smale (1974). The converse of this theorem is not true.

7 An $n \times n$ matrix $A = [a_{ij}]$ is said to have a dominant diagonal if there exist positive constants $K_1, K_2, \ldots, K_n$ such that

$$K_j \cdot |a_{jj}| > \sum_{i \neq j} K_i \cdot |a_{ii}| \qquad j = 1, 2, \ldots, n$$

8 It has thus been shown that by confronting the household with consistent price changes, the sum of the positive entries in each column of matrix V.3.16 is smaller than the absolute value of the negative entry on the diagonal in the same column. This is sufficient to prove stability of prices in the upward direction. Because the marginal utility of consumption is always positive, it is not possible for the price vector to collapse onto the zero vector; hence, we also have downward stability of prices in the general nonlinear system of equations V.3.9, V.3.10, and V.3.11. This argument is then taken to justify the assumption that the negative off-diagonal elements in columns 2 and 3 of matrix V.3.16 are small enough to allow the diagonal elements to dominate.

9 For a definition of the degree of a nonconvexity and a general discussion of the approach outlined in this section, see the work of Arrow and Hahn (1971).

10 This approximation theorem was first rigorously proved by Starr (1969) and has been proved for sequence economies by Heller and Starr (1976).

11 If, for example, the cross section of a transactions technology with respect to $C_M(t)_i$ is shaped

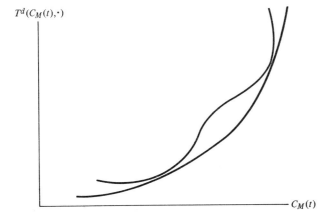

then the convexified transactions technology is given by the convex hull.

12 In the context of IS-LM model it can be inferred that Hicks perceived an increasing marginal cost of transacting in the goods market and a decreasing marginal cost of transacting in the assets markets. Hence, Hicks specified the demand functions in the goods market as continuous-flow demand functions and approximated the equilibrium conditions in the assets markets, where stock-shift transactions take place, by requiring that the outstanding stocks of money and bonds be willingly held at the equilibrium price vector. From the evidence presented in this section it is apparent that the equilibrium concept appropriate in the LM sector is the approximate equilibrium, with demand functions specified as flow demand functions.

13 For simplicity of exposition it is assumed that the changes in $b_M(t)\Pi(t)$ do not change sign on $[0, T]$. This assumption is justified, because the sign of the change in the total amount of real bonds purchased with money is as indicated in equation V.4.1. Furthermore, if prices change consistently, then the changes in the choice variables $C_B(t)$, $C_M(t)$, and $b_M(t)\Pi(t)$ will not change sign on $[0, T]$.

Chapter VI: Optimality of intertemporal equilibria and the role of government

1 Because $\lambda_M(t) = \mu_M(t)\exp(-\rho t)$ and $d\lambda_M(t)/dt = (d\mu_M(t)/dt)\exp(-\rho t) - \rho\mu_M(t)\exp(-\rho t)$. Furthermore, $d\lambda_M(t)/dt = \hat{P}_{CM}(t)\lambda_M(t)$; hence, $(d\mu_M(t)/dt)\exp(-\rho t) - \rho\mu_M(t)\exp(-\rho t) = \hat{P}_{CM}(t)\mu_M(t)\exp(-\rho t)$ and $d\mu_M(t)/dt = \rho + \hat{P}_{CM}(t) \mu_m(t) \ \forall \ t \in [0, T]$. Equations II.2.8 and VI.2.9 can be derived in a similar manner.

2 In an economy with continuously overlapping generations but constant age structure, $\hat{P}_{CM}(t)$ equals zero.

3 As long as all households have identical discount rates (i.e., as long as $\rho^i = \rho \ \forall \ i = 1, \ldots, m$), Pareto optimality can be attained (Friedman, 1969; Niehans, 1975).

4 In this case, condition VI.2.7 changes to $\hat{\mu}_M(t) = \rho + \hat{P}_{CM}(t) - r_M(t) \ \forall \ t \in [0, T]$.

5 This unstable policy rule has been derived and advocated by some writers. The rule of thumb often used for determining the optimal supply of money requires that $r_M(t) = P_{MB}(t) \ \forall \ t \in [0, T]$. First, this is correct only if $\hat{P}_{MB}(t) = 0 \ \forall \ t \in [0, T]$, because $r_M(t) = \rho + \hat{P}_{CM}(t)$ and $P_{MB}(t) = \rho + \hat{P}_{CB}(t)$ and $\hat{P}_{CM}(t) + \hat{P}_{MB}(t) = \hat{P}_{CB}(t) \ \forall \ t \in [0, T]$. Second, this rule also produces an instability (Feige and Parkin, 1971).

6 See the work of Samuelson (1958) and Gale (1973) for statements of the problem of intergenerational nonoptimality.

7 In a one-good economy, consumption and investment goods are identical.

8 In a production economy, condition VI.2.8 changes to $\hat{\mu}_M(t) = \rho + \delta - g(C(t)) \ \forall \ t \in [0, T]$.

9 Define $C_B(t)_H = \Sigma_{i=1}^{n} C_B(t)_i$, $C_M(t)_H = \Sigma_{i=1}^{n} C_M(t)_i$, and $B_M(t)_H = \Sigma_{i=1}^{n} B_M(t)_i$.

Chapter VII: A theory of disequilibrium adjustments

1 See the work of Grossman (1977) and Hellwig (1980). The effects of monopolistic competition on market clearing have been discussed by Negishi (1978) and Iwai (1974). In a production economy the costs of adjusting output levels and prices also retard the instantaneous movements of prices and quantities toward their

equilibria (Barro, 1972; Phelps and Winter, 1970). Because all prices are spot prices, we do not have recourse to long-term contracting to motivate the finite rate of change of prices in situations of market disequilibrium.

2 The subscript i, which indicates that the price and quantity expectations are formed by the ith household, has been omitted.

3 The existing literature on disequilibrium theory follows the tradition of Clower and equates notional and Walrasian demands. However, if the household has been constrained at any time $s \in [0, t]$, or if its expected prices are not equal to actual future spot prices, then its notional plans formed at time t will be different from the Walrasian demands (Benassy, 1975).

4 This initial endowment of information also permits the household to form the price and quantity expectations at $t = 0$.

5 From the continuity assumption of equation VII.2.3 it is apparent that the limit of this expression exists as τ approaches 0. We admit the possibility that $P(t + \tau, t)^e$ is adjusted downward for $\tau \in S$ only and remains unchanged everywhere else on $[t, T]$. However, $P(t + \tau, t)^e$ must not increase anywhere on $[t, T]$.

6 Thus, even though the household enters all markets simultaneously, a quantity constraint in one of the three markets affects its behavior in the other two (Fisher, 1978).

7 Hence, on introduction of expected constraints on future demands, the household's behavior conforms to Clower's dual-decision hypothesis (1965) only when its expectations are incorrect. Accurate expectations make remaximization unnecessary. In Clower's model, households always expect to be able to obtain their notional demands. Households do not learn when their expectations are unfulfilled, and thus they remaximize every period.

8 If the quantity constraints $C_B(\tau, t)^e$ and $B_M(\tau, t)^e$ are also binding, then the upward shift of $C_M(\tau, t)^e$ may not affect $C_B(\tau, t)^e$ and $B_M(\tau, t)^e$.

9 This is the voluntary-exchange assumption.

10 The voluntary-exchange assumption rules out $S(t, t)^a > S(t, t)^N$.

11 The decrease in $d(\tau, t)^e$ makes the quantity constraint less binding on $(t, T]$ and hence results in a decrease in $d(\tau, t)^N$ (see Section VII.2). The increase in $P(\tau, t)^e$ also decreases $d(\tau, t)^N$ directly.

12 Assumptions VII.2.7 and VII.2.8 are sufficient but not necessary, because a very rapid adjustment of prices and quantities in excess-demand situations may dominate those shifts in demand and supply functions that aggravate disequilibrium situations.

13 Examples of models of markets that are unstable because of nonconverging expectations-adjustment mechanisms can be found among the various classes of cobweb models and asset-accumulation models with saddle-point instability.

14 Because the transactions flow constraints must be valid even when effective demands are constrained, the household's excess demands in all markets must add to zero, and hence Walras's law holds with respect to effective, notional, and Walrasian excess demands. These are among the relations that F must satisfy (Cass and Shell, 1976).

15 F confines the admissible variations in demand space to a lower-dimensional subspace.

16 See the equation system VII.3.20, VII.3.21, and VII.3.22 and $F(\cdot) = 0$.

Bibliography

Akerlof, G. A. 1973. "The Demand for Money: A General-Equilibrium Inventory-Theoretic Approach." *Review of Economic Studies* 40:115–30.

Ando, A., and Modigliani, F. 1963. "The 'Life-Cycle' Hypothesis of Saving: Aggregate Implications and Tests." *American Economic Review* 53:55–84.

Arrow, K. J. 1959. "Towards a Theory of Price Adjustment." In *The Allocation of Economic Resources,* edited by M. Abramowitz, pp. 41–51. Stanford: Stanford University Press.

Arrow, K. J., Block, H. D., and Hurwicz, L. 1959. "On the Stability of the Competitive Equilibrium, II." *Econometrica* 27:82–109.

Arrow, K. J., and Hahn, F. H. 1971. *General Competitive Analysis.* San Francisco: Holden-Day.

Arrow, K. J., and Hurwicz, L. 1958. "On the Stability of the Competitive Equilibrium, I." *Econometrica* 26:522–52.

Arrow, K. J., and Kurz, M. 1969. "Optimum Consumer Allocation over an Infinite Horizon." *Journal of Economic Theory* 1:68–91.

⸻. 1970. *Public Investment, the Rate of Return and Optimal Fiscal Policy.* Baltimore: Johns Hopkins Press.

Athans, M., and Falb, P. L. 1966. *Optimal Control.* New York: McGraw-Hill.

Barro, R. J. 1972. "A Theory of Monopolistic Price Adjustment." *Review of Economic Studies* 39:17–26.

⸻. 1974. "Are Government Bonds Net Wealth?" *Journal of Political Economy* 82:1095–118.

⸻. 1976. "Output and Employment in a Macro Model with Discrete Transaction Costs." *Journal of Monetary Economics* 2:297–310.

Barro, R. J., and Grossman, H. I. 1971. "A General Disequilibrium Model of Income and Employment." *American Economic Review* 61:82–93.

Baumol, W. J. 1952a. "The Transaction Demand for Cash—An Inventory Theoretic Approach." *Quarterly Journal of Economics* 60:545–56.

⸻. 1952b. *Welfare Economics and the Theory of the State.* Cambridge: Harvard University Press.

Becker, G. 1965. "A Theory of the Allocation of Time." *Economic Journal* 75:493–517.

Bellman, R. 1957. *Dynamic Programming.* Princeton: Princeton University Press.

Benassy, J. P. 1975. "Neokeynesian Disequilibrium Theory in a Monetary Economy." *Review of Economic Studies* 42:503–24.

⸻. 1976. "The Disequilibrium Approach to Monopolistic Price Setting and General Monopolistic Equilibrium." *Review of Economic Studies* 43:69–81.

⸻. 1977. "On Quantity Signals and the Foundations of Effective Demand Theory." *Scandinavian Journal of Economics* 79:147–68.

Berge, C. 1962. *The Theory of Graphs and Its Application.* New York: Wiley.

Blinder, A., and Solow, R. 1974. "Does Fiscal Policy Matter?" *Journal of Public Economics* pp. 85–99.

Borodin, A., and Munro, I. 1975. *The Computational Complexity of Algebraic and Numeric Problems.* New York: American Elsevier.

162

Brainard, W. D., and Tobin, J. 1968. "Pitfalls in Financial Model Building." *American Economic Review* 58:99-122.

Brock, W. A. 1971. "Sensitivity of Optimal Growth Paths with Respect to a Change in Final Stocks." In *Contributions to the Von Neumann Growth Model,* edited by G. Brockmann and W. Weber, pp. 340-69. New York: Springer-Verlag.

—— 1972. "On Models of Expectations that arise from Maximizing Behavior of Economic Agents over Time." *Journal of Economic Theory* 5:348-76.

—— 1973. "Some Results on the Uniqueness of Steady States in Multi-Sector Models of Optimum Growth When Future Utilities are Discounted." *International Economic Review* 6:65-79.

—— 1974. "Money and Growth: The Case of the Long Run Perfect Foresight." *International Economic Review* 15:750-77.

Brock, W. A., and Scheinkman, J. A. 1976. "Global Asymptotic Stability of Optimal Control Systems with Applications to the Theory of Economic Growth." *Journal of Economic Theory* 12:164-90.

Brunner, K., and Meltzer, A. H. 1971. "The Uses of Money: Money in the Theory of an Exchange Economy." *American Economic Review* 61:784-805.

Bryson, A. E., and Ho, Y.-C. 1969. *Applied Optimal Control Theory.* Waltham, Mass.: Blaisdell.

Burmeister, E., and Dobell, R. 1970. *Mathematical Theories of Economic Growth.* New York: Macmillan.

Burmeister, E., and Turnovsky, S. J. 1976. "The Specification of Adaptive Expectations in Continuous Time Dynamic Economic Models." *Econometrica* 44:879-906.

Cass, D. 1965. "Optimum Growth in a Model of Capital Accumulation." *Review of Economic Studies* 32:233-40.

Cass, D., and Shell, K. 1976. "The Structure and Stability of Competitive Dynamical Systems." *Journal of Economic Theory* 12:31-70.

Cass, D., and Yaari, M. 1966. "A Re-examination of the Pure Consumption Loan Model." *Journal of Political Economy* 74:353-67.

Clower, R. W. 1965. "The Keynesian Counterrevolution: A Theoretical Appraisal." In *The Theory of Interest Rates,* edited by F. H. Hahn and F. P. R. Brechling, pp. 103-25. Proceedings of an IEA conference. London: Macmillan.

—— 1969. "Foundations of Monetary Theory." In *Monetary Theory,* edited by R. W. Clower, pp. 202-11. Baltimore: Penguin.

Debreu, G. 1959. *Theory of Value.* New York: Wiley.

Dhrymes, P. J. 1971. *Distributed Lags: Problems of Estimation Formulation.* San Francisco: Holden-Day.

Diamond, P. 1971. "A Model of Price Adjustment." *Journal of Economic Theory* 3:156-68.

Dixit, A., Mirrlees, J., and Stern, N. 1975. "Optimum Saving with Economies of Scale." *Review of Economic Studies* 42:303-26.

Dreyfus, S. 1965. *Dynamic Programming and the Calculus of Variations, Vol. 21, Mathematics in Science and Engineering Series.* New York: Academic.

Edgeworth, F. Y. 1932. *Mathematical Psychics: An Essay on the Application of Mathematics to the Moral Sciences.* London: London School of Economics and Political Science.

Feige, E. L., and Parkin, M. 1971. "The Optimal Quantity of Money, Bonds, Commodity Inventories and Capital." *American Economic Review* 61:335-49.

Fisher, F. M. 1972. "On Price Adjustment without an Auctioneer." *Review of Economic Studies* 39:1-16.

—— 1974. "The Hahn Process with Firms but No Production." *Econometrica* 42:471-87.

—— 1978. "Quantity Constraints, Spillovers, and the Hahn Process." *Review of Economic Studies* 45:19-32.

Foley, D. K. 1975. "On Two Specifications of Asset Equilibrium in Macroeconomic Models." *Journal of Political Economy* 83:303-24.

Foley, D., and Sidrauski, M. 1970. "Portfolio Choice, Investment and Growth." *American Economic Review* 60:44-63.

——— 1971. *Monetary and Fiscal Policy in a Growing Economy.* New York: Macmillan.

Friedman, M. 1957. *A Theory of the Consumption Function.* Princeton: Princeton University Press.

——— 1969. *The Optimum Quantity of Money and Other Essays.* Chicago: University of Chicago Press.

——— 1970. "A Theoretical Framework for Monetary Analysis." *Journal of Political Economy* 78:193-237.

Gale, D. 1960. *The Theory of Linear Economic Models.* New York: McGraw-Hill.

——— 1973. "Pure Exchange Equilibrium of Dynamic Economic Models." *Journal of Economic Theory* 6:12-36.

——— 1978. "A Note on Conjectural Equilibria." *Review of Economic Studies* 45:33-8.

Gale, D., and Nikaido, H. 1965. "The Jacobian Matrix and the Global Univalence of Mappings." *Mathematische Annalen* 159:81-93.

Gould, J. P. 1968. "Adjustment Cost in the Theory of Investment of the Firm." *Review of Economic Studies* 35:47-55.

Grandmont, J. M. 1973. "On the Short-Run and Long-Run Demand for Money." *European Economic Review* 6:99-115.

——— 1977. "Temporary General Equilibrium Theory." *Econometrica* 45:535-72.

Grandmont, J. M., and Laroque, G. 1973. "Money in the Pure Consumption Loan Model." *Journal of Economic Theory* 6:382-98.

Grandmont, J. M., and Younes, Y. 1972. "On the Role of Money and the Existence of a Monetary Equilibrium." *Review of Economic Studies* 39:355-71.

——— 1973. "On the Efficiency of a Monetary Equilibrium." *Review of Economic Studies* 40:149-66.

Green, J. R. 1973. "Temporary General Equilibrium in a Sequential Trading Model with Spot and Futures Transactions." *Econometrica* 41:1103-24.

Grossman, H. I. 1971. "Money, Interest and Prices in Market Disequilibrium." *Journal of Political Economy* 79:943-61.

——— 1972. "A Choice-Theoretic Model of an Income Investment Accelerator." *American Economic Review* 62:630-41.

Grossman, H., and Policano, A. 1975. "Money Balances, Commodity Inventories, and Inflationary Expectations." *Journal of Political Economy* 83:1093-112.

Grossman, S. 1977. "The Existence of Future Markets, Noisy Rational Expectations and Informational Externalities." *Review of Economic Studies* 44:431-49.

Guillemin, V., and Pollack, A. 1974. *Differential Topology.* Englewood Cliffs, N.J.: Prentice-Hall.

Hadley, G. 1964. *Non-linear and Dynamic Programming.* Reading, Mass.: Addison-Wesley.

Hadley, G., and Kemp, M. C. 1971. *Variational Methods in Economics.* New York: American Elsevier.

Hadley, G., and Whitin, T. M. 1963. *Analysis of Inventory Systems.* Englewood Cliffs, N.J.: Prentice-Hall.

Hahn, F. H. 1962. "On the Stability of Pure Exchange Equilibrium." *International Economic Review* 3:206-13.

——— 1965. "On Some Problems on Proving the Existence of an Equilibrium in a Monetary Economy." In *The Theory of Interest Rates,* edited by F. H. Hahn and F. Brechling, pp. 126-35. London: Macmillan.

bibliography

1971. "Equilibrium with Transactions Costs." *Econometrica* 39:417–40.

1973. "On Transaction Costs, Inessential Sequence Economies and Money." *Review of Economic Studies* 40:449–62.

1978. "On Non-Walrasian Equilibria." *Review of Economic Studies* 45:1–17.

Hahn, F. H., and Brechling, F. P. R. (eds.) 1965. *The Theory of Interest Rates*. Proceedings of an IEA conference. London: Macmillan.

Hahn, F. H., and Negishi, T. 1962. "A Theorem on Non-Tatonnement Stability." *Econometrica* 30:463–9.

Hansen, B. 1970. *A Survey of General Equilibrium Systems*. New York: McGraw-Hill.

Hawkins, D. 1948. "Some Conditions of Macro-economic Stability." *Econometrica* 16:309–22.

Hawkins, D., and Simon, H. A. 1949. "Note: Some Conditions of Macro-economic Stability." *Econometrica* 17:245–9.

Heller, W. P. 1972. "Transactions with Set-Up Cost." *Journal of Economic Theory* 4:465–78.

Heller, W. P., and Starr, R. M. 1976. "Equilibrium with Non-Convex Transactions Costs: Monetary and Non-Monetary Economies." *Review of Economic Studies* 43:195–216.

Hellwig, M. 1975. "The Demand for Money and Bonds in Continuous Time Models." *Journal of Economic Theory* 11:462–5.

1980. "On the Aggregation of Information in Competitive Markets." *Journal of Economic Theory* 22:477–98.

Hestenes, M. R. 1966. *Calculus of Variations and Optimal Control Theory*. New York: Wiley.

Hicks, J. R. 1935. "A Suggestion for Simplifying the Theory of Money." *Economica* 5:1–19.

1937. "Mr. Keynes and the Classics." *Econometrica* 5:147–59.

1946. *Value and Capital* (2nd ed.). Oxford: Oxford University Press.

1965. *Capital and Growth*. Oxford: Oxford University Press.

Hirsch, M., and Smale, S. 1974. *Differential Equations, Dynamical Systems, and Linear Algebra*. New York: Academic.

Ho, Y.-C. 1975. *Applied Optimal Control*. New York: Halsted.

Intriligator, M. D. 1971. *Mathematical Optimization and Economic Theory*. Englewood Cliffs, N.J.: Prentice-Hall.

Iwai, K. 1974. "The Firm in Uncertain Markets and Its Price, Wage, and Employment Adjustments." *Review of Economic Studies* 41:257–76.

Johansen, L. 1977. "Price-taking Behavior." *Econometrica* 45:1651–6.

Kemp, M. C. 1976. *Three Topics in the Theory of International Trade*. Amsterdam: North-Holland.

Keynes, J. M. 1936. *The General Theory of Employment, Interest and Money*. London: Macmillan.

Koopmans, T. C. 1965. "On the Concept of Optimal Economic Growth." In *Econometric Approach to Development Planning*, edited by T. C. Koopmans, pp. 225–87. Amsterdam: North-Holland.

1972. "Representations of Preference Orderings over Time." In *Decisions and Organization*, edited by C. B. McGuire and R. Radner, pp. 79–100. Amsterdam: North Holland.

Kurz, M. 1974. "Equilibrium with Transaction Cost and Money in a Single Market Exchange Economy." *Journal of Economic Theory* 7:418–52.

1976. "Equilibrium in a Finite Sequence of Markets with Transactions Costs." *Econometrica* 42:1–20.

Laroque, G., and Grandmont, J. M. 1976. "On Temporary Keynesian Equilibria." *Review of Economic Studies* 43:53–68.

Leijonhufvud, A. 1968. *On Keynesian Economics and the Economics of Keynes*. Oxford: Oxford University Press.

Levhari, D., and Patinkin, D. 1968. "The Role of Money in a Simple Growth Model." *American Economic Review* 58:713–53.

Lighthill, M. J. 1958. *Fourier Analysis and Generalized Functions.* Cambridge: Cambridge University Press.

Lucas, R. E. 1967. "Optimal Investment Policy and the Flexible Accelerator." *International Economic Review* 8:78–85.

1975. "An Equilibrium Model of the Business Cycle." *Journal of Political Economy* 83:1113–45.

1978. "Asset Prices in an Exchange Economy." *Econometrica* 46:1429–47.

Lucas, R. E., and Sargent, T. J. 1979. "After Keynesian Macroeconomics." *Federal Reserve Board of Minnesota Review* pp. 1–16.

Malinvaud, E. 1953. "Capital Accumulation and Efficient Allocation of Resources." *Econometrica* 21:233–68.

1977. *The Theory of Unemployment Reconsidered.* Oxford: Blackwell.

Mangasarian, O. L. 1966. "Sufficient Conditions for the Optimal Control of Non-Linear Systems." *Journal of SIAM Control* 4:275–87.

May, J. 1970. "Period Analysis and Continuous Analysis in Patinkin's Macro-Economic Model." *Journal of Economic Theory* 2:1–19.

McKenzie, L. W. 1957. "An Elementary Analysis of the Leontief System." *Econometrica* 25:456–62.

1960. "Matrices with Dominant Diagonals and Economic Theory." In *Mathematical Methods in Social Sciences,* edited by K. Arrow, S. Karlin, and F. Suppes, p. 2. Stanford: Stanford University Press.

Merton, R. 1971. "Optimum Consumption and Portfolio Rules in a Continuous Time Model." *Journal of Economic Theory* 3:1051–127.

Metzler, L. A. 1945. "Stability of Multiple Markets: The Hicks Conditions." *Econometrica* 13:277–92.

1951. "Wealth, Saving and the Rate of Interest." *Journal of Political Economy* 59:150–71.

Mills, E. 1962. *Price Output and Inventory Policy.* New York: Wiley.

Modigliani, F., and Brumberg, R. 1954. "Utility Analysis and the Consumption Function." In *Post-Keynesian Economics,* edited by K. K. Kurihara, pp. 388–436. New Brunswick, N.J.: Rutgers University Press.

Mossin, J. 1977. *The Economic Efficiency of Financial Markets.* Lexington, Mass.: D. C. Heath.

Mundell, R. A. 1965. "A Fallacy in the Interpretation of Macro Economic Equilibrium." *Journal of Political Economy* 73:61–6.

Nadiri, M. I., and Rosen, S. 1969. "Interrelated Factor Demand Functions." *American Economic Review* 59:457–72.

Negishi, T. 1961. "On the Formation of Prices," *International Economic Review* 2:135–51.

1978. "Involuntary Unemployment and Market Imperfection." In *Equilibrium and Disequilibrium in Economic Theory,* edited by G. Schwödiauer, pp. 497–510. Boston: Reidel.

Niehans, J. 1969. "Money in a Static Theory of Optimal Payment Arrangements." *Journal of Money, Credit, and Banking* 1:706–26.

1971. "Money and Barter in General Equilibrium with Transactions Costs." *American Economic Review* 61:773–83.

1975. "Interest and Credit in General Equilibrium with Transactions Cost." *American Economic Review* 65:548–66.

Patinkin, D. 1965. *Money, Interest, and Prices* (2nd ed.) New York: Harper & Row.

Peleg, B., and Yaari, M. 1970. "Efficiency Prices in an Infinite Dimensional Space." *Journal of Economic Theory* 2:41–85.

Phelps, E. S. 1969. "The New Microeconomics in Inflation and Employment Theory." *American Economic Review* 59:147–60.

Phelps, E. S., and Taylor, J. B. 1977. "Stabilizing Powers of Monetary Policy under Rational Expectations." *Journal of Political Economy* 85:163–90.

Phelps, E., and Winter, S. 1970. "Optimal Price Policy under Atomistic Competition." In *Microeconomic Foundations of Employment and Inflation Theory,* edited by E. S. Phelps, pp. 309–37. New York: W. W. Norton.

Pontryagin, L. S., Boltyanskii, V. C., Gramkrelidze, R. V., and Mishehenko, E. F. 1962. *The Mathematical Theory of Optimal Processes.* New York: Wiley.

Roberts, J., and Sonnenschein H. 1977. "On the Foundations of the Theory of Monopolistic Competition." *Econometrica* 45:101–14.

Ryder, H. E., and Heal, G. M. 1973. "Optimal Growth with Intertemporally Dependent Preferences." *Review of Economic Studies* 40:1–31.

Samuelson, P. A. 1947. *Foundations of Economic Analysis.* Cambridge: Harvard University Press.

1958. "An Exact Consumption-Loan Model of Interest with or without the Social Contrivance of Money." *Journal of Political Economy* 66:467–82.

1965. "Proof that Properly Anticipated Prices Fluctuate Randomly." *Industrial Management Review* 6:41–9.

Sargent, T. J. 1978. "Estimation of Dynamic Labor Demand Schedules under Rational Expectations." *Journal of Political Economy* 86:1009–44.

1979. *Macroeconomics.* New York: Academic.

Sargent, T. J., and Wallace, N. 1975. " 'Rational' Expectations, the Optimal Monetary Instrument, and the Optimal Money Supply Rule." *Journal of Political Economy* 83:241–54.

1976. "Rational Expectations and the Theory of Economic Policy." *Journal of Monetary Economics* 2:169–84.

Shell, K. 1969. "Applications of Pontryagin's Maximum Problem to Economics." In *Mathematical Systems, Theory and Economics, Vol. 1,* edited by H. W. Kuhn and G. P. Szego, pp. 325–59. Berlin: Springer-Verlag.

Sidrauski, M. 1967. "Rational Choice and Patterns of Growth in a Monetary Economy." *American Economic Review* 57:534–44.

1969. "Rational Choice and Patterns of Growth in a Monetary Economy." *Journal of Political Economy* 77:575–85.

Solow, R. M., and Stiglitz, J. E. 1968. "Output, Employment and Wages in the Short Run." *Quarterly Journal of Economics* 82:537–60.

Starr, R. M. 1969. "Quasi-Equilibria in Markets with Non-Convex Preferences." *Econometrica.*

1972. "Exchange in Barter and Monetary Economies." *Quarterly Journal of Economics* 86:290–302.

1974. "The Price of Money in a Pure Exchange Monetary Economy with Taxation." *Econometrica.*

Stein, J. 1969. "The Optimum Quantity of Money." *Journal of Money, Credit, and Banking* 1:35–49.

Stigum, B. 1973. "Competitive Equilibrium with Infinitely Many Commodities II." *Journal of Economic Theory* 6:415–45.

Takayama, A. 1974. *Mathematical Economics.* Hinsdale, Ill.: Dryden.

Tobin, J. 1956. "The Interest Elasticity of the Transactions Demand for Cash." *Review of Economic Statistics* 38:241–7.

1959. "The Demand for Money." Unpublished manuscript.

1965. "Money and Economic Growth." *Econometrica* 33:671–84.

1967. "Life-Cycle Saving and Balanced Growth." In *Ten Economic Studies in the Tradition of Irving Fisher,* edited by W. Fellner, pp. 128–53. New York: Wiley.

1969. "A General Equilibrium Approach to Monetary Theory." *Journal of Money, Credit, and Banking* 1:15–29.

Turnovsky, S. J. 1977. "On the Formulation of Continuous Time Macroeconomic Models with Asset Accumulation." *International Economic Review* 18:1–28.

Turnovsky, S. J., and Burmeister, E. 1977. "Perfect Foresight, Expectational Consistency and Macroeconomic Equilibrium." *Journal of Political Economy* 85:379–94.

Uzawa, H. 1968a. "Time Preference, the Consumption Function and Optimum Asset Holdings." In *Value, Capital and Growth,* edited by J. N. Wolfe, pp. 185–219. Edinburgh: Edinburgh University Press.

1968b. "The Penrose Curve and Optimum Growth." *Economic Studies Quarterly* 3:210–23.

Veendorp, E. C. H. 1975. "Stable Spillovers Among Substitutes." *Review of Economic Studies* 42:445–56.

Walras, L. 1954. *Elements of Pure Economics.* New York: Augustus M. Kelley.

Witte, J. 1963. "The Microfoundations of the Social Investment Function." *Journal of Political Economy* 71:441–56.

Younès, Y. 1975. "On the Role of Money in the Process of Exchange and the Existence of a Non-Walrasian Equilibrium." *Review of Economic Studies* 42:489–502.

Index

169